Self-Gamification
Happiness Formula

How to Turn Your Life into Fun Games

Victoria Ichizli-Bartels

Self-Gamification Happiness Formula
How to Turn Your Life into Fun Games
1st Edition

Copyright © 2019 Victoria Ichizli-Bartels

The moral right of the author has been asserted.

All rights reserved.

This book and the content provided herein are for informational and educational purposes only. They do not constitute medical, legal, financial, or similar professional advice. They are based on the author's opinion and personal experiences and observations. Every effort has been made to ensure that the content provided in this book is accurate and helpful. However, the author, who is also the publisher of this book, does not assume any liability whatsoever for the use of or inability to use any or all information contained in this book. Thus, she accepts no responsibility for any loss or damages of any kind that may be incurred by the reader as a result of actions arising from the use of information found in this book. The purchaser of this publication assumes full responsibility for the use of these materials and information. Please consult applicable laws and regulations and competent counsel to ensure your use of this material conforms with all applicable laws and regulations.

The author reserves the right to make any changes she deems necessary to future versions of the publication to ensure its accuracy.

No part of this publication may be reproduced, stored in or introduced into a retrieval system or transmitted, in any form or by any means (electronic, mechanical, photocopying, recording or otherwise), without the prior written permission of the author.

Cover art © Heike Werntgen

Cover design by Alice Jago and Victoria Ichizli-Bartels

All trademarks and brands mentioned in this book are for clarifying and reference purposes only. Rather than putting a trademark symbol after every occurrence of a trademarked name, the names are used in an editorial fashion and to the benefit of the trademark owner, with no intention of infringement of the trademark. Where such designations appear in this book, and where the author (and publisher) was aware of that claim, they have been capitalized. The trademarks and brands are proprietary to their owners and are not affiliated with this document in any way.

The sources to the quotations made in the book are given before, after, or in the same places as the quotes in the text.

For Michael, Niklas, and Emma,
My three favorite gamers.

Self-Gamification Happiness Formula
Table of Contents

A Quote About Happiness 9

Preface 11

More on Self-Gamification 15

Introduction 17

Part I. Reasons, Examples, Definition, and Formula 41

    Chapter 1. Why Turn Our Lives Into Games? 41

    Chapter 2. What Can Be Turned into Games? 61

    Chapter 3. From a Project to a Whole Life 74

    Chapter 4: Self-Gamification and the Happiness Formula 92

Part II. Anthropology and Non-Judgmental Seeing 105

    Chapter 5. Awareness and Anthropology 105

    Chapter 6. Observing What We Do and Don't Do Non-Judgmentally 125

Part III. Kaizen and the Small Steps 155

    Chapter 7. Kaizen and Why It Works 155

    Chapter 8. The Magic of an Effortless Step 174

    Chapter 9. The Starting Point and the Next Step 203

Part IV. Self-Gamification in Design and Practice 219

    Chapter 10. Games, Game Design, Gamification, and Self-Gamification 219

Chapter 11. Seeing and Designing What We Do as Games 231

Chapter 12. Definition and Design of Self-Motivational Games 252

Chapter 13. Fun in Self-Gamification 298

Chapter 14. Let's Talk About Rewards 313

Chapter 15. Practicing Self-Gamification 330

Chapter 16. Sharing Self-Gamification 391

Part V. Self-Gamification Framework Examples 409

Chapter 17. Introduction to Optimist Writer's Self-Gamification Frameworks 409

Chapter 18. 5 Minute Perseverance Game 414

Chapter 19. Project ("Crush") Management Game 424

Chapter 20. Balance Game 443

Conclusion 464

Two More Quotes About Happiness 467

Recommended Reading 468

Dear Reader, Thank You! 471

Acknowledgments 473

About the Author 479

Also by Victoria Ichizli-Bartels 480

Self-Gamification Happiness Formula

A Quote About Happiness

"Happiness is not a destination. It is a way of life."

— Anonymous

Preface

"True happiness arises, in the first place, from the enjoyment of one's self." — Joseph Addison

I used to wonder for a very long time why successful people are so happy, motivated and have so much fun with what they do. I couldn't figure it out until I looked at it from another angle. I realized that people who have fun are also happy and motivated, and they are also successful with what they do. Shortly after that epiphany, I discovered that about myself too. The more fun I had with a task at hand, the more motivated and happier I was, the more engaged I was in the process, and the more successful I was at carrying out and finishing it.

So if fun is a great tool for motivation and success, where would be the best place to look for it? Games, of course! The main reason people spend time playing games is that they make us happy and are supposed to be fun. So why not turn anything we want or have to do into fun and engaging games?

Is it even possible? Yes, it is. The approach of bringing game design elements and concepts into day-to-day contexts is called gamification*.

This book is about "self-gamification," a new term, which I apply to the unique approach of turning our own lives into games; that is designing our own happy, motivational, and engaging games for ourselves, and playing them.

At the time of writing this book, I have been turning my life into games for several years now. Or rather, for the past three years I have done so deliberately. I now realize that I have been applying game-design principles to my life for much longer, unwittingly. Since September 2017, I have been turning all areas of my life into games. While doing that, I found myself experiencing happiness more and more often, and having enormous fun with what I was doing, regardless of what that was.

When I first heard the word "gamification," I was already turning my life into games. So I was sure that I would find someone else who had had similar experiences to me and who had come to the same conclusions. I hoped to learn more from them because I assumed that these unknown people would have practiced similar approaches for a much longer time than I had. But I couldn't find anyone. The more questions I asked, and the more I was sharing what I was doing, the more it looked like the approach I was applying to uplift and motivate myself was unique.

In my search for an existing example of the personal application of gamification, I was also looking for another non-gamer like me — that is a person who plays video or board games only occasionally — who was also turning his or her life into games. But I couldn't find that person either.

As a non-gamer, I was looking for a simple and highly practical way to turn my life into games. I wanted to identify the tools that would help me to get out of the "lows" in my day and get back into the flow** and experience fun, regardless of what I was doing.

Now, as the interest in my approach to turning my life into fun and happy games — which brings three established techniques into one strong synergy — grows, I would like to share all the knowledge and experience I have gathered so far, in this book.

I hope you enjoy reading this book as much as I enjoyed writing it.

I also hope that as you read this book, you begin viewing and treating your dreams, goals, project plans, and to-do lists, not as some crazy or annoying necessities but as design plans and score sheets for exciting games that you design yourself. And that, just like the most brilliant game designers do who want to create the best game they can for their players, you would do the same and ensure that you, as the player in your own life, have the greatest amount of fun possible!

Glossary and references:

* Gamification is "the use of game design elements in non-game contexts" — Deterding, S., Dixon, D., Khaled, R., & Nacke, L. (2011). *From game design elements to gamefulness: defining gamification.* In Proceedings of the 15th international academic MindTrek conference: Envisioning future media environments (pp. 9-15). ACM.

** "There is virtually nothing as engaging as this state of working at the very limits of your ability — or what both game designers and psychologists call 'flow'. When you are in a state of flow, you want to stay there: both quitting *and* winning are equally unsatisfying outcomes." — Jane McGonigal, *Reality is Broken: Why Games Make Us Better and How They Can Change the World*

More on Self-Gamification

Book
5 Minute Perseverance Game: Play Daily for a Month and Become the Ultimate Procrastination Breaker is a short, fun book, which I wrote before I had heard about gamification and kaizen, two of the approaches self-gamification brings together. But it was after I had discovered and practiced living in the moment— the starting point and the first step in self-gamification — for a couple of years. I structured this easy-to-read book as a description for a board game. The little game it introduces, the 5 Minute Perseverance Game, is ideal when you start turning your life into games or want to see whether that is something for you.

I invite you to check it out here: https://www.victoriaichizlibartels.com/5-minute-perseverance-game/

Online course
Motivate Yourself by Turning Your Life Into Fun Games: Practice Self-Gamification, a Unique Self-Help Approach Uniting Anthropology, Kaizen, and

Gamification is an online course on Udemy with a couple of hours of content.

As a reader of *Self-Gamification Happiness Formula: How to Turn Your Life into Fun Games*, you have the opportunity to enroll in this online course for a considerable discount. Go to "Self-Gamification" or "Motivate Yourself by Turning Your Life Into Fun Games" on Udemy.com and choose the first course in the list (with my name) to preview it. Enter the coupon "SGBOOK" to get your discount. You can also click on this link (if you are reading this on an e-reader) or type in the following address to get there right away: https://bit.ly/2QDpbbw.

Self-gamification community

I am also busy building the self-gamification community. To find out how you can join, go to this link: www.victoriaichizlibartels.com/community/.

Introduction

"Lessons learned in games have a greater impact than lessons learned any other way." — Richard Garfield, inventor of the game "Magic: The Gathering," quoted by Brian Tinsman in *The Game Inventor's Guidebook: How to Invent and Sell Board Games, Card Games, Role-playing Games & Everything in Between!*

1. What is this book about?
We all want to live happy lives. Not just experience happiness for one moment, but to do so continuously. I am no exception. I wish that too. Which is why, some time ago, I bought a little plaque and put it in the small home office where I work most of the time and write my books. Most of us will have heard variations of the message on this plaque before, and, because of its brilliance, I already quoted it at the start of this book. Here it is one more time:

"Happiness is not a destination. It is a way of life." — Anonymous

We all want to find that happy path. Every person must find his or her own means of having a happy life. We might not recognize it at first, and we often step away from it. Time and time again we find our way back to it. But we are all eager to recognize this path so that we can return to it when we feel low and when we "mistakenly" step away from it.

I realized some time ago that I had found this happy path for myself. And as you might have guessed, it is a lifestyle, which I practice every day.

Here is my map to that path: I turn my life into fun games. I treat my life as though it is my all-time favorite game.

I find this path rewarding and new every time I design my self-motivational and uplifting games, and especially every time I play them (which is basically all the time, even when I sleep or am upset about something). The constant presence of these fun, gameful tools at my fingertips and in my head is one of the most significant discoveries I have made in my life.

Self-Gamification Happiness Formula: How to Turn Your Life into Fun Games is a combination of a guidebook, memoir, reference book, and essay/case-study anthology.

It will show you how by turning your life into fun and engaging games you can brighten your day and find your way back to the flow, happiness, and fun that you sometimes experience but will now do so intentionally and repeatedly. It will show you how to do so without having to study gamification or psychology in detail.

It can also pave the way for you to follow up reading this book with the more in-depth studies of the disciplines and approaches mentioned and referred to in this book.

When you are in the flow and enjoy what you do, you don't need help. You simply have fun with whatever you do. This book offers you tools to come back to that happy state of mind when you are out of balance, and you feel like the light around you has dimmed a little.

You will discover that you can only be happy if you become aware of the fact that you are both the designer and the player of your life games. This is the main message of this book. This circumstance includes and requires being simultaneously kind and honest with yourself. And only you can design games that will satisfy your changing, continually learning, and thus growing, player's mind. This book will make you aware of all the tools that are already in your hands and your head.

2. Who is this book for?

This book is for anyone who wants to bring fun and joy into various projects and activities they take on, and if they wish so, to all aspects of their lives.

Since I am a non-gamer, I initially had all my fellow non-gamers in mind, or those who play games very occasionally and prefer spending their free time doing activities other than games, but who, like me, want to enjoy life regardless of how it turns out. This book will help non-gamers lose the suspicion and fear they might hold against games, as I did in the past (especially for video games), and find a natural starting point for turning their lives into fun games without having to delve into gamification design or psychological research.

But if you are a gamer (that is someone who spends many hours playing various games, often video and online games, in your free time) then this book is also for you. It will show you that experiencing fun doesn't have to stop with switching off your video game. You will learn that you can take your favorite games and apply their elements to every-day life and become the super-hero yourself.

If you have already tried to consciously turn some activities into games and wonder how you can extend gamification principles to other or every area of your life, then this book will help with that too.

Gamification designers can also profit by discovering techniques and skill sets to enable the users of their frameworks to obtain maximum benefit from their products.

A few words about age. The approaches in this book are applicable to both children and adults. I had adults, including young adults, in mind when I wrote this book, but I would like to urge you to share the possibility of turning your life into fun games with your children or your younger siblings and friends. This will enrich the experiences of the whole family or community.

3. Who is this book *not* for?

This book is *not* for someone who:
- Is looking for the results of scientific studies on gamification,
- Wishes to study the psychotherapeutic effects of gamification,
- Wishes to learn advanced game or gamification design techniques, or
- Seeks a scientific book on self-therapy, self-counseling, or self-help therapy*.

Nor is it for those who:
- Want to escape everyday challenges,
- Want to give up their current jobs, companies, or relationships,
- Seek a quick-fix, one-time happiness "pill" to solve all their problems,
- Think that hard work and being serious are essential and that having fun is a flaw, or

- Despise games and believe there is nothing worth learning from them.

Speaking of despising games and their primary goal of bringing fun and making us happy, do you perhaps think all this gamification "stuff" is nonsense and that life is not a matter of enjoyment? That life is a torment, through which we must fight until the end? That life is unfair?

Then this book is not for you.

But since you've read this far, perhaps you are looking for a way to change your mindset from serious and hard, to light and joyful.

In that case I invite you to continue reading.

But here are four more disclaimers for this book:

First of all, this book doesn't promote the development of games that place their participants in scary or uncomfortable situations, like experiences shown on "Candid camera"** or the like. I won't be advising you to go bungee jumping, if that is not already your dream or wish. Most of the self-motivational and uplifting game examples discussed in this book are about making everyday activities and projects (i.e. those we have already committed to doing or want to address, and which we already have on our to-do or wish lists) fun, enjoyable, and achievable.

Second, although I share my self-motivational game designs with you here, as well as many examples of how I have used those game plans, I am not suggesting that you use them. You are free to do so. But my main message is that you are the designer of your own games. No one but you lives — and that is designs and plays — your life. So ultimately, even if you try out one or more of my game plans, you will still put your own personal stamp on them as they become an integral part of your daily, monthly, and so on, games.

Third, this is not the description of an app. There is no self-gamification app, and I hope there never will be. After all, there could be many. And the same person would require countless versions, since we humans need a frequent change in occupation to feel alive. As Winston Churchill once brilliantly said, "To improve is to change; To be perfect is to change often."

Fourth, this book does not show the way to eternal bliss. I can guarantee that after reading this book, you will still experience discomfort and be upset and desperate from time to time. But you will feel more in control and have the tools at your disposal to make those periods of distress shorter. You will also learn how to shift your focus from complaints to creativity, and be able to bring yourself back into the flow without too much effort. And most importantly, you will learn to be both honest and kind to yourself.

4. Who am I?

My name is Victoria Ichizli-Bartels. My last name is hard to pronounce, so two of my friends call me Itsy Bitsy Bartels. My other friends and family call me Vica or Victoria.

I was born and grew up in the Republic of Moldova, part of the former Soviet Union. I am now a German citizen and have lived in Aalborg, Denmark since 2008, with my husband and two children.

I am a writer, self-publisher, teacher, coach, and consultant. In October 2015 I started my own business, which I called Optimist Writer.

My work experience includes semiconductor physics and engineering (with a Ph.D. in electronic engineering), secretary, personal assistant, interpreter, coach, consultant, language teacher, a specialist in business development and information technology, project manager and team/working group leader (some of them for over ten years).

At the time of writing this book, I have written and self-published eleven books, varying in length from short stories to a novel, and from booklets to over a five hundred page guide to implementing an international standard. The work on and completion of most of these book projects were turned into a game, or in other words, I approached them as if they were games.

There have also been many large and small consulting and teaching projects that profited from my use of game design elements.

I created my business and called it Optimist Writer because I was on a mission to explore and share the possibilities that open up when we have fun and bring positivity into every aspect of our lives.

I wrote and published the following passage less than six months after starting my business, and just around the time I started systematically turning my life into games:

"Whatever your project is, you have the ability to turn it into a valuable and enjoyable game, gathering many unforgettable experiences. Every project, however tiny, if given enough attention and peeled off worries, can bring inspiration and eagerness to do more, to create more." — Victoria Ichizli-Bartels, *Turn Your No Into Yes: 15 Yes-Or-No Questions to Disentangle Your Project*

5. Why am I qualified to write this book?
The fact that I am probably the first person to use the term "self-gamification" and to define it, is not the only reason I am qualified to talk about it.

As mentioned above, I initially planned this book for non-gamers. I am a non-gamer myself without any qualifications in software, game, or gamification design, nor in psychology. I may well be the first person of this kind to explore gamification and apply it to herself. And to teach it.

I have to admit that when I heard that what I was doing not only had a term but was also a scientific topic of its own, I wondered if I had any right to say anything on the topic. Was I, a non-gamer, with little background in programming, really qualified to not only talk about gamification but even gamify (= turn into games) my life?

A non-biased answer, one stripped of fear of being judged, was a definite "Yes." Especially the right to turn my own life into games, despite not having studied gamification or game design in detail. If gamification of my life was not only fun but also increased the quality of both my life and those of my family and friends, then it was something worth pursuing and sharing.

My lack of a game-design background is, in fact, an advantage. Because if I can turn my life into fun games without having studied gamification or psychology in detail, then so can you.

I believe my primary qualification for explaining and teaching self-gamification is the enormous fun I have had turning my life into games; experiencing happiness multiple times every day while doing so; and never wishing to stop designing and playing my self-motivational and uplifting games.

6. My experience with self-gamification

My background as an experimental physicist probably led to me launching straight into experimenting with self-gamification, without researching the topic too much beforehand. In fact, I started consciously gamifying various projects, of which writing was the first, even before I had heard the word "gamification." I shared the writing game (which I learned from my writing teacher and best-selling author, Menna van Praag) and saw how it inspired others. A little later, I started calling an extended variant of the writing game the "5 Minute Perseverance Game" and published a little book with the title *5 Minute Perseverance Game: Play Daily for a Month and Become the Ultimate Procrastination Breaker*, about that experience. Inspired by board games, I structured the book as if it was a board game description.

Bit by bit I extended the game to other areas of my life and soon observed myself developing and practicing three skill sets, which I address in this book.

These skills are: observing myself non-judgmentally (as an anthropologist would); making small and effortless steps; and applying game design elements to appreciate the small steps in a fun way. I was and am today using these three skill sets together. I might be the first to claim that these skills are mutually supportive and can result in fantastic synergy when applied together.

Here is my experience in developing those skill sets. Towards the end of 2011, I learned about the work of award-winning authors and international seminar leaders Ariel and Shya Kane, who developed an anthropological approach to living in the moment. Inspired by their work, I practice being here and living in the moment, as well as the application to myself of what I call "anthropology of now"; in other words, I strive to see and study myself, the world around me, and my thought processes non-judgmentally. About three years later I began applying small steps to all medium and long-term activities without being aware of kaizen and the concepts behind it. I gamified the writing of a book for the first time at the start of 2014, in Spring 2016 I started conscious gamification of various projects and activities as well as sharing it, and since September 2017 I have been gamifying all areas of my life, both work and personal.

Almost three quarters of a year later (on May 31, 2018) I published my first online course on Udemy — one of the most popular platforms for online teaching and learning — titled *Motivate Yourself by Turning Your Life Into Fun Games: Practice Self-Gamification, a Unique Self-Help Approach Uniting Anthropology, Kaizen, and Gamification*. If you are reading this in e-book format, then you can find the link to it at the beginning (just before the introduction) and at the end of this book; in "More on Self-Gamification" and "Also by Victoria Ichizli-Bartels," correspondingly.

7. Why is this book unique?

One of the unique aspects of this book, but not the only one, is that it introduces a new term, "self-gamification," which means turning one's own life into a game.

Since I am not a gamer, the perspective of this book is different from other books on gamification. Most of the advanced and brilliant books on gamification are written by game designers who either are or were passionate gamers.

I am also not providing a new approach to gamification. I am not inventing something new. Instead, I bring three approaches together and show how their application can mutually support each other to help you live a fulfilled, happy, and fun life.

In addition to gamification (the application of game elements to everyday life), I will demonstrate how an anthropological approach to living in the moment and kaizen (the philosophy of continuous improvement by making small, effortless steps) make it possible to turn our lives into games that are sustainable and easy to maintain.

I will address each component of this combined approach I call "self-gamification," and their various aspects, in the subsequent sections of this book.

Self-Gamification Happiness Formula: How to Turn Your Life into Fun Games is also a self-help book. Because it suggests treating our lives as our favorite game, you could say that it is a gameful self-help book.

Another new aspect of the approach described here is that through continuous application of self-gamification to oneself, carrying out various projects and activities (whatever stage these projects and activities are at), as well as the management of these, becomes not only effortless but also immensely fun.

8. What might happen during and after you read this book?

Honing the three skill sets outlined in this book will equip you with the necessary tools to get back on your happy path, regain motivation if you feel like you lost it, bring fun to whatever you are up to, and be successful in what you do.

You will still have so-called "setbacks" and step away from your happy path, but you will discover that these setbacks become shorter and shorter with time and you will more easily return to your happy mode. Before I started turning my life into games I would procrastinate over things I wanted or needed to do for weeks, months or even years. Today, the longest I will delay something is a couple of days.

You will remain a normal human being with ambitions and dreams, continually looking for a way to progress with your plans and projects and, if possible, have fun in the process. The difference will be that after reading this book you might feel there are infinite possibilities for having fun in whatever you are up to.

You might find yourself trying out some or all of the self-motivational and uplifting games I have designed, as well as games of your own making, and through this start to enjoy the projects you have initially found daunting or annoying.

Besides which, you might find yourself recording your points and perhaps even sharing the self-motivational games with your family and friends, motivating them with tips and tricks, sharing jokes and celebrating the progress of both your projects and theirs.

You might discover that all it takes to stay happy, motivated, present and engaged is to be aware, to make small steps, and appreciate each of these steps as you would in a game by getting points, badges, treasures, or something else. The *Self-Gamification Happiness Formula: How to Turn Your Life into Fun Games* can help you with that.

By the end of this book you will observe yourself as an anthropologist would, identify your big goals and make small, effortless steps towards them, and design and continuously develop self-motivational games that engage you as a player. You will reduce the duration of the "low" periods in your life without trying to resist or change them. And you will start experiencing your life as if you were playing your favorite game.

9. Conventions used in this book
Chapter length

The standard copyright statement on the copyright page of this book states: "Every effort has been made to ensure that the content provided in this book is accurate and helpful."

For this reason the length of each chapter varies, since some topics required more attention than others. It didn't feel right to break them down into several chapters. This especially applies to chapters 12 and 15, which address the definition and design of self-motivational games and the practice of self-gamification. To make them more digestible, all chapters contain sections, which cover one or other specific aspects of the topics discussed in each chapter.

Examples

Since this book is primarily based on my experiences and the lessons I've learned while turning my life into games, many of the examples are of episodes from the life of a writer and entrepreneur. I have tried to include instances of gamifying as many areas of life as possible, but I hope you won't mind the examples about writing books (especially this book), articles, reports, blogs, social media posts and e-mails. I am sure you will be able to draw parallels from these to your own long and short term projects and activities.

Quotes

This book brings three widely known approaches together. Thus, it builds upon the wisdom accumulated by many amazing people over the years. I didn't want to paraphrase the beautiful pearls of wisdom, both from the authors of these approaches and other inspiring people, so I have quoted them directly at the beginning of each chapter (and even in Recommended Reading) as well as within sections of the book.

To keep the book readable, I haven't formatted the quotes as block quotes or emphasized them in any way. Instead, I have used quotation marks and indicated the source before or after the quote. Where there are several quotes listed one after another from the same source, then the latter is shown after the last quote.

This approach felt as though the quotes were part of a dialog that might have taken place between myself and the authors of the words. That is how I feel when I read these brilliant books — as if the authors are talking to me. I hope you will feel the same way and that you will join the conversations in this book by reading and doing the exercises (more on that below).

I made an exception for larger excerpts from my other books, articles, or posts. To avoid putting quotation marks around each paragraph, I made these visible by preceding the extracts with "(The beginning of the excerpt/comment/answer/blog post)" and succeeding with "(The end of the excerpt/comment/answer/blog post)."

Side-notes

There are fourteen side-notes in this book, which I added either for your enjoyment or for clarification purposes. I marked them in the following way:

[A side-note: This is the text of the side-note.]

In most cases, you will find the side-notes on a new line. There are two occurrences where a side-note appears within a bulleted item or a paragraph.

Things to draw your attention to

I tried to emphasize as little as possible in the text. I used *italic* where the emphasis was needed.

The only exceptions are the quotes at the beginning of each chapter and the self-gamification happiness formula, and its components, in chapter 4, section 5, charts/diagrams in chapter 9, section 1, as well as some sub-titles when they needed to be distinguished from the ones emphasized with italic. These appear as ***bold and italic***.

The *italic* emphasis was used to mark the titles of books I have quoted, section sub-headings, words I wished to enhance, and some statements that I wanted to draw your attention to when you browse the book.

Trademarks

As mentioned in the copyright, all trademarks and brands are used in this book for clarifying and reference purposes only. Instead of putting a trademark symbol after every occurrence of a trademarked name, I have capitalized them. Although the titles of my self-motivational game frameworks and some of the terms and tools I use also have initial capital letters, they are not trademarks. You will be able to recognize when I talk about a brand or when I talk about a game I have developed.

10. How to use this book

When reading the book for the first time, I suggest that you read it as you would a novel. That is from beginning to end.

And as you would with a novel, I recommend that you read it without taking the suggestions as strict instructions and instead observe yourself non-judgmentally while reading it, to see what resonates with you as you go along.

Since it is also a guidebook, I will provide questions for contemplation in many of the chapters and even activities to allow you to study your habits and thought processes non-judgmentally, explore the methods described, and try your hand (and head) at designing and playing self-motivational and uplifting games. The first activity is at the end of this introduction.

I would also like to suggest that you take short breaks between the sections in the chapters, or at least between the chapters, to allow yourself time to digest the information you have read. Give yourself time to become aware of and experience the epiphanies ignited here and observe how your state of mind and perception of the world transforms.

11. How this book is structured

Here is, for your convenience, a summary of what each part of the *Self-Gamification Happiness Formula: How to Turn Your Life into Fun Games* covers.

Self-Gamification Happiness Formula

Part I. Reasons, Examples, Definition, and Formula

In this part I share the reasons for turning our lives (including all its various projects and activities) into fun games.

I will demonstrate how any project or activity we commit to is a game (of sorts) already, because they contain all the basic components of a traditional game and can be designed in such a way as to make them engaging and fun.

I will also demonstrate how various projects and activities can be turned into games, and provide examples of different inspiring personalities approaching their lives gamefully and playfully. I will also share how I turned my life into games, starting with one activity until every area was covered by my newly-formed "self-gamer's" mind.

You will learn about self-gamification, the three skill sets it brings together, and the happiness formula attempting to quantify the success of practicing these three skill sets on their own and together.

Part II. Anthropology and Non-Judgmental Seeing

Here, you will start to see yourself non-judgmentally and become aware of how you subconsciously differentiate between various projects and activities through your behavior and in your thoughts.

Part III. Kaizen and the Small Steps

The chapters in this part of the book build upon the observations made in part II. Based on that, you will take a look at your goals and aspirations and learn how to identify the smallest and most effortless steps you can do right here, right now, toward your goals. And you will witness how by seemingly slowing down you will be accelerating your progress in comparison to how you handled your projects before.

Part IV. Self-Gamification in Design and Practice

This part is about designing your games with the help of the skills you have developed in the previous sections, that is based on your non-judgmental observations and identification of the smallest, most easily manageable steps towards your goals.

You will learn how to use fun as a tool and a parameter to measure the success of your self-motivational game designs, so that you come up with the best and most captivating games for yourself in any circumstances of your life.

I will also provide the lessons I have learned and tips to help you turn the above three skill sets into intentional habits for the various areas of your life. You will also discover different ways of sharing self-gamification with others.

Part V. Self-Gamification Framework Examples

The last part of the book is about three self-motivational game frameworks (including some of their possible tactical variants), which I have developed and played so far. In addition to the definition of the goals, rules, and feedback systems for these frameworks, you will also find photographs of my feedback systems, the template for a daily game plan, and examples of my scores for each of these frameworks, along with the lessons learned.

12. What are your expectations?

Now that you have had a glimpse of what this book is and is not about, what are your expectations of it? How do you expect to see yourself once you have finished the book and are in the process of turning your life (or parts of it) into games?

Use the lines below (or a notebook, if you are reading this on an e-reader) and a pen to jot down your expectations and visions:

_____
_____
_____
_____
_____
_____

Glossary and references:

* "Merriam Webster defines self-therapy, …, as follows: 'Therapeutic treatment of oneself especially for the purpose of coping with one's personal or emotional problems.'" (In addition to this definition of self-therapy, you can find ones for self-counseling and self-help therapy, and how they all relate to each other, here: https://positivepsychologyprogram.com/self-therapy-anxiety-depression/)

** https://en.wikipedia.org/wiki/Candid_Camera

Part I. Reasons, Examples, Definition, and Formula

Chapter 1. Why Turn Our Lives Into Games?

"Do not take life too seriously. You will never get out of it alive."
— Elbert Hubbard

1. Looking for happiness
Most of us want to live happy lives. Many people say that they play games because games make them happy. So why not turn every day of our lives into a fun game? By doing so, we might just turn every day into a happy one.

This answer might seem too simple. Thus, before looking into how we can turn our lives into games, let's explore why chores, projects, activities, free time, and any- and everything in our lives is worth turning into games.

When I asked myself why I think it makes sense to approach our lives as games, I reached the conclusion that the reasons are based on both the occasional discoveries, and the cumulative experiences I gathered while turning my life into games.

In the preface I mentioned one of the reasons: the fact that most successful people are successful and happy because they have fun in their lives and with what they do.

Yes, games are a great resource for fun. So it seems logical to learn from and be inspired by games to increase the engagement and fun factor of what we want or need to do.

Additionally, many successful companies bring numerous game elements* either into their products and services, their operational procedures, or both. If you think of progress bars, countdown timers, stars for reviews, you will immediately recognize those game elements, as well as the more obvious ones such as points, badges, leaderboards, treasures gathered, "lost lives," collected "energy" and others.

The above reasons might be a factor, but there's more to it.

2. We are not (or are less) afraid of games
If I look at what I want or have to do as a game, then the stakes are not that high, are they? It's just a

game, isn't it? So the drama, that seriousness I used to require in order to succeed, falls away. But if I add drama to what I do, then the stakes become enormous.

In most cases, the stakes are not high. Some projects or activities can be life-changing or even life-saving, but they don't have to carry the burden of either guilt (for not attending to them enough), or blame (that if it weren't for them, the people around you or specific circumstances, then you would be a better person or have a better life).

Furthermore, I found I was more at ease with fully engaging in a game than I would a real-life project. Yes, drama and seriousness might be one reason. But the limited length of a game is another. We are often more aware that games (or game rounds) end sooner rather than later, while we expect to "suffer" the real-life project for a more extended period.

Yes, being present, excellent (that is giving your best), and engaged seems to happen more easily in games. In games, especially in video games, you have only a limited time to make your next move. You need to assess the situation quickly and do so. Otherwise, the moment is gone. This is it! There is only one moment. If you are present and fully engaged you have a better chance of making a successful move and getting the next badge, treasure or more points. When you are playing, you don't discuss or complain about having to make a move.

Also, if you miss your moment in a game, and don't get the points, you just move on to the next one, without moaning. You become aware of the situation and move on. And if you do groan a little, then those complaints are often short and often uttered playfully, just adding to the fun. If not then the game is no longer fun, in which case you merely stop and leave it, and possibly return to it another time, when you get the "appetite" for the game again.

Imagine how much easier seeing, handling and engaging with your daily projects would become if you treated them like games?

Another reason is that when you view what you are doing as a game, you are less likely to forget what the goal is. The goal is always clear and visible in a game. In a real-life project, we often get lost in complaints and forget why we started doing something in the first place (see also chapter 12, section 7).

Beyond that, we are more willing to follow the rules in a game and to practice it to become better at it (chapter 12, section 8).

If you see your life, projects, and activities as games, which you design yourself, you realize that you have control. That by playing continuously and adjusting your game plan for each round, you can practice both the game design and playing it. So that moving from one level of the game to another ceases to feel like being pushed by life in the direction you think you don't want to take, and instead, you dive into the adventure of your life games by designing, playing, and enjoying them.

There is another reason which is by no means the least significant. Any game has a feedback system with one of various ways of keeping score. By giving yourself points, badges, magic treasures, or other non-material rewards for your efforts, you can document your progress for multiple projects in a fun way. By doing so, you will have a more reliable record of your achievements than your tired or fretful mind might otherwise suggest to you at the end of a long day. We will discuss feedback systems in more detail in chapter 12, section 9.

And here is probably the most beautiful byproduct of recording the score for each bit in a project we tackle. I discovered that by giving myself points, I take the time to appreciate what I have done (more on this in chapter 14, section 3). This helps me to slow down and not give in to the automatic urge to hurry forward, and instead become aware of what the next move should be in my games.

3. It's easier to wholeheartedly commit in games

"Life is not a game," we often hear. "You have to be serious when you want to achieve or be good at something."

But what is this "seriousness" needed to achieve something? Is it really the concentration and full engagement we need in order to make progress and be successful in a project? Or is this seriousness in fact the drama, the complaint we express before actually doing something, so that we can prove to others that we are "serious" about that thing?

Athletes in Ninja Warrior or Olympic games are brought to mind now. I remember many interviews in which journalists ask famous athletes about the effort and dedication they have to invest. And in many cases it is not the effort, or seriousness, that they describe. I don't recall any drama in their accounts. Any reference to hardship is usually met with a shrug. Yes, they express dedication, but there is often that phrase, "This is what I love doing. It's fun."

Have you noticed that in games, you enjoy the challenges the games pose, you don't really think of them as an effort or a hardship, and you just give your best to achieve the next level?

You are in the moment and concentrate on achieving that level, to get that treasure.

And you give your best in games. It is much easier to do so in games. Again, less dramatic, less at stake.

We are less afraid to fail in games than in real-life activities. Studies show that we are more willing to try again and again, to practice in games, and even work harder than in real-life studies or for work.

Jane McGonigal, one of the most well-known gamification advocates and game designers, has addressed this particular characteristic of games in detail.

In her acclaimed book *Reality Is Broken: Why Games Make Us Better and How They Can Change the World*, McGonigal quoted the playwright Noël Coward, who said, "Work is more fun than fun."

She supported this statement by referring to a psychological research method known as the experience sampling method (ESM), which concentrates on finding out "how we really feel during different parts of our day."

These studies show that the widely agreed relaxing or indulging activities, such as eating sweets, watching a movie, or just doing nothing, don't improve our mood as much as we might expect. On the other hand, events that challenge us, where we see the task as doable, do bring about happiness.

Jane calls this kind of work "hard fun."

She says, "Hard fun leaves us feeling measurably better than when we started [playing, added by the author]. So it's no surprise, then that one of the activities from which ESM subjects report the highest levels of interest and positive moods both during and afterward is when they're playing games — including sports, card games, board games, and computer and video games. The research proves what gamers already know: within the limits of our own endurance, we would rather work hard than be entertained. Perhaps that's why gamers spend less time watching television than anyone else on the planet." — Jane McGonigal, *Reality Is Broken: Why Games Make Us Better and How They Can Change the World*

This fun, hard work might be one of the reasons that bringing game elements into education and the work environment is so popular nowadays. When he was in first grade my son would get a glittery or brightly-colored sticker for more than 100 minutes of reading at home a week (either with us parents or by himself). Or if he and his school friends behaved well without disturbing the lesson for a certain length of time (over several weeks), they got a pure-play-hour during the lecture time and were allowed to bring a toy from home for this hour.

Studies of classrooms with older students also show the use of more and more game elements than the simple taking of notes, memorizing, and repetition that were once the norm. The same can be said of work environments. I have seen adult employees smile brightly after being given a glittery sticker on a postcard by their employers, testifying their excellent work. And you have probably tried to win a book or a trip or a weekend at a hotel or a free dessert from a physical or online shop or service. You might also have an app on your smartphone or a voucher for your favorite coffee shop (I have both for two different shops). You get a stamp or sticker on the voucher card or a specific mark in the app for each coffee, tea or other drink of your preference. When you collect a certain amount of these stamps or marks, you get a free drink.

So if our professors, employers, shops, restaurants, and other companies use game design elements and principles to increase our motivation to learn, work, or buy something, why don't we do similar things with ourselves?

If we want to be in control of our lives, why do we still talk about the necessity of working hard to learn or achieve something, when studies on games, and experiences in education and in the workplace show the opposite?

The answer is simple. We grew up in cultures that taught us that hard work comes first and fun second, that we should put ourselves and our well-being on the back-burner and first achieve something "meaningful" in life.

Only recently with the spread of the urge to be aware, present and mindful, do we hear more and more often, "Be kind to yourself."

Turning our lives into fun games is the next natural and logical step from being kind to ourselves. Wouldn't we think of a sweet and engaging game to uplift the mood of a sulking child? Why not treat ourselves as we do the children we love and care for? (See also chapter 15, section 25.)

4. It's easier to handle upsets in a game

Mindfulness and being in the moment raise the question of positivity. I've come across several articles on social media, in the press, and online discussing false positivity**. The concern is that there is a tendency to turn everything into a positive and that we might suppress negative feelings, which have their reasons for cropping up.

I can understand this concern. Denying or suppressing an upset doesn't make it go away. Doing so can, in fact, make it grow stronger and lead to an ex- or implosion of emotions, if fought for too long.

Self-gamification has nothing to do with false positivity or an attempt to avoid unwanted feelings.

Just consider, do you avoid your feelings in games? Do you not get angry if something doesn't go your way in a game? You do.

The clue here is that you don't stay upset for too long. If you do, then you stop playing the game. To continue playing you need to put your upset aside and focus your attention on the next move in the game. Or to another game.

Again, imagine how much easier real-life projects can become if you proceed with them in the same way. Acknowledge the upset and move on.

So, I would like to invite you to become inspired by games. In those you don't dwell on bumping a car into a wall if you want to continue playing that game. Instead, you notice what happened, turn the car around, and carry on. We can do the same in our life games.

5. It's easier to be less judgmental toward ourselves

When I started sharing the self-gamification approach with others, some people told me that I was tricking my mind. My immediate answer was a cheerful "Yes."

Only in retrospect did I consider that the statement about tricking my mind could be seen as an accusation of being dishonest with my brain, or in other words being dishonest with myself. That I hadn't solved or overcome my procrastination, but had tricked my mind into doing what I wanted to do.

After contemplating this possible argument, I had to agree with some of these statements.

No, I hadn't overcome my procrastination and probably never would. And yes, by playing my self-motivational games and giving myself, for example, a daily point for each step in each project of the game, I was tricking my mind into forgetting or bypassing fretful thoughts and into fulfilling what I wanted and had to do. Moreover, I tricked it into doing this step-by-step, with less drama around each task and with more fun.

Was I being dishonest with myself when I did so? I don't believe so. I was more and more willing to look honestly at my thought processes. And I was able to see them with humor and not to judge myself for what I was seeing.

Besides which, my increased motivation and an increasingly positive attitude provided arguments in favor of such a "cheating-the-brain" game. But let us for a moment consider who is who in this game.

What is the difference between me and my brain? Is there any?

Ariel and Shya Kane wrote the following in their acclaimed book *Practical Enlightenment*:

"If you want to be clear about what is a thought and what is 'you,' it's simple. Any sentence that you say to yourself containing the word 'I' is a thought:

"I like / I don't like
I don't understand
I can't
I want
I won't
I am

"Most people think that they are their thoughts. They believe that the voice they listen to, the voice that speaks to them about how they are doing, about how life is showing up, what they want or don't want, is really them. They don't think that they are listening to some disembodied commentary, one that is sometimes accurate and sometimes not."

Later in the same chapter, the Kanes wrote the following eye-opening and enlightening words:

"You are not your voice. *You have a voice. And when you can make the distinction between the one who listens and the voice, you get control over the mechanical nature of life.*" — Ariel and Shya Kane, *Practical Enlightenment*

This means that anything concerning how I was doing or who I was, were thoughts produced by my brain.

Then what about my heart's desires? What were those visions I longed for and which drew my attention, left me sleepless at night, and eager to achieve those visions in the mornings? Who or what produced them?

A well-known American brain researcher, Jill Bolte Taylor, who experienced a stroke and shared her experiences shortly before, during and afterwards in her acclaimed book *My Stroke of Insight: A Brain Scientist's Personal Journey*, wrote the following intriguing words in this respect:

"Many of us speak about how our head (left hemisphere) is telling us to do one thing while our heart (right hemisphere) is telling us to do the exact opposite. Some of us distinguish between what we think (left hemisphere) and what we feel (right hemisphere)."

And a little before that in the same paragraph she wrote,

"It appears that many of us struggle regularly with polar opposite characters holding court inside our heads. In fact, just about everyone I speak with is keenly aware that they have conflicting parts of their personality." — Jill Bolte Taylor, *My Stroke of Insight: A Brain Scientist's Personal Journey*

This means that everything produced inside me, either thoughts or feelings, whether they appear in my head or my heart or anywhere else in my body, either creative and uplifting or depressive and dragging, are all produced by my brain. By different parts of it, but still by the same physical entity of my human body.

So, it was my brain that was doing all the struggling, and waging all the wars in my head!

As I became aware of that, I had an idea.

We all learned about the ancient Olympic Games at school, and the idea behind them. We've heard that all wars and conflicts were stopped so that the opponents could step into peaceful competition within the framework of the Olympic games. They got points, scores, and laurels.

So, I thought, if creativity was fighting a battle with fear in my head, why not let them put their war aside and organize games for them instead. Why not give each of them points as they progress, as well as laurels and applauds for the winner of each round and praise for the other half who gave her best but lost?

Yes, why not? In doing so, I showed respect to both opponents in my head, the one driving forward and the one hitting the breaks. I showed them this regard by organizing "Olympic" games for them. And not only for a short time, but again and again. Beyond that, I varied the types of games to keep them going and having fun, and me along with them.

The results of these "brainy Olympic Games" were brilliant. If war erupted again between the competitors in my head for any reason, then it didn't last long, because these wars were not fun at all, while playing games was.

6. Any project is already a game

And now let's consider probably the most surprising reason that it makes sense to turn our lives into games.

But first the simple truth about turning our lives into games:

To turn our projects and activities into games, we need to see them as games. Otherwise, how can we "play" something if we don't call it a game?

Real-life projects are rarely considered to be games even if we do sometimes use metaphors like "it's a tough game" or similar.

I hadn't seen the parallels clearly between what I was doing at home or work and games until I read the following definition by Jane McGonigal, even if I was turning my life into games by that time:

"What defines a game are the goal, the rules, the feedback system, and voluntary participation. Everything else is an effort to reinforce and enhance these four core components." — Jane McGonigal, *Reality Is Broken: Why Games Make Us Better and How They Can Change the World*

So let's repeat this quote and put this into bullet points. The primary components of a game are:
1. The goal,
2. The rules,
3. The feedback system,
4. Voluntary participation.

I am a business owner, so after reading this, I could immediately see parallels between the projects I was working on for my customers, and games. A contract or an agreement, which my customer and I both sign, contains all four of these components. Each project has a goal, there are specific rules, like how I shall do it and by when. There is a reporting and evaluation system in each contract, which is indeed a feedback system even if the progress is not recorded by getting points or badges. And finally, when my client and I sign the contract and make an agreement, we both demonstrate the free will to participate in that project's "game."

The same applies to job contracts which lead to your job "games," with their goals, rules, feedback system (the regular meetings you most likely have with your boss, before or after which you and your employer provide some kind of evaluation of each other), and both sides demonstrating the voluntary participation by signing the employment contract.

Other activities, like sports to stay in shape, also have all four components. The goal could be to live a healthy life. The rules are then the allocation of time you commit to it, the feedback system might be your step counter or an app where you record your workout results every day. Some people take on thirty, one hundred or another amount of days challenges and have social media as their feedback system. Each post recounting a successful workout session is cheered about by their friends and followers.

Voluntary participation might be difficult to see in such cases when we think we don't want to do sports or to develop other healthy habits, but if we end up working out or doing yoga without someone forcing us, then that is still voluntary participation.

So any project or activity is already a game. We just rarely see them that way.

Here is a brilliant quote confirming this, by one of the most respected experts in gamification:

"Work is actually very similar to play and even more like games. The main difference is perception." — Andrzej Marczewski, *Even Ninja Monkeys Like to Play: Unicorn Edition*

In that case, if a game can be designed to bring fun and happiness to its players, can't then any project or activity be re-designed to make them both fun and successful? Yes, they can.

Moreover, as both their designer and player, who is better placed than you to make them fun and engaging?

I'll address the reasons discussed above again throughout this book, and go into more detail on how to tackle each of these aspects when you turn your life into games. But first I have a few questions for you.

7. What would be your reason for turning your life into games?

Now it's your turn. Take a minute and contemplate what your reasons would be for turning your life into games. Are they the same as the ones discussed above, or are they something else?

Use the lines below (or a notebook, if you are reading this on an e-reader) and a pen to record your reasons and other related thoughts:

_____
_____
_____
_____
_____
_____

Glossary and references:
* "*Game Elements/Components:* These are bits that are taken from games, such as progress bars, missions, points, badges etc." — Andrzej Marczewski, *Even Ninja Monkeys Like to Play: Unicorn Edition*
** For instance: http://positivefabulouswomen.com/say-no-to-false-positivity/

Chapter 2. What Can Be Turned into Games?

"She made the most of a mundane situation. She turned misery into fun."
— Ian Bogost, *Play Anything: The pleasure of limits, the uses of boredom, & the secret of games*

1. What to turn into games

I have been asked many times what can be turned into games and what cannot. There were times when I thought that my personal life, such as for example spending time with my husband and children, would be unethical to see as a game.

My answer today, the hint of which you might have seen in the previous chapter is:

You can turn anything into a game.

I am not alone in this opinion. The gamification specialist and award-winning game designer Dr. Ian Bogost wrote a book with the following title, *Play Anything: The Pleasure of Limits, the Uses of Boredom, and the Secret of Games*. He claims that you can "play anything" if you add rules (that is limits) to how you can perform the task. These limits can often be uncomfortable and not obvious, like brushing your teeth holding the brush with your left hand if you are a right-handed person, walking only on the lines of the plaster on the sidewalk or similar. In chapter 12, section 8, we will address the aspect of rules in self-motivational games, and also how defining them makes games and real-life projects and activities more exciting and fun.

Yes, you can turn anything into a game. Both at work and at home. Also when it comes to taking care of your loved ones. I observed that I don't play with my children to gain more points in my self-motivational games. I just enjoy playing with my children. But at the end of the day, I sit down with my notepad and record the points. Recording the points helps me to become aware that I do take care of my children, that I play with them and pay attention to them, that I spend time with my husband and value it. By turning my life into a game and applying metrics to my actions, I become more aware, mindful of, and responsible (without guilt) for what happens in my life and what I do with that.

There is another aspect to what we can or maybe should gamify (turn into games). I discovered that most satisfaction comes when I turn those tasks into games that appear tricky and tough. A task seems tough and overwhelming when I resist it. Turning those tough tasks into enjoyable and fun activities helps me melt my procrastination and increase my desire to "play" them. That is the actual fun of self-gamification.

2. Possible self-gamification examples

Without realizing it I'll bet that you encounter gamification (bringing game design elements into real-life contexts) on a fairly regular basis. You gave five stars to one product and only one to another, while posting a customer review on an online shop's site; you invested a little more time than planned to gain a higher percentage on the progress bar of your profile on a professional network.

There are also many examples of self-gamification, however new the term might be. And you might have already subconsciously turned parts of your life into games too.

Today, I realized that before I gamified my writing, I already gamified or brought playful elements into everyday tasks and chores. I danced and sang while cleaning, played a memory game while matching clean and dry socks from the rest of the laundry. Before and after I had heard the word "gamification" I read stories of other experiences of turning one's life into a game, without realizing that this was indeed what was occurring.

Sportsmen gamify their lives, and not only those who train and take part in the Olympics and other high-profile games. Weight Watchers and similar programs employ gamification too. All the metrics in these — including the number of calories you consume — are the score, the feedback systems, utilized in games.

In the next four sections of this chapter, I share the results of my search for examples that come close to what I mean by "self-gamification." That is, examples of how people consciously treat their lives, and its challenges, in playful and gameful ways.

I have divided these examples into four groups:
- Gamifying big challenges,
- Turning self-learning into games,
- Big "silly" quests that turn into life lessons,
- Approaching life (especially "work") playfully.
- Just a reminder, when I was looking for examples of self-gamification I was looking for both designers and players of their games.

Other criteria were that these persons showed signs of possessing and practicing the three skills:
1. Being aware and non-judgmental towards themselves and others (demonstrated by their compassion),
2. Taking small steps towards their goals (based on the time they invested in achieving those

goals and the multidimensionality of what they were doing), and
3. Bringing game-like, playful, or humorous elements into their lives (their humor and playfulness speak for themselves).

3. Gamifying big challenges

People in critical situations often find power in not taking their circumstances too seriously and finding uplifting solutions instead.

Jane McGonigal, the game designer and gamification pioneer, who was "the first to earn a Ph.D. studying the psychological strengths of games and how those strengths can translate to real-world problem solving," and whom I quote often in this book, used gamification during her recovery from a severe concussion. As with many patients who've suffered a brain injury, she struggled with its consequences.

Then "thirty-four days after I hit my head — and I will never forget this moment — I said to myself, *I am either going to kill myself, or I'm going to turn this into a game.*"

So she created a game, she later called *SuperBetter*, where she took on the *secret identity* of "Jane, the Concussion Slayer." Her sister and her husband became her *allies*. Everything she needed to avoid, such as bright light and crowded spaces became *bad guys,* and anything that was helping her, like cuddling her dog or eating walnuts or going for a walk with her husband, were her *power-ups**.

In her acclaimed book *SuperBetter: How a Gameful Life Can Make You Stronger, Happier, Braver and More Resilient*, Jane McGonigal wrote, "The game was that simple: adopt a secret identity, recruit allies, battle the bad guys, and activate power-ups. But even with a game so simple, within just a couple days of starting to play, that fog of depression and anxiety went away. It just vanished. It felt like a miracle to me. It wasn't a miracle cure for the headaches or the cognitive symptoms — they lasted more than a year, and it was the hardest year of my life by far. But even when I still had the symptoms, even while I was still in pain, *I stopped suffering*. I felt more in control of my own destiny. My friends and family knew exactly how to help and support me. And I started to see myself as a much stronger person."

After her recovery, she created a framework and an app with the same name *SuperBetter***. Her system has helped many people to overcome little and significant challenges and to do so in a much lighter and more gameful way than they would have managed otherwise.

4. Turning self-learning into games

Other examples of self-gamification are set by gamification pioneers who research this relatively new science and create frameworks and resources for themselves and others to grasp. One of the most prominent is Yu-kai Chou, who created a framework to study gamification called Octalysis. He uses it himself, and if you watch videos of him presenting it, you will not doubt his deep passion for it. The Octalysis framework is based on thorough psychological research and years of game design and game playing by its originator. And at the same time, it is a game.

There is another game and gamification designer who researches, works and creates knowledge on gamification, which I am sure he uses himself. This is Zac Fitz-Walter, who earned one of the world's first PhDs in gamification design. He created GamificationGeek.com where he offers, among other resources, a free book with four chapters on gamification, he calls *quests*. Through his work and blog posts, you see that he uses those resources too.

I have also seen other gamification designers developing their websites as virtual reality worlds where you get information by traveling within them. They enjoy making those worlds grow by developing them, and themselves, further. Where is the distinction between the game and their work on these websites? The border is not clear to me.

5. Big "silly" quests that turn into life lessons

Another possibility for gamifying your life is to embark on a journey that might seem silly. There are two authors I enjoy reading, who did just that.

First is Tony Hawks, a British comedian who started by hitching around Ireland with a fridge. Then a couple of years later he continued by playing tennis against all eleven national soccer players from the country I come from, the Republic of Moldova (my homesickness helped me to discover him and his books), then went to Albania in an attempt to land a top twenty musical hit. And all of these were the result of bets with his friends in a pub or at a party.

During those adventures, Tony gathered many lessons that changed his life. He learned how to be more humble while at the same time being more humorous in life, not taking himself too seriously, appreciating people and the world around him more, and increasing his sense of compassion. Particularly dear to me is what he did following his adventure in Moldova:

"In August 2000 we opened The Hippocrates Children's Centre (now called The Tony Hawks Centre), run by Diana Covalciuc, the doctor with whom I'd lodged during my Moldovan sojourn."***

Another author who turned his life into an experiment — and wrote a book about it: *My Life as an Experiment* — is A.J. Jacobs****. He is a journalist and author who read the whole *Encyclopaedia Britannica*, lived a year following the rules of the Old Testament, and has taken on many other fun quests, such as for example the meaningful approach of uni-tasking, observing himself and the world around him (including his wife's reactions) in the process. He still practices many of the habits he picked up during these quests, and I expect he will continue to discover more.

6. Approaching life playfully

Then there are of course the successful people who treat themselves and their lives very playfully.

The first person I would like to mention and quote is Heidi Klum, a German-American supermodel, and television personality, and one of the four judges on *America's Got Talent* (AGT) between 2013 and early 2019.

After the results show of the AGT 2017 finals, a reporter asked Heidi what advice she would give to the winner, Darcy Lynn, a twelve-year-old ventriloquist. Without hesitating, Heidi answered, "Always to have fun. If you don't have fun, it shows in your performance. That is always the key number one."

And fun is evident in all the projects Heidi initiates, produces and participates in. It is true of the reality shows she produces and hosts in Germany and the USA, and also of her intricate, sophisticated and always surprising Halloween costumes. Seeing her in those costumes***** generates the thought, "Her life must be a fun game."

The same applies to Tom Jones, who can't stop producing more and more brilliant music, and who said to Graham Norton on May 18, 2012, as they talked about Tom's thirty-eighth studio album, that he "hasn't worked since 1962." Since that show and to the present day he has produced another two studio albums.

I can also see Whoopi Goldberg "falling into this category." In her current job as a co-host of *The View* — an ABC morning show that discusses various events of the day — she is both passionate and compassionate, as well as whimsical, with her fun footwear that she sometimes lets her fans choose for her.

What do all these people have in common? These and many other brilliant people unfailingly inspire me to live my life in a gameful and playful way and to share this possibility with others.

I am sure they all view themselves and others (at least sometimes) non-judgmentally, that they move toward set goals by taking small steps at a time, and enjoy the ride by not taking themselves and others too seriously.

7. Now, take a look at those you admire

Think of one or more successful people you admire and answer the following questions with a "Yes," "No," or "I don't know:"

The name of the person(s):
_____

1. Do they have fun with what they do? _____
2. Are they passionate about it? _____
3. Do you think they are compassionate to themselves? _____
4. Do you think they are compassionate to others? _____
5. Do they do what they do to serve others? _____
6. Do you think of them as being non-judgmental in general? _____
7. Do you think they are both kind to and honest with themselves? _____
8. Do you think they are fully present and engaged in whatever they do, including the interviews they are giving? _____

9. Do you think they managed to be masters in what they are successful at by making small but steady steps? _____

10. Do you think they approached at least something in a playful way? What was that?_____
_____
_____

Did you answer five or more questions with a "Yes"? Then the person you admire practices non-judgmental seeing of themselves and the world around them, making progress with small steps, and being humorous and gameful while they do those steps, often deliberately honing these three skill sets, even if they might not have heard of any of the approaches brought together by self-gamification.

Glossary and references:
* A power-up is "(in a video game) a bonus which a player can collect and which gives their character an advantage such as more strength or firepower." — https://en.oxforddictionaries.com/definition/power-up
** https://janemcgonigal.com/ and https://www.superbetter.com/
*** http://www.tony-hawks.com/index.php
**** http://ajjacobs.com/

*****   http://www.vogue.co.uk/gallery/heidi-klum-halloween-costumes

Chapter 3. From a Project to a Whole Life

"Life can be easy and will support you if you let it."
— Ariel and Shya Kane, *Being Here…Too*

1. How I started turning my life into games
Today, I gamify my life and help others turn their lives into fun games. But it wasn't planned. It happened more or less by itself.

The very first part of my life that I gamified — even before I knew what gamification meant — was writing*.

Being an avid reader, I started to wonder if I could write something interesting too. I started diving into books and blogs about the craft of writing, and I found out what many aspiring writers hear when they begin their adventure: that writing is a difficult job. I would certainly agree with that. Undoubtedly, writing a book is not a one-day assignment. It takes weeks, months, or even years.

That is why at first I decided to write short pieces and share them on my blog.

But there was a story inside me that wanted to be told. One that couldn't be told in just a short blog post. It needed an entire book. And being dear to my heart – it was the story of my late father trying to locate the family he lost during World War II – the story kept reminding me that I needed to tell it.

So, like many people before me, I realized I wanted to write that book with my whole heart. And like so many others too, I felt I didn't have the time to do it.

What was I to do?

I decided I would start writing it without putting any pressure on myself to finish it. I would just test out how it felt to write, and see where it might lead.

I wrote a few chapters, then shared them with a friend and my niece. They loved what they read. But then I stopped writing the story. Reasons for it were plenty, and all the typical culprits. Full-time job, a family with a small child, voluntary work, the story being too sad, and my telling of the story too slow, thinking it wasn't good enough, etc., etc.

Joining a writing course with my dear friend and best-selling author Menna van Praag helped to boost my energy for writing again. Every month for about a year I sent her three pages of the story and then got her feedback both in written form and on the phone during a one-hour telephone seminar, together with her other students.

Just a few months into the course, and particularly in between the monthly phone calls, my writing energy would ebb again. My fellow students and I complained to Menna that we just couldn't find the time to write, so Menna suggested playing a game. She proposed that each of us write for just a few minutes a day for a month, and share our experiences in the Facebook group created by one of the students.

It was a fantastic experience. We cheered each other through the process, and my writing just flew. Sometimes I only wrote for five minutes or less, but still, it was progressing. In the subsequent months, I forgot about the game, but I continued to write.

2. Sharing the writing game with others

In 2015, even with two small children, I managed to finish my first book: revising it, having it professionally edited, and then publishing it. Doing all of it in small steps between taking care of my family, maintaining a household, and blogging.

At the end of that year, I published another book. Shortly before that, I joined a writers' club in Aalborg, Denmark, where I live. At that time I was already working on several writing projects in parallel, continuing the voluntary work in a technical community, moved to a new house with my family, and had started a business. At some point, my fellow writers in the writers' club asked me how I managed to pursue so many projects in parallel, along with taking care of a business and a family with two small children.

As I was contemplating how to summarize and explain how I did it, I recalled the game introduced to me by Menna. So, I suggested that my friends give it a go. I organized a Facebook group called "Procrastination Breakers Club" where we played this game with rounds going for one month.

The rules of the game were straightforward. We had to introduce the project we wanted to take into the game. It didn't have to be writing; it could be learning a language, practicing a musical instrument, planning a big event, such as a wedding, working out, renovating a house, or anything else that we wanted or had to do but didn't think we had time for. Then we had to pursue the project for at least five minutes a day. If we did it, we earned a point. If we didn't, then we lost the point to our procrastinating selves. And if we persevered for less than five minutes, we got half a point with the other half going to the procrastinating part of ourselves (read more on this game in chapter 12, section 8 and chapter 18).

At the end of the month we counted up our points, and if it was a writing project we also counted the words we had written.

That first round of the game I moderated for the Procrastination Breakers' Club was one of the most significant revelations in my life as a writer. In that month I wrote more than six thousand words, by writing for five minutes a day, sometimes more (but never longer than twenty minutes) and sometimes less. Six thousand! If I continued to write the book at the same pace, I would have a full manuscript within a year. By writing for only five minutes a day!

Many traditionally published authors sign contracts with publishers where they commit to writing one book a year. So, by writing in small chunks every day, I would be able to write a manuscript a year and manage such terms too.

That was one of the most beautiful discoveries for me as a writer.

I didn't proceed with that book further but finished writing and published several other books of various length that year and in the years after.

And another marvelous thing happened. During one of the rounds of our game, a writer friend wrote me a personal message on Facebook. She told me that a sentence I often like quoting and which I mentioned at the writers' panel we both attended helped her to break her writer's block. She was late with sending a book manuscript to her publisher, and it seemed unlikely that she would manage to get it done. The sentence she referred to was: "You can't edit an empty page." (See also chapter 15, section 4.)

I was delighted when she shared this experience with me, and I invited her to play the game with us. She accepted the invitation.

She commented on the page of our group that the game was helping her, and she expressed her surprise with much color and enthusiasm. Sometime later she posted a message with multiple exclamation marks announcing that she had finished the manuscript and sent it to her publisher.

This author's name is Sasha Christensen, and she is an award-winning Young Adult fantasy author in Denmark. She allowed me to quote her and even suggested that I put the cover of her book (the one she'd been struggling to finish) on my website. Before sending the picture, she wrote, "This [book] is the one you helped break my block on, btw ;)."

Seeing the effect the game could have, and how much fun could come of it, I decided to dedicate a little book to it, which, as described in the introduction, I named *5 Minute Perseverance Game: Play Daily for a Month and Become the Ultimate Procrastination Breaker.* The board game I got from my husband as a gift for Christmas the previous year inspired me to structure this little book as if it were the description for such a game. Writing this little book was a unique and fun experience in itself.

3. Gamifying other areas of my life

The writing of *5 Minute Perseverance Game: Play Daily for a Month and Become the Ultimate Procrastination Breaker* became a game too. It was one of the projects I took into a game-round and regularly reported on to the Procrastination Breakers' Club I mentioned in the previous section.

At some point, I started taking other projects into the game and reporting on them too.

In May 2016, I took on a project that I thought would be annoying to finish. "I am going to prepare my novelette *Nothing Is As It Seems* for publishing," I wrote in the comments to that month's game-round.

I had the idea that formatting and preparing a book for publication was complicated and tedious. I wanted to have finished it already, so each step in doing so was an effort. And since the 5 Minute Perseverance Game had previously helped me to combat my procrastination, I took this into the game too.

With time I forgot that the project was not supposed to be fun. Here is what I wrote on the last day of the May 2016 round, May 31: "I've spent more than 5 minutes [on the project] today. I guess I was caught up in the fun. This process of formatting was probably the most relaxing of all four paperbacks I have formatted [so far]. I love this game. I now even have a game book on 'playing' other projects."

So, the project I expected to dislike became fun. I even "got caught up in the fun."

This was my first time experiencing the possibility of an activity I thought was tedious (and that there was no way I would like it) becoming fun.

Another memorable project that I initially thought of as unwanted, was applying for new passports. In the past three years of self-gamification, I have had to do so three times: the renewal of my son's and my own passports, and obtaining the first one for my daughter.

Fortunately, I turned the project into a game with the first one, for my son. It was also after I had discovered kaizen, so I didn't spend five minutes on the project, but did just one little thing towards it each day. On the first day, I searched for links that provided the rules on getting a new passport. On the next day, I read through the rules and made notes about which documents I needed to prepare. On the following day, I prepared one document or filled in the first page (or part) of the form. And so on. Each time I gave myself a point.

On one of the days of preparing the documents, I discovered myself taking on this project before the others. It became so straightforward to do just one step of it at a time (and fun to earn the point), that I started looking forward to attending to it. By the time I applied for the third passport and went to the German embassy to give them the documents, I even found myself enjoying the conversation with the official there. We discovered that we both used to live in Bonn and enjoyed each other's company through the process of filling in more of the documents, copying, and other parts of the standard procedure.

Through all that, I discovered that my little perseverance game not only helped me make time for and progress with the projects I liked but couldn't find the time for previously, but it also ignited fun for the tasks I thought I didn't like.

4. Turning project management into games
I will provide more examples of turning life into games throughout the book, more so in part IV (specifically chapters 15 and 16). But here I would like to address one more activity, which I discovered accidentally, and which I used to hate prior to the birth of self-gamification.

Sometime after publishing the *5 Minute Perseverance Game: Play Daily for a Month and Become the Ultimate Procrastination Breaker* and while sharing the game with other people, a friend told me, "Oh, there is a well-known term for what you do. It's called gamification. We learned about it in college."

"Gamification? I have never heard of it," I answered. As soon as I was back at my computer that day, I started researching it. I discovered that this was the method of bringing games and a game-design approach into non-game areas of our lives, for example, work.

So, I started researching to see what areas have been gamified in the world. I was awestruck by the area of research, of its broadness, and also potential.

A little later, I read about kaizen – the technique by which large goals are achieved through the taking of smaller steps and breaking down of more significant problems into smaller and less terrifying ones. Or in other words by breaking down substantial challenges into smaller ones, without posing obstacles for our brains to overcome.

"So," I told myself then, "This is what I am doing with my 5 Minute Perseverance Game: I am gamifying various projects and activities, and applying kaizen. In other words, I make progress in my projects by taking tiny steps and by gathering points."

There was something else too. When I started consciously applying kaizen and gamification to my life, I had already been practicing living in the moment for five years. Inspired by the work of Ariel and Shya Kane, I had learned to observe myself non-judgmentally, as if I was an anthropologist studying myself as a culture of one person. There will be more on this in chapter 5.

Based on these non-judgmental observations, I started designing monthly rounds of my project games. Inspired by the occasional invitations from friends to play Candy Crush Saga, I started lovingly calling this planning game in my thoughts "Project Crush." (Today I call this game "Project ('Crush') Management Game," see chapter 19.) I sat down at the end of each month and planned which projects I would take into the next month's game, how many points I would give for each small step in every project, whether there would be limits or bonus points and how many, etc. I loved (and still do) these creative sessions, and looked forward to the end of each month when I would adjust the design of my self-motivational games, and the beginning of each month when I could test them out and adjust them if necessary.

As each monthly round progressed, I found myself taking notes about what I wanted to improve for the next round. For example, in September 2017,

I made a note, "Next month bonus for all areas —> 10 points." By that I meant that if I managed to attend to all project areas I had planned for that month, on any given day, then I would get ten bonus points instead of the previously allotted two points. You can read more on this in chapter 12, section 9. Later, these game design sessions took place each week, due to the reduction of the game rounds from a month to a week long. Now my game rounds are a day long, and when I get the idea for a design adjustment I test it either the next day, or the same day, if I've had the new idea in the morning.

I also recorded points for each accomplished task, then each morning took a look at how many points I had gathered in total the previous day, and for the various areas of my life. I did the same on a weekly and monthly basis. This analysis, along with the feelings and thought processes I observed along the way, gave me an idea of how balanced my life had been in the past month, and whether I felt the same way as the scores would suggest.

At some point, after designing many monthly rounds of my game, I discovered something astonishing: the game design I had been doing at first once a month, and then on a weekly and daily basis, and which I was enjoying so much, was nothing less than project and time management, and… it was fun!

That was yet another activity I used to think I hated, which now having turned it into a game, I loved. I'd always despised project and time management activities, thinking of them as difficult chores: jotting down to-do lists, making priority lists, and recording progress. Now I was enjoying recording them, measuring progress in points, and always eager to score more. If the steps were too big or overwhelming, I made them smaller, and I caught myself smiling broadly whenever I recorded a score for each of them.

My life had become a fun game.

And I didn't want to stop playing it.

5. What examples of playfulness and gamefulness are there in your life?

Before we continue, I would like you to pause here and contemplate a little.

You may not have intentionally gamified your life or some parts of it, but you are sure to have done so subconsciously. Or perhaps you have done so on purpose, but without considering it to be an application of game design elements to your life.

I don't only mean playfulness here, such as when you dance while cleaning or tidying up, or turn a piece of vegetable on a fork into a rocket to entice your baby to eat it.

Take a look at whether you ever set a timer for a task and tried to accomplish it within that time; whether you have rewarded yourself or your children with small pieces of chocolate, self-made stars, tablet or computer play time or small change, for doing some household chore.

But yes, also think about playfulness in your life. Become aware of it.

Here are some of my examples of self-gamification, to give you more clues as to what to look for here.

Some time ago, I faced the challenge of motivating my then three-year-old daughter to leave the house and go to kindergarten. So my children and I had a competition every morning for several months as we were heading out. We ran from the living room door through the dining area in our kitchen to the entrance area. Surprisingly, after almost a hundred of these races, I didn't win, even once. Now we rarely have the race, but motivating them to leave the house in time is no longer a challenge.

Another example is that I put on music and dance while cooking, doing dishes, or tidying and cleaning my house. I was tired of my thought processes complaining about cleaning the house or other household "chores," and simply wanted to have a good time, whatever I was up to. The choice to take responsibility for my good mood helped me to be creative in finding a solution that would make the cleaning or similarly previously "hated" chores fun.

And one last example of a growing number, as I continue to turn my life into games. Often, I put the timer on, or give myself bonus points, to ensure that I take regular breaks and don't sit at my desk for hours. The reason is probably well-known to you. Office jobs inevitably lead to low movement during the day, and I, like most people, wish to stay motivated and form healthy habits in a fun way. I also noticed that my creativity and flow decrease the longer I sit in front of a computer screen, and get interrupted by complaints or other unproductive thoughts. A break, whatever it is used for — a nap, a cup of coffee and reading a few pages of a novel or an inspiring non-fiction book, lunch break, household chores, attending to other projects that have to be done away from my computer — often results in increased motivation when I come back. Thus limiting the time and using a timer along with bonus points turned out, as I discovered, to be a great and fun tool to pep up an activity. My son and I use the timer sometimes to see if we can clean his room in the time we allocate. Or we compete at tidying two different rooms to see who can accomplish the task in the time set.

Now look back (it doesn't have to be very far) into your past and identify anything you might have deliberately or subconsciously turned into a game or a game-like activity. Think of at least one example.

Use the lines below (or a notebook, if you are reading this on an e-reader) and a pen to record your examples of turning your life or parts of it into fun games:

_____
_____
_____
_____
_____

Now consider who or what inspired you to turn that particular activity into a game? Was it someone else or yourself? What were the circumstances that 'nudged' you into doing it?

Use the lines below (or a notebook, if you are reading this on an e-reader) and a pen to write down who inspired you to turn these parts of your life into games:

_____
_____
_____

_____
_____
_____

If you like, you can keep the notes on these discoveries. For example, you could return to these notes to see how your game- and playfulness, and your awareness of them, change with time and how you change yourself. You don't need to aspire to change, you will do it anyway without intending to. But being aware of what's happening and appreciating each step on the way can make your life more and more rewarding.

Additional thoughts and references:
* While revising the manuscript of this book and preparing to send it to my editor (March-April 2019), I have noticed an ad for the book which was soon to be published. That book is *Level Up: Quests to Master Mindset, Overcome Procrastination and Increase Productivity* by Rochelle Melander and is a guide for "writers and entrepreneurs, professionals, and creatives who write as part of their business." It was published on April 2, 2019, so I didn't have enough time to read it through and give you a precise account on its content and my experiences with testing its approach.

But the description suggests that it is something like Jane McGonigal's SuperBetter approach (introduced in chapter 2, section 3) for writers: *"In Level Up: Quests to Master Mindset, Overcome Procrastination, and Increase*

Productivity, you'll tackle quests to help you discover your ideal work rhythms, design a life that supports your productivity, and overcome any obstacle you face. Instead of playing someone else's game, you get to design the game, create your own playbook, define the rewards, and reap them all! You'll also adopt a secret identity, recruit allies, identify villains, and celebrate your epic wins. Because you'll be using a gameful approach to shaping your creative life, taking on these quests won't be a chore. You'll relish investigating your life and playing with possibilities."

After a quick search in the book, I found that Jane McGonigal's SuperBetter approach and the book dedicated to it are quoted in Rochelle Melander's *Level Up* book and served as one of the inspirations for her gameful approach for writers.

I love turning my writing into games, so I am looking forward to trying this approach and using its elements in my self-motivational games. I am also utterly excited that more and more authors provide their guides on how to approach our lives or parts of them playfully and gamefully, which was not the case a couple of years ago when I started on my self-gamification adventure. I especially like that Rochelle Melander aims to help you to design your own game. See more at https://writenowcoach.com/level-up/.

Chapter 4: Self-Gamification and the Happiness Formula

"Now and then it's good to pause in our pursuit of happiness and just be happy."
— Guillaume Apollinaire

1. What is self-gamification?
So, what is this new approach to increasing self-motivation and bringing ourselves back on our happy path? And why the need for a new term?

First of all,

Self-gamification is the art of turning our own lives into games.

Self-gamification is not the same as gamification, although, as the name suggests, the former is based on the latter.

Gamification has become a buzzword, but many people, especially non-gamers but sometimes gamers as well, are still confused when they hear it. They recognize the "game" part, but not the word in its entirety.

I address the terms "gamification" and "self-gamification" often throughout this book, but we need to stop briefly to define them in more detail and examine the differences between the two, before we dive into the components of self-gamification.

Let's start with gamification and what it means.

One of the most common gamification definitions, which I quoted in the glossary and references of the preface, is "the use of game design elements in non-game contexts."*

Following on from this, therefore,

Self-gamification is the application of game design elements to one's own life.

You could also say that,

Self-gamification is a self-help approach showing you how to be playful and gameful.

I felt the need to coin this new term for gamifying one's life when I realized through self-observation that there is more at stake here than just learning from games and game design.

One of the gamification pioneers, Yu-kai Chou, pointed this out when he said that gamification is "more than points, badges, and leaderboards." — Yu-kai Chou, *Actionable Gamification: Beyond Points, Badges, and Leaderboards*

The same applies to self-gamification.

Beyond this, there is an essential feature that distinguishes self-gamification from gamification as it is currently known. Here it is:

In self-gamification, you are both the designer AND the player of your self-motivational games.

So as a designer you take responsibility for how the game is developed. On the other hand, as the dedicated and highly interested player, you are responsible for playing the game, as well as giving the designer feedback on how it could be improved.

The design part is critical — which is taking responsibility for how fun and engaging your games are for yourself as a player. Without judging the player, you must create the best games for them, i.e. for yourself.

This is the primary difference between the self-gamification approach and the games and gamification frameworks designed by others. In self-gamification YOU, and no one else, have to develop your short (minutes or hours long), also daily, weekly, monthly, yearly, etc. games. You'll do well playing other people's games, but you will inevitably give your personal touch to each of the games when you play them, and it is your choice and responsibility how you mix these games with those of your own design. Nobody else could do it for you even if you or they wanted to.

Now, let's consider the three approaches self-gamification brings together to help you turn your life into fun games and have fun with everything or anything you are up to.

2. Three components of self-gamification

Self-gamification brings three well-known and popular techniques together.

The first is *being here and living in the moment*. There are various approaches to being present and living in the present moment. But for me, the most straightforward and most fun approach is to study myself *anthropologically* and then learn from it. I discovered this possibility through the work of award-winning authors Ariel and Shya Kane, who have dedicated many books to the various aspects of living in the moment. For over ten years they have hosted the radio show *Being Here* (the popularity of which grows steadily all over the world), as well as offering many free and paid resources on how to enjoy our lives moment by moment. They suggest that we study ourselves, those around us, and the circumstances we are in, the same way that anthropologists would do while exploring a foreign culture — without judgment.

The second approach is *kaizen*. One of the most popular interpretations of kaizen is continuous improvement, and it is a philosophy and method by which set goals can be achieved by making very small, effortless steps.

And finally, *gamification* itself: that is the application of game design principles to everyday life. And especially one of the four main elements of games, voluntary participation in games. For self-gamification, that means a will to see various real-life activities as games, to make games out of them, to play them, be curious about and inspired by existing games, to improve your own self-motivational games, and to eventually embark on continuous development of these from one round to another. This development means defining the feedback systems for your games, which will help you to establish the habit of appreciating and enjoying every step you make toward your goals, however small (such as an entry on the to-do list) or big (such as your dreams) they might be.

3. Why these three approaches together and not just one of them?

You might ask, why the need to apply these three approaches together? People have been developing and using them for decades in some cases. Isn't each one enough on its own?

Absolutely. But together these techniques allow amazing synergy to take place. This synergy and the potential resulting from it can help you to emerge from any upset or challenge not only as a winner, but as a winner enjoying your life, and each step in the process.

There are several articles addressing gamification and kaizen together. Many scholarly and business articles discuss how gamification can facilitate the application of kaizen in the corporate world**.

But I haven't seen any article or book addressing all of the three approaches together. I have found mentions of being present in separate books on kaizen and gamification, but it was described more as a byproduct of the two approaches.

On the other hand, I think it is crucial to emphasize living in the moment. In fact, I am convinced that being here, living in the now and observing ourselves and the world around us non-judgmentally is not part of the outcome or a byproduct of kaizen or gamification, but rather the starting point, without which neither kaizen nor gamification is possible in the long run.

I might be the first to write about bringing these three well-known techniques together, but I doubt I am the first to apply them all. Applying the anthropological approach to living in the moment, making tiny, effortless steps, and appreciating each of them in a humorous and gameful way, is a fundamental wisdom held by happy and successful people. They probably just never thought to define what they do in this way.

I gave examples of approaching life playfully in chapter 2. Feel free to read it now if you haven't done so already, or if you need a reminder of what doing so can mean in practice.

4. Self-gamification is like building a house

When you apply the three approaches together, they become mutually supportive. When you look non-judgmentally you might find your thought processes amusing, since they often go in very unexpected ways when we feel unsettled. Humor lets you be more playful and bring at least some lightness to difficult situations.

In addition, when you strive to see a task as a game, you are reminded to look non-judgmentally at what is happening. This can help you to become aware of whether the next step toward your goal is too big, in which case you might break it down further so that it becomes effortless. This will boost your motivation and "shift your thinking into this frame — *I've started being productive, so I'm going to keep being productive.*"*** The small steps can help you to find your way back into the flow and the current moment and make whatever you are doing feel like a fun game.

Each of the three approaches could remind you or help you to practice the other two, but in my experience, self-gamification always starts with awareness. It continues with the ability to concentrate on what you can do effortlessly, right now and with what you have at hand, and it ends with the appreciation of that step, and celebrating the achievement as you would in a game (by gaining points and a fist pump with a cheerful "Yes!", or similar).

When I was preparing the online course *Motivate Yourself by Turning Your Life Into Fun Games: Practice Self-Gamification, a Unique Self-Help Approach Uniting Anthropology, Kaizen, and Gamification*, I contemplated how I could visualize this relationship, and a picture of a beautiful house with turrets and intricate roof-line appeared in my mind.

I realized that self-gamification is like building a beautiful house.

It starts with awareness, which is the foundation of it all. Without seeing yourself non-judgmentally, you won't be able to identify how many bricks (i.e. small steps) you need to build your house.

Then the building of the walls follows, while you continually remain aware, so that you don't build your walls in the wrong place (such as, for example, beyond the foundations), or as crooked as the Leaning Tower of Pisa. So you build your house brick-by-brick, step-by-step while being aware of every step along the way.

And then finally, you add the fun bits to your house, which make it appealing, cozy, and just perfect to enjoy. This is where you design your projects and how to manage them as games. Don't dismiss this as unnecessary. You wouldn't want to live in an ugly house. So why omit these final touches to the way you do what you need or want to do? This last part is significant to your well-being.

But neither building the walls nor adding the fun elements would work without the foundation being in place. Learning and practicing self-gamification start with awareness; that is observing yourself, your thought processes, the world around you and how you react to it, non-judgmentally.

Which is why I defined the self-gamification happiness formula as follows.

5. The self-gamification happiness formula

The empirical self-gamification happiness formula (that is, one based on my observations and experience) is as follows:

$H = A + K*A + G*A*K$

Where:

$*$ — Multiplication symbol when related to this formula,

H — Happiness,

A — Awareness,

Self-Gamification Happiness Formula

K — Kaizen,
G — Gamification.

If we put it in words, happiness is not possible without awareness and observing yourself non-judgmentally. So if A (Awareness) equals zero, then your happiness equals zero as well. As the quote at the start of this chapter suggests, you need to pause, look around and become aware of happiness, or, simply, be happy. That is why each addend of the sum in the happiness formula contains the A (Awareness).

With awareness in place, you can identify the next step you can make right now toward your dream and enjoy making that step. So you will be happier if you make small steps towards your goals, where they are what you want to do or what you committed to (promised). That is why K (for kaizen) in the second addend ($K*A$) of the sum above needs only awareness to add to your happiness.

And finally, you will be even happier if you see what you do as games, make these games exciting and uplifting by setting goals, rules, and designing a fun feedback system, as well as recording your points or badges for each of those steps. As many gamification veterans point out, points, badges, and leaderboards are not enough. We've established that without awareness, you won't be able to notice your happiness. But also without making small steps, you will miss the fun. That effect is shown by the presence of *A* and *K* in the third addend (***G*****A*****K***) of the happiness formula, where ***G*** (for Gamification, that is bringing game-design elements into real life) is present.

This formula might seem strange at first glance. But if you look closer, you will see that if you try to achieve your goals (write a book, learn a language, apply for a passport, renovate a house) in one go (which is, of course, not possible) then you will procrastinate because it overwhelms you. No fun and no happiness in sight.

As you continue reading this book, you will see that the following parts reflect the self-gamification happiness formula above. Part II concentrates on the awareness and non-judgmental seeing (*A*), part III on kaizen along with awareness (***K*****A***), while part IV introduces gamification, but it does so along with awareness and kaizen (***G*****A*****K***). This structure appeared almost by itself as I explored the synergy of the three methods and tried to describe each of them. Initially, I intended to introduce the three approaches separately and then summarize them together in another part. But it didn't work. When I described kaizen in part III, I came back again and again to the need to be aware of where we are, and of our thought processes. When I attempted to introduce games and gamification in part IV, I found myself referring again and again to awareness and kaizen. That is when the formula appeared clearly.

Now it is time to look closer at each of the three addends (A, $K*A$, and $G*A*K$) of the self-gamification happiness formula. We will start with awareness (A) in the next part (part II) of this book.

6. What would be your happiness formula?

Before we continue, please consider what would be your happiness formula. Would it resemble the one defined in this chapter, one from other resources****, or something entirely different?

Use the lines below (or a notebook, if you are reading this on an e-reader) and a pen to record your happiness formula and thoughts on this topic:

_____
_____
_____
_____
_____
_____

Glossary and references:

* "The use of game design elements in non-game contexts" — Deterding, S., Dixon, D., Khaled, R., & Nacke, L. (2011). From game design elements to gamefulness: defining gamification. In *Proceedings of the*

15th international academic MindTrek conference: Envisioning future media environments (pp. 9-15). ACM.

** An example of such an article is "GamifiKAIZEN – Gamification and Kaizen – using gamification for continuous process improvement," Gal Rimon, Game Effective, April 23, 2013, https://www.gameffective.com/gamification-continuous-process-improvement/

*** "Micro-Progress and the Magic of Just Getting Started," Tim Herrera, Smarter Living at *The New York Times*, Jan. 22, 2018, https://www.nytimes.com/2018/01/22/smarter-living/micro-progress.html

**** Here is one of the articles you can find on the Happiness Formula: https://www.brevedy.com/2013/12/18/the-happiness-formula-h-s-c-v/

Part II. Anthropology and Non-Judgmental Seeing

Chapter 5. Awareness and Anthropology

"Self-discovery isn't meant to be painful. If it is, then you're working on yourself, lost in the story of your life, or simply resisting what is." –Ariel & Shya Kane, *Practical Enlightenment*

1. Introduction to awareness

In the previous chapter we established that to play fun, self-motivational, and uplifting games you first need to design them. You need to be the designer of your games.

Great game and gamification designers have one thing in common. They don't judge what they see in themselves and the players of their games. Instead, they observe and learn to be *aware* of what their players want, like, and need in games to experience them as fun, and to fortify happiness.

Let's see what awareness means and how you can tap into its power of enlightenment.

Awareness occurs when you observe yourself non-judgmentally. Award-winning authors, Ariel and Shya Kane*, whose work I quote many times in this book, define awareness as follows:

"A nonjudgmental, non-preferential seeing. It's an objective, noncritical witnessing of the nature or what we call the 'isness' of any particular circumstance or situation. It can be described as an ongoing process in which you are bringing yourself back to the moment, rather than complaining silently about how you would prefer this moment to be." — Ariel and Shya Kane, *Practical Enlightenment*

So to be aware, you don't have to do anything complex or difficult. All you need to do is to look around and observe. This observation includes seeing and listening without validating what you see or hear. It is about discovering anew without comparing to what you already know. Such seeing and listening bring to any moment a newly experienced crispness and freshness (read more on this in chapter 15, section 2).

Let's see how you can enable such non-judgmental seeing for yourself, the world around you, and your thought processes when you respond to what life brings your way.

2. Be your own anthropologist

Ariel and Shya Kane suggest something quite brilliant in their award-winning books, radio show *Being Here,* and live seminars. They invite the readers, listeners, and participants of their workshops to study themselves, those around them, and the circumstances they are in as *anthropologists* would do, non-judgmentally.

This suggestion is utterly simple and at the same time extremely profound.

Here is what they say in their award-winning book *How to Have A Match Made in Heaven: A Transformational Approach to Dating, Relating, and Marriage,* "Practice your anthropological approach. Pretend you're a scientist observing a culture of one — yourself. The trick is not to judge what you see, but to neutrally observe how you function, including your thought processes. Awareness and kindness are key."

Before we discuss this in more detail, let's see what anthropology is.

Anthropology is "the scientific study of the origin, the behavior, and the physical, social, and cultural development of humans."**

When anthropologists study and talk about a culture they mean "the whole set of information a human mind uses to describe what the world is like and what's appropriate behavior for living in that world. Cultural differences are basically different conceptions of what is appropriate in a given situation." — Cameron M. Smith, *Anthropology For Dummies*

I believe that the best game and gamification designers must also be anthropologists. Because as I suggested above, they don't judge what they see. They learn as much as they can about the players of their games because they are utterly invested in the interests and needs of their players.

Here is what I discovered about anthropology:

"One foundation of anthropology is the *comparative approach*, in which cultures aren't compared to one another in terms of which is better than the other but rather in an attempt to understand how and why they differ as well as share commonalities. This method is also known as *cultural relativism*, an approach that rejects making moral judgments about different kinds of humanity and simply examines each relative to its own unique origins and history." — Cameron M. Smith, *Anthropology For Dummies*

Maybe that is why anthropologists are:
- Non-judgmental,
- Utterly curious about what's in front of them,
- Often diving into and actively engaging with the culture they are studying,

- Immensely interested in understanding the culture they are studying, as well as its motivations, without judging or labeling them.

Now imagine being like that towards yourself!

It *is* possible.

The recipe for this is again a little pause and non-judgmental observation. It can help and works wonders.

As I learn more about gamification in general, I have the growing feeling that the field could tremendously profit from the anthropological, that is non-judgmental, observation and study of those who play a particular game or use a specific gamified system. Independent of age, gender or any other social group. Each generation, each group of people, is a "culture" of its own.

And each age group could learn from another. So, even games for the smallest children could inspire creative mechanisms for gamification design for adults, making various activities as effortless and enjoyable as possible.

In fact, Mitchel Resnick, the LEGO Papert Professor of Learning Research, Director of the Okawa Center, and Director of the Lifelong Kindergarten group at the MIT Media Lab insists in his acclaimed book *Lifelong Kindergarten: Cultivating Creativity through Projects, Passion, Peers, and Play* that traditional kindergarten play should be introduced into the "adult" and corporate world to make it more productive, efficient, welcoming, and creative. ***

However, not only are there differences between groups of people and every person in general, but each of us also differs depending on circumstances, situations, and states of mind. Therefore, observe and learn from what you see about yourself. You might discover something you never expected.

For example, I discovered at some point that when doing arithmetic calculations in my head, I wasn't using the languages I expected. I applied neither my mother tongue, Romanian (still used with my mother, sister, and niece), nor Russian (the language I spoke during my school, kindergarten and university years), nor English (which I predominantly used to communicate with my colleagues at work). Instead, I was using German, the language I was only just starting to learn (being just one or two years after I'd moved to Germany, and while I was still attending language lessons). I can't recall now which language I had used previously for such mental sums, but it must have been either Romanian, Russian or English, the languages I spoke fluently at the time. I couldn't believe it when I became aware of it, and tried to guess the reason. I think it is because the German system of putting the units before the tens when naming the numbers was so unusual to me that I practiced it over and over, and in so doing it then became automatic for me to use German when making simple calculations. Even today when I speak to my mother, and we both need to add or subtract in our heads, each of us does it in a different language, she in Romanian and I in German, even if we use Romanian for the rest of the conversation. This discovery was a big shock both for me and those who observed me calculating quickly out loud in German for the first time.

At this point, I would like to ask you to take a couple of moments and reflect on whether you have had a similar "self-revelation."

Use the lines below (or a notebook, if you are reading this on an e-reader) and a pen to write down these "surprises" when you try to observe yourself non-judgmentally. Record the first revelations that come to your mind.

_____
_____
_____
_____
_____
_____

I invite you to do this exercise now and again. You might discover abilities and potential that you didn't think you possessed, by just being here and being interested in what is happening inside and outside yourself.

So when you turn your life into games, don't be "only" the designer and the player — first and foremost you should start by being your own *anthropologist*.

3. Kindness and honesty as keys to anthropological seeing

In a motivational book for writers I named *Cheerleading for Writers: Discover How Truly Talented You Are*, I told the story of discovering that this non-judgmental observation meant — and also resulted in — being simultaneously kind and honest to ourselves.

Here is a section from chapter "T — Tell It Like It Is" of this book, titled "Honesty and kindness are mutually inclusive and cannot be true without one another":

(The beginning of the excerpt)

For a long time, I erroneously thought that being kind to myself meant claiming time and space for myself away from others. Aspiring writers often hear, "Protect your writing time." Which makes it sound like somebody is attacking our writing time, or is eager to steal it. Sure, we get interrupted, but the same happens in every other job. In those jobs, even if we sometimes complain about interruptions, we try to go back to the task as soon as possible afterwards. Or we ask others not to disturb us for some time. But this complaint about the lack of time is so frequently mentioned when it comes to writing. At least, I have never heard interruptions spoken of more often or with a more negative tone than since I became a writer.

For me, the brightest lightbulb in this respect went off one evening when I complained to my husband about my lack of time for writing. "Other authors take one hour or more in the evenings to write, or even go to writers' retreats with the sole purpose of writing their books. I also want this! Even if it is just for five minutes every day."

His answer was short and couldn't have been more honest, direct and, I must admit, fair. He said, "So go to your desk, close the door behind you, and write."

I was speechless. All I could do in response was go to our little home office, shut the door, put the timer on for five minutes and write.

I managed to write three short paragraphs during those five minutes. I did edit them heavily later, but the ease with which they'd flowed struck me. I realized that the whole heaviness of the task didn't come from the lack of time I had to write but from the drama I had created around taking this time. The drama had not contained even an ounce of either kindness or honesty, to myself or those around me.

I observed myself "testing" honesty and kindness towards myself and others, and tried to apply them separately, but I realized that they stopped existing without each other.

When I tried being kind to myself without seeing that I was the one preventing myself from doing what I wanted to do, and instead trying to put the blame on others, I stopped being kind altogether. Blaming others for my inability to take time for my writing didn't buy me a ticket to feeling good as I thought it would. I thought that by putting the responsibility for this on others would relieve the guilt I felt inside. It didn't.

After that, I decided to blame myself instead, expose my "mistakes" (almost) publicly. That was my idea of being honest. But soon after, I felt miserable and started whining and asking people around me for mercy. To my surprise, many did have compassion and understanding. The one without compassion, who had been unable to see the truth, was me.

Grasping that honesty and kindness cannot fully bloom without each other was a big relief. There was suddenly both calmness and time to do what I wanted to do. I had neither to beat myself up nor to lie to myself. All there was to do was become aware that I was in discomfort, and then make a choice about what to do next without trying to fix myself, anybody or anything. All there was to do was move forward. And people around me seemed not only to accept but also understand me more than they ever had before.

(The end of the excerpt)

4. Observe how you observe yourself

I have a question for you. How do you feel when you try to look at yourself non-judgmentally? That is, both kindly and honestly at the same time. If you haven't attempted to do so, then go ahead, take a few minutes or even put a timer on for let's say three minutes and try to look at what you do and don't do non-judgmentally. In the next chapter, we will discuss what you might observe while doing that. But right now I would like you to look at how you feel when you try to consider that:

1. Are you completely comfortable with what you see?
2. Or did you judge yourself for procrastinating over what you want or have to do, and for doing something else instead, which doesn't bring you further towards your goals?

Use the lines below (or a notebook, if you are reading this on an e-reader) and a pen to record your thoughts and feelings when trying to observe yourself non-judgmentally. Record the first things that come to your mind.

_____
_____
_____
_____
_____

Now put your notes and this book aside for some time — a couple of minutes or an hour, whatever works best for you. Do something else during that time. Then take your notes and read them. How do they sound? More like option (1) above, that is non-judgmental, kind, like simple facts or interesting observations? Or more like option (2), resentful, judgmental, and worrisome?

Here's how you can recognize judgmental thoughts. When your notes concentrate on what you haven't achieved, have qualifiers and comparison, or contain the words "should" or "shouldn't have," then it is likely that you are regretting the way your life is unfolding or has unfolded so far.

Don't worry if you observed yourself choosing the second, judgmental, option. Even after more than seven years of practicing seeing myself non-judgmentally, I still watch myself selecting the second option from time to time. But I also find myself picking the first, more relaxed way as well, more and more often. And you will too.

Let's go back to the non-judgmental approach to living in the moment. Ariel and Shya Kane defined three simple and enlightening ideas in this respect:
1. "What you resist persists and grows stronger."
2. "No two things can occupy the same you at the same time."
3. "Anything you allow to be, allows you to be."

— Ariel and Shya Kane, *Practical Enlightenment*

Here is what I learned over the years of practicing non-judgmental seeing and living in the moment as inspired by the three simple ideas formulated by Ariel and Shya Kane.

First, I realized that if I resisted something or tried to get rid of something — a thought, a habit, a person, a task, or anything else — I didn't get rid of it at all. This person or thing just kept on sticking around, dominated my life and often became overwhelming.

Then, I learned that I couldn't be anywhere else or anyone else at any given moment — I could only be who and how I was (and couldn't be who I wasn't), whether I liked it or not. And whether I judged my situation or not.

Finally, anything that I allowed to be exactly as it was without judging or trying to change it completed itself in an instant.

5. Other "being here" techniques

You might not have heard about the possibility of studying yourself anthropologically before. And you might wonder if there are other techniques to non-judgmental seeing and living in the moment.

There are. For example, if you are acquainted with or are practicing mindfulness, then the ideas defined by Ariel and Shya Kane might remind you of that.

Here is a definition of mindfulness from one of the sites that gives advice on how to practice it:

"Mindfulness is the practice of purposefully focusing all of your attention on the current moment, and accepting it without judgment. This is a great place to start if you are looking for the key element in happiness."****

Today, many people have heard at least something about mindfulness. I discovered many other blog posts, articles, books, and online courses on this now popular discipline.

Mindfulness is very popular in Denmark (where I live). There are meet-ups for mindfulness meditation, and they even teach it in school. My son has been taught mindfulness at school since zeroth grade (preschool year), and my four-year-old daughter practices yoga with some meditation elements every Friday in kindergarten.

I am happy that my children are learning to be here and self-aware in kindergarten and school.

A few more words on mindfulness. Here is how Wikipedia defines it:

"Mindfulness is the psychological process of bringing one's attention to experiences occurring in the present moment, which one can develop through the practice of meditation and through other training."*****

So mindfulness relies among other things on meditation.

"Meditation is a practice where an individual uses a technique, such as focusing their mind on a particular object, thought or activity, to achieve a mentally clear and emotionally calm state."******

Thus meditation promotes slowing down and observation of both bodily reactions and thought processes.

I don't practice either mindfulness or meditation, and I wouldn't do so in order to achieve something or to manipulate my thought processes, as many people attempt, and as Wikipedia's definition of meditation above would suggest.

I find the idea of studying myself non-judgmentally as an anthropologist would more natural.

What I am interested in is *Practical Enlightenment*, which is the title of one of Ariel and Shya Kane's latest books. In other words, I am looking to achieve a "mentally clear and emotionally calm state" in this moment of now by being aware and observing myself, the world around me and my thought processes in reaction to it, non-judgmentally. And by engaging actively in each moment of my life.

But if mindfulness and meditation are more practical and more helpful for you, then use them to become aware of the present moment. The most important thing is that you don't judge yourself and the world around you, and instead become interested in the processes you observe. Like anthropologists do when they study a culture.

I enjoy taking on the role of an anthropologist when I observe my thought processes and my interactions with the world around me non-judgmentally, as if I were a culture or a country. It is like a game in itself. It helps to reduce the drama that might be building in my head due to resistance of the way my life is unfolding.

6. Discovering who you are in each moment

I want to emphasize something here before we go on.

Non-judgmental observation is not meant to analyze and mark you with any labels like "good" or "bad," "extrovert," "introvert," "agile," "calm," "slow," "quick-tempered" and so on.

I am not judging the use of those words either. To grasp something and communicate about it, we need to give various things we observe and feel a name.

Feel free to use them when you observe something, but try to do so non-judgmentally. For example, in the following way, "Oh, I just validated it as bad. I wonder why?"

Always be curious and interested. Remember that with your brain you have a fantastic piece of nature's (and if you believe in God then also divine) creation right at your disposal and no one else can research it the way you can.

What you have experienced so far, all the people and circumstances you were touched by along the way, all the books you have read, all the games you have played, all the meals you have tasted, all the fights you have fought, all the jokes you have shared, combine with what you genetically inherited. This also applies to what you *don't* learn, see, hear, touch, smell, and taste (especially if you act in opposition to the things you don't do).

Don't you think it's insane that we try to put this fantastic, evolving, sparkling, constantly changing mass into one single box that we try to label with a specific type of identity or personality?

However, we often try to build and construct something of ourselves. In other words, to manipulate and shape ourselves into whatever we think makes a great, successful person.

We all probably agree that none of us wants to be manipulated and forced into something. So why do we do it to ourselves?

Here is an idea. Let's do the following. Instead of trying to mold our identity or personality into something we vaguely imagine, let's study and discover what happens in our brains when interacting actively with the world around us.

Now, having learned about the possibility of studying myself and the world around me anthropologically, I like thinking that my identity doesn't have to be built, but instead discovered in each moment.

It is like the pressure that is put on writers when they are starting out, to "find their voice." I certainly felt it. But when I found my way back into the moment and just wrote, and later read what I had written, I discovered that I had my own voice.

Here is what I advised to writers in chapter "V — Voice (Discovering It in Each Moment Rather Than Finding It)" of the previously mentioned book *Cheerleading for Writers: Discover How Truly Talented You Are*:

(The beginning of the excerpt)

So my advice to you and myself is to sit down, *just* write and let's discover our voices in the process. And *yes*, read, go to the movies, talk to your loved ones and people you don't know, go for a walk, engage in stimulating discussions, enjoy your meals, and absorb all this. Absorb also what you feel inside at any given moment. Observe your feelings without judging them. And then sit down and write again, and again. And then some more.

After some time, pick up what you have written and read it. Discover your voice in that particular moment from the recent or long gone past. Experience the feelings generated by this reading, as well as the anticipation of new creations to come from the near or far-off future. This will lead you to a new shade of your voice in the present moment.

(The end of the excerpt)

The same is true of identity and personality. I believe we all have both our identity and personality at birth. Moreover, they unfold in each moment. They are never static. We just need to discover each of them, moment by moment. That is why we are able to surprise ourselves, at least from time to time.

Our identities and personalities are building themselves on their own with each experience we make. We don't need to force them. We just need to be there to discover them. Both for the ups and downs. Our interactions and being with whatever comes our way in each moment comprise the colorful building blocks of our identities and personalities.

In the next chapter, we will consider what you might observe when you look at what you do and don't do, non-judgmentally, as an anthropologist would.

References:
* https://www.transformationmadeeasy.com/
** http://www.thefreedictionary.com/anthropology
*** https://web.media.mit.edu/~mres/
**** https://www.developgoodhabits.com/how-to-practice-mindfulness/
***** https://en.wikipedia.org/wiki/Mindfulness
****** https://en.wikipedia.org/wiki/Meditation

Chapter 6. Observing What We Do and Don't Do Non-Judgmentally

"At times you will live in the moment. Other times you will repeat old behaviors from the past. Expect it and don't judge it!" — Ariel and Shya Kane

1. How we treat our tasks

Our days as humans, or as living beings, are full of action. Even when we say we aren't doing anything, we are. We look out of the window, watch TV, surf in the sea, surf the internet, take a nap, work in the garden, do housework, play with our children, play an online game, write a book, play an instrument alone or in public, etc.

And there are also things that we aspire to do.

Many of us have learned at various points in our lives to classify our projects and tasks into urgent and non-urgent, important and unimportant. I learned and tried to apply this system multiple times too.

While turning my life into games, and by observing myself and the world around me non-judgmentally, I discovered that there are only two types of projects and tasks depending on how I treat them.

I either:
1. escape *from* them, or
2. escape *to* them.

That is it. Nothing more.

There is, of course, psychological research about how and why we behave in various situations. In the area of gamification, one of its pioneers, Yu-kai Chou (whom I have mentioned in chapter 2, section 3 and chapter 4, section 1) has performed extensive and remarkable research in this area. In his book *Actionable Gamification: Beyond Points, Badges, and Leaderboards*, he described a gamification design framework, which he created and named Octalysis, and where he identified eight core drives of human behavior based on interdisciplinary research.

Here is how Yu-kai Chou defines effective gamification:

"Effective gamification is a combination of game design, game dynamics, behavioral economics, motivational psychology, UX/UI (User Experience and User Interface), neurobiology, technology platforms, as well as ROI-driving business implementations." — Yu-kai Chou, *Actionable Gamification: Beyond Points, Badges, and Leaderboards*

This shows the multidimensionality of human behavior, motivation, and drives. Thus, it is even

more amazing to realize that independent of the causes for our actions, we treat whatever we want or have to do in only two ways:
1. We either avoid them (in other words, we don't do them), or
2. Do them while escaping from other things.

As we take a more detailed look at these two types of what we do or don't do and as I give you examples, you might observe yourself wondering which of these apply to you. There is space for this exercise at the end of the chapter, rather than after each example. The reason being that I would like to reveal to you many (but probably not all, because that is impossible) of the tricks that our minds use to judge and mislead ourselves; the results of these actions by our brains are byproducts of our survival mechanisms and underlying fear. As I suggested in section 10 of the Introduction, you should read this chapter as a fictional story too, without taking the epiphanies described in it personally. Just observe all that resonates with you without judging or doing anything about it, relax, and enjoy the read.

2. *Escape-from* tasks

Let's now take a closer look at the tasks and projects from which we tend to escape — that is procrastinate about before attending to, or avoid forever. What are these?

When I considered what these were for me, I realized that there were again two types of projects and tasks, independent of whether they had to do with work, my family and friends, or myself.

My thought processes determined these two types of *escape-from* tasks, and this is how I thought of them:
1. I either felt that I wanted to do them very much, but didn't have time for them, or
2. I thought I didn't want to do them but had to do them.

Here are some examples of the *tasks I wanted to do but thought that I didn't have time for* (type 1):
- I wanted to spend more time writing my works-in-progress during the day but I couldn't because I had so many other things to do.
- I wanted to learn and speak better Danish.

Here are examples of the *tasks I needed to do because I had committed to them, but claimed or thought that I didn't want to do them* (type 2):
- I didn't like doing book-keeping for my business, but I had to.
- I didn't like working out or doing any kinds of sports, but I had to because it was better for my health.

3. *Escape-to* tasks

Now, let's consider the things that we *escape to*. The things that we choose to do before those discussed in the previous section. Let's take a look at the tasks we blame for our procrastination of escape-from tasks.

I discovered that here there are also two sub-types. There are *obvious* and *productive* escape-to tasks.

The *obvious* are those we describe as, "I deserve a break, so I'll do that instead of what I planned to do."

These could be, for example, watching TV or random videos on YouTube, reading a book for leisure, playing an online game, staying in bed, spending time on social media, surfing the internet, etc.

And the second type is *productive* activities, but not necessarily those that are urgent or necessary to reach our set goals. Instead these are beneficial but non-urgent, and things we might attend to when we "should" be doing other more pressing activities or those we claim we want to do.

For me, that used to be doing laundry (or in the absence of it, other household chores). If I was finding it a challenge to write an article or a blog post or a book chapter or to compile advertising copy for my books and services, I sometimes followed the impulse to go and check if there were enough dirty clothes to wash or any clean and dry laundry to fold.

Others might choose, for example, gardening before any other things they have to do. Or if you work in an office, you might find yourself restructuring the folders on your shelves or some similarly useful but not necessarily urgent activity.

4. What seeing *escape-from* tasks can teach us

The judgmental answers to why we don't do things we want or have to do and instead do those we seemingly didn't intend or want to do, always have at least one of two sources. We either blame ourselves for being lazy and incapable, or we blame other people and circumstances for hindering us in doing what we wanted or intended to do.

But if we look non-judgmentally instead, the answer is simple. We are merely saying "No" to those things we aren't doing in those moments, including those we supposedly want to do very much. So, if we aren't writing the book we said we wanted to write, then we are saying "No" to it. That is neither good nor bad. It is simply happening. It means that we've said "Yes" to something else.

While practicing self-gamification, I discovered something surprising that now sounds logical and revealing to me. The tasks we "have" to do must also be something we "want" to do, otherwise we wouldn't keep them around but would give them up entirely after some time. We can become aware of this by recognizing that they are in fact parts of the more significant projects or goals we want to achieve. Such as preparing for exams to get the degree we want.

Sometimes without noticing it, we keep tasks on our to-do lists that lead us to goals we don't want to pursue right now or ever. Perhaps we do them because someone else said or wrote that it would be good for us (or those like us) or our work. In which case we are pursuing someone else's goals. Or they are goals from another time, such as our past, which we often remember erroneously, or our future, which we fantasize about or describe with "Someday I want to."

A note of clarification: I'm not saying that it doesn't make sense to follow someone else's advice, or pursue plans that we made a long time ago. It does make sense to try many things out before finding what resonates with you and what's right for you (there will be more on this in chapter 15, section 2). This applies to foods, books, approaches, places, apps, other tools, and many other things. And even to people when you think of dating.

What I mean here are the tasks that we escape from and procrastinate about. Those we are often afraid to give up and therefore keep around in our to-do lists (and minds) as something we will do later, thinking that a perfect moment will someday miraculously arrive.

But you have no doubt heard before, and experienced many times, that there is no better time than now.

One example for me is the intention to read books or articles on genres I do not write in currently but might at some future point (I have many print-outs waiting to be read).

Becoming aware of this can help identify whether we genuinely want to do what is on our to-do lists. We might become aware that we want to do them but are afraid of failure. Or we are scared to succeed. So we procrastinate about them instead. On the other hand, we might equally realize that we don't really want to do these tasks, in which case this awareness will help us to let go of those "unwanted" goals in a much easier way, and without guilt.

Turning de-cluttering into a game (and attending to it in small steps whenever I think of it — a few minutes or even seconds are enough) proves to be of great help to me with the many articles waiting to be read. We will address the magic of small steps and how to turn various chores into games in the subsequent parts (parts III and IV) of this book.

5. Learning from *escape-to* tasks

Let's recall what those tasks are, which we are "guilty" of doing instead of those we want or have to do.

These are either *obviously* "unnecessary" activities such as surfing on the internet, spending time on social media, watching TV or videos online, playing video games, or *productive* activities that are non-urgent, such as attending to household chores if you are working from home, or re-structuring your file-system on the computer at home or your workplace, and so on.

We often blame these for "overpowering" us ("I just can't stop being on Facebook. It's like a drug!") or "threatening our well-being" if not done ("If I don't do the laundry now, then I will have many loads on the weekend, or my children won't have their favorite T-shirts to wear, and that will stress me out.")

Let's take a look at what happens when we switch from an escape-from to an escape-to task.

In the beginning, these escape-to activities might feel like fun. Yes, even laundry, although we might not say it out loud. The reason for that fun feeling could be that the escape-to tasks appear more straightforward or easy than what we want or have to do. Here's why. We attach drama to the escape-from tasks. (Do you remember the story of how I dramatized my lack of writing time and how I discovered who was really responsible, in chapter 5, section 3?) The escape-to tasks don't have that drama. They are merely there whenever we choose to pay attention to them.

In the next part (part III) of this book, and especially in chapters 8 and 9, we will discuss why escape-to tasks are easier to switch to and do than those other daunting things we want or have to do.

But for now, let's come back to the feeling of fun when we switch to the escape-to tasks. You might argue that it is not the case because, for example, taking a mobile out of a pocket, activating it and tapping on one of the social media icons and scrolling is not always fun, especially if the posts there are depressing. Yes, it is easy to do, but not always fun. It could be just a habit, this is true. However, have you observed your stubborn satisfaction (of comfort, for example) at the very beginning of this whole process of activating your social media presence? Or satisfying the curiosity you have about what your friends and the rest of the world are up to?

So yes, there is this first moment of fun and ease. Whatever the cause might be. But after some time (which can be either short or long) the feeling of pleasure at escaping diminishes. Thoughts about whatever else you should or could be doing start interrupting your concentration while surfing social media, or the cozy and merry scrubbing of your bathroom floor. Instead of stopping what you are doing and following the impulse to return to the activities you are procrastinating over, you might observe yourself stubbornly thinking, "No, I won't do that. What I'm doing now is easier. I deserve a break." or something similar. And you might try to resist and push away those images of you writing that book or report or practicing a musical instrument, or any other of your escape-from tasks and projects.

Recognizing this without judging what you see is the key. Not the fact that you have been escaping something, or your thought processes with the touch of guilt or any other feelings you might observe yourself having.

There is something else to these escape-to projects and activities. They are also a solution. The solution for escaping the tasks to which we want or need to say "Yes." I heard this for the first time from Ariel and Shya Kane and later saw for myself that my "problems" are often "very clever solutions"* to escape what makes me uncomfortable.

Yes, we hear often,

"Great things never came from comfort zones."**

or

"Life always begins with one step outside of your comfort zone."***

And of course, we want both to live great lives and achieve great things.

But we love being comfortable too.

So what are the possible solutions to this dilemma?

I am convinced that self-gamification, and the three approaches brought together in this book, are one of the successful solutions to it.

We will address kaizen and gamification in the subsequent parts of this book.

But let us emphasize awareness again as the main component of self-gamification.

If you consider yourself as a player of your project games, look at yourself and your thought processes non-judgmentally, and through that become aware of your dynamics as a player, then you can adjust the rules of your self-motivational and uplifting games, as well as the projects you take into those games. So as soon as you recognize your escape-to activity, you can plan to give yourself fewer points for attending to it in your next daily, weekly, or monthly round of your self-motivational games. The natural wish to be better in a game and gain more points will help you to make more room for your escape-from projects and activities.

For example, if I gained a point for laundry on a particular day, trying to do more of it wouldn't earn me another point. But writing a paragraph for my book or working on another escape-from project would. So writing that paragraph or working on the other escape-from project become more attractive.

The trick here is to see the whole process as a game and be aware when you stop doing so. And if you come to a halt, then as a designer you can figure out a creative twist to how your project and self-motivational games are configured, so that the player in you feels compelled to start playing again.

6. When *escape-from* and *escape-to* tasks switch places

There is another quite curious thing about *escape-from* and *escape-to* tasks.

The activities we escape from can become those we escape to and vice versa, depending on whether we have fun attending to them and also on how much effort we think they would cost us.

For example, laundry is not always my favorite activity. I have caught myself more than once procrastinating about it, letting it pile up into considerable mountains and instead finding myself entering expenses and income into my book-keeping system.

But wait! Didn't I claim earlier in this chapter that this task was one of my escape-from ones? I did; in section 2.

Here's what happened.

Becoming aware of my prejudice against bookkeeping helped me to make progress by taking small steps towards it every day. So the discipline was no longer a challenge, because I was not forcing myself to do what I had committed to doing. I merely made progress one tiny step after another.

After some time, I stopped leaving my business's books unattended and recorded the entries as often as they came. This activity didn't take much effort and even became fun because I was accomplishing it so easily and getting points in my self-motivational games along the way.

But there was a downside to that. The laundry was piling up! Instead of leaving my desk and attending to it, I found myself checking my bank accounts almost daily, even if there were no entries to record.

So, what to do?

Yes, the next game-design twist was in order. This one was for the task and time-management "games." I have reserved a spot on my calendar for each Friday to check my business and private accounts and update my business books and personal expenses. Until Friday came, I wouldn't get any check mark (or point) for doing this task. Now I was free to do the other tasks I had on my to-do list. Like laundry, for example, which had become an escape-from task.

The next logical step here is to talk about the importance of various projects and activities and whether it is indeed possible to differentiate between what we want and have to do in terms of importance.

7. Important and unimportant tasks

My friend Auria, who enrolled in the online course *Motivate Yourself by Turning Your Life Into Fun Games: Practice Self-Gamification, a Unique Self-Help Approach Uniting Anthropology, Kaizen, and Gamification*, wrote the following after she assessed her projects and activities without judgment: "The new thing is the sense of satisfaction because all the projects are important in terms of priorities."

I loved this statement because it reminded me of how I made a similar discovery while turning my life into games. At some point, I realized that I couldn't honestly classify projects and activities I planned to do as more or less important or critical. They were all equally important because I wanted to engage in all of them. At different times, but in all of them.

This is similar to my relationship with my children: I love my son and daughter equally, but of course, they are different and unique. As are the projects I commit to. They are all important, but they are different, so I address them differently. When I am present and non-judgmental I don't treat them as more or less important because they are all important. If they are not important, then why do them at all?

"But," you might say, "do you always want to do what you have committed to? What about the things you promise to do but resent because they are not your heart's desire? Didn't you mention something above about doing what others want and not what we want?"

Let's talk a bit more about that now.

8. What do we really want?
We all have things to do that (seemingly) stand in the way of the things we want.

But we have also established that we often don't give up some of the projects we "hate" because they are necessary parts of the bigger dreams and goals that we want to achieve. So what is it that we really want?

Ariel and Shya Kane give the following hint: "If you want to know what you really want, look at what you've got." — Ariel and Shya Kane, *Being Here...Too: Short Stories of Modern Day Enlightenment*

And this one too: "You know what you want by how you act." — Ariel and Shya Kane, *How to Have A Match Made in Heaven: A Transformational Approach to Dating, Relating, and Marriage*

We often judge the circumstances we are in and the lives we live as not good enough. However, many of us, when offered the possibility of being in another situation, would still choose what we've got, one of the reasons probably being that we know what our circumstances are, whereas the unknown can be scary.

We also forget that we made choices that brought us to where we are. And many of those choices were good. In fact, they were perfect for the moments we made them in, even if we might not like them as much in retrospect.

Our fear that we are doing something wrong, and our resistance to that fear, distort our view of the fact that if we do something and don't stop, then chances are it is something we want to do, even if publicly we might claim otherwise.

Here is what the Kanes have to say on that (where "it" could be anything): "If you do it, then you want it. If you don't want to do it, then you stop doing it." — Ariel and Shya Kane, *How to Have*

A Match Made in Heaven: A Transformational Approach to Dating, Relating, and Marriage

Simple, right? Kindness and honesty applied simultaneously allow us to become aware of what we have, and to be thankful for it. This awareness can also help us to stop doing something we don't want to do, in any given moment — even if we might have wanted to the moment before — just like we stop playing games when we are no longer enjoying them.

It can also help us to move forward. We all want to learn something new because we all have curiosity programmed in us. In which case, it is worth remembering that, "life is fleeting. If you have the idea you want to do something, you should go for it." — Shya Kane in the "Transformation in the New Year" video by Ariel and Shya Kane****

So with the knowledge we gathered above, let's take a look at what we think or say we really want.

First and foremost, most of us say we want to live happy, healthy and long lives. But how to achieve that?

Ariel and Shya Kane have a brilliant answer to this. They say:

"The secret to happiness and well-being is interacting with your life as though your life is your idea." — Ariel and Shya Kane, *Practical Enlightenment*

If we follow their advice and treat the way our lives turn up as if it was our idea, does it mean that the lives we live will feel like exactly what we wanted? Or even something beyond what we wanted?

Yes, this is my experience. When I relax into the moment and make the best of it, life feels like a fantastic and fun roller-coaster. An utterly exciting and pleasant roller-coaster. Each day becomes full of events and colorful experiences.

Here is something else I discovered. If I don't manage to give up something, or it reappears in my thoughts or reminders from outside, then I probably wanted it in the first place. I have discovered this in various areas of my life, and continue to do so. This applies to both my professional and personal life.

You might think that the reappearance of what we want in our thoughts, even if we are resisting it, is a good thing. At least in the end. "This sticking thought might someday nudge me into attending to my heart's desire or towards what is really good for me," you could say.

I have an example from my life, which at first might sound like proof of this.

About ten years ago I stumbled upon something, without which I wouldn't have started blogging, and wouldn't have met many of the wonderful and supportive friends I have from all over the world. Without this something, I wouldn't have written the many books I have to date, including the one you are holding and reading right now.

This something was a book. Its title is *Being Here: Modern Day Tales of Enlightenment* and it was written by Ariel and Shya Kane.

I first saw it when an online retailer generated a recommendation based on my previous orders of many self-help and motivational books.

After buying it in October 2009, I resisted reading it for almost two years, although the beautiful butterfly on its cover often caught my eye, as well as the spine when I tucked it between the other books on my bookshelf.

Now I realize that one of the reasons for my resistance was my assumption that this book would be like any other self-help book I had read before, which, as I saw it then, had failed to solve my problems or to fix me, since I considered myself a failure. It was beyond my realm of imagination to consider that there was nothing to be repaired or changed. That there was another way.

Then in September of 2011, I surrendered and read it. My life took a turn I had never expected, but for which I am immensely grateful.

So all was well in the end, you could say.

But there is a clear downside to resisting. If we oppose what we really want to do or how our lives show up, we start resisting other things as well, including those that might have been easier to do previously. Many activities become a struggle. Because resistance becomes our lifestyle.

That was true for me during those two years (as well as before). Somewhere in the middle of those two years, one of my biggest dreams came true. After six long years and various failed attempts (including IVF treatment and considering adopting a child), I became pregnant with our son, Niklas, who was born in October 2010.

But, strangely enough, I still found myself feeling miserable. Others seemed happier than me, more satisfied. How could that be? I had what I always wanted — a loving husband, a child, an amazing and supportive family and friends, a job — but I was still unhappy? So I concluded I was doing something wrong. Despite everything I had achieved in life (including a Ph.D. in electrical engineering), I thought I was incompetent at almost everything. Whatever idea or wish I had and contemplated trying out, like writing, for example, I discarded it. I hid the short story away for a while, which I had written while going through the fertilization process.

Now in retrospect, I see that this cycle of the wish appearing and me saying, "Not now, next year" only reinforced the desire and the growing frustration that I was denying myself that wish. Because next year, tomorrow, etc. don't exist for human brains. If an idea appears, then we want to action it right now. And if we deny ourselves this wish, we get bitter, with ourselves and with everyone and everything around us.

With the tools that anthropology offered, I realized that being self-critical was totally normal, and that many people were. I learned to observe myself and the world around me non-judgmentally, and to treat both myself and others with kindness. I also learned that awareness (and practicing being here) is not a one-time happiness pill. I lose it many times a day, but I learned to find my way back into this moment again and again. Saying "Yes" to life became a fantastic adventure.

I discovered that for some tasks, jotting down my intention on a to-do list was the first step in saying "Yes" toward its completion. But I learned that if my thoughts returned to it again and again, then there was often a deeply-ingrained wish to spend at least a little time on it now and then, rather than defer it for too long.

I was also surprised to observe the following. I expected that adding another item to my to-do list and then doing it would cause me stress. Especially if that additional item was a recurring one that would take a long time to complete. But something else happened. Resolving a "No" and saying "Yes" to a wish didn't overwhelm me. Instead, clearly seeing what my wish was and giving at least a little time to it boosted productivity and motivation in other projects. And I felt amazingly relaxed and content. (We will address the magic of small, effortless steps in the next part (part III) of the book and, in particular, in chapter 8.)

As I read Ariel and Shya's books and articles, listened to their *Being Here* internet radio show, and participated in their live seminars, I experienced what it meant to let myself and others be just as we were. I discovered how to breathe and savor my life moment by moment, completely and freely. I came to understand what I truly wanted, what was my heart's desire.

Yes, reading *Being Here: Modern Day Tales of Enlightenment* was the moment when this beautiful journey I am now on began. It is a journey of curiosity about what is happening at any given moment of now, and what can happen if I surrender to my wishes and do what my heart calls me to do, instead of what I *think* others want me to do.

When talking about our heart's desires, I would like to share with you a story I had written in a blog post long before I started turning my life into games and became aware of kaizen and gamification. It was also before I published my first book. The epiphany I had back in December of 2014 remains fresh, and I rediscover it again and again. A note beforehand: I had practiced being present, non-judgmental, and aware (as inspired by the work of Ariel and Shya Kane) for about three years by then.

9. Heart's desires and dreams
*(based on a blog post, Which way to go?, published on December 30, 2014*****)*

(The beginning of the updated blog post text)

Many of us have heard one of these incitements, or a version of them: "Follow your heart!" or "Listen to your heart!"

I had too, but I wondered, what does my heart sound like? How do I recognize when I am following my heart?

As I was wondering that, I discovered a quote in German that gave me a clue:

"Welch eine *himmlische Empfindung* ist es, seinem Herzen zu folgen." — Johann Wolfgang von Goethe

My interpretation:

"What a *heavenly feeling* to follow one's own heart." — Johann Wolfgang von Goethe

As I read those beautiful words, I realized that this "heavenly feeling" or, in other words, happiness, when I experienced it, showed me that I was following my heart.

Which was an intriguing discovery because if well-being was an indicator of listening to my heart, then it became clear that following my heart was not the same as following my dreams. I became aware that I used to mistakenly attribute following my dream with following my heart. I could suddenly see that the dream was something I hoped to achieve in the future, but that I was capable of experiencing many happy moments before doing so.

Just a few days before writing the blog post on which this section is based, I felt tired and considered that everything I had done that day was something I hadn't wanted to do. As a result, a thought kept occurring: "I am not following my dream. I did nothing to work towards my dream today!" *The dream* was to become a published novelist.

But the fact was that these thoughts were not accurate. I had done something that day, by editing some of the chapters of my novel. And I had also done many other things, including things related to a dream that came true four years earlier: having a family.

It was quite funny to discover how easily we can forget those dreams that have already come true.

They fall out of focus. But weren't they supposed to make us eternally happy? Why do they fail to do so?

Or was it just my inability, in that moment, to look around and see the beauty of what was already there, which made me unhappy?

Then in a bright light of recognition, I saw where my heart was. It was right there, right in that moment with me. I didn't have to go anywhere to follow it. I just had to be there in that moment with everything that made up a part of me, including my actual heart, eyes, my ears, my brain, my thoughts, me, and the world around me as it was and not as I imagined or expected it to be.

(The end of the updated blog post text)

10. What is our truth?

I hope you enjoyed reading about this small but significant memory. The truth I discovered then and rediscover today, again and again, is that I can find out what I really want in any moment, by making myself aware of where I am and what draws my attention.

Here again is a quick reminder: honesty and kindness are the keys to non-judgmental seeing and successful anthropological observation.

You won't be able to identify whether the path you follow is your heart's desire or not if you continue to blame yourself, people around you, or the circumstances you are in for what is happening in your life.

And on top of that, you won't be able to have fun in the games you play if you continue to complain about your life and how it turns out. But don't be tempted to judge yourself for judging. Because you also then tear yourself out of the game flow.

After quoting Ariel and Shya Kane in this and the previous chapter so many times, I would like to conclude this chapter with their words on our truth and what can happen if we try to resist, escape or deny what we see in it:

"When you have chipped away at the edges of your truth and life applies a little pressure, things easily fall apart. But when you operate with integrity, it is far easier to withstand life's pressures." — Ariel and Shya Kane, *Practical Enlightenment*

So I invite you to look honestly and with kindness at what your *escape-from* and *escape-to* tasks, projects, and activities are.

11. What are your *escape-from* and *escape-to* tasks?

Probably by now, you have had thoughts popping into your mind with realizations about what your *escape-from* and *escape-to* tasks are. They might have been the same as the examples above, or something else entirely.

As I mentioned in section 1 above, I waited to ask you about these until now because I wanted to make you aware of various clever and judgmental "traps" our, as Ariel and Shya Kane call it, "insatiable mind" uses when we try to look at our lives and where we are in this moment. I hoped that you would see this, relax and find humor in all these tricks your mind is playing on you.

But now I think you have all the tools to answer the following questions non-judgmentally, as a curious and engaged anthropologist would do when studying a new culture.

Don't worry if you notice that you can't identify your examples of escape-from and escape-to tasks clearly, since depending on circumstances they can switch places and roles. That is natural. We've discussed this briefly above, and with time you will learn to recognize these dynamics more and more easily.

What are your escape-from tasks?
That is:
What are the projects that you really want to do but simply don't find the time for?
Your answer (at least one example):

_____

_____

Self-Gamification Happiness Formula

_____
_____
_____

What are the things you committed to or were told to do, but you think you don't want to do and consider tedious and annoying?
Your answer (at least one example):

_____
_____
_____
_____
_____

What are your escape-to tasks?
And more concrete:

What are the *obvious* escape-to tasks (that don't appear to be too productive) for you? Your answer (at least one example):

_____
_____
_____
_____
_____

What are the *productive* escape-to activities for you?

Your answer (at least one example):
_____
_____
_____
_____
_____
_____

References:
* Ariel and Shya Kane in *Being Here: Modern Day Tales of Enlightenment*
** Anonymous
*** Shannon L. Alder
**** https://www.youtube.com/watch?v=0JV03rpPPSw
***** https://www.victoriaichizlibartels.com/which-way-to-go/

Part III. Kaizen and the Small Steps

Chapter 7. Kaizen and Why It Works

"Just as a record-setting marathon runner will continue to search out ways to shave another second off his or her best time, you can seek out strategies to constantly sharpen your life's game."
— Robert Maurer, *One Small Step Can Change Your Life: The Kaizen Way*

1. What we have covered so far
Here is a quick reminder of what we have covered so far. You learned about self-gamification and what approaches it embraces. You learned about awareness and how you can observe yourself non-judgmentally as an anthropologist would. And you assessed your projects and activities in terms of whether you escape from or to them.

In this part of the book, you will continue the practice of observing yourself as an anthropologist would, that is non-judgmentally. This corresponds to the second addend of the self-gamification happiness formula, which we defined in chapter 4, section 5. There, I claimed you first need to be present and aware before you can identify your next smallest, most effortless and appropriate step, the kaizen way.

You will also learn about kaizen and why making progress by taking one small step at a time is so efficient. You will get to know your brain and to better understand your behavior.

With that knowledge, you will understand why you procrastinate over various things, even those that you want to do. Then you will learn to identify and make the smallest, and most effortless steps toward your goals, which will help you to bypass the fear of more significant tasks.

With these tools it will become more natural for you to practice seeing both your dreams or goals and where you are in any given circumstance so that you can identify the next, most appropriate step to make.

But before we look at the definition of kaizen and the philosophy of breaking things into small bits, whether it is a problem or a task, I would like to share with you how I discovered kaizen.

2. How I discovered kaizen and why I was inspired

I didn't know about kaizen when I first played the game I later named the 5 Minute Perseverance Game (see more on this story in chapter 3, section 1). And indeed, I wasn't seeking to understand why the game was so much fun, I simply enjoyed playing it.

An activity that has always been fun to me since my school and university years is reading. So it was reading, or rather my curiosity about a book, which led me to discover kaizen.

I lived in Denmark (as I still do today) and was about to start a project for a big Danish company on behalf of another Danish company. So when I heard about a seminar called "Danish Workplace Culture," I immediately wanted to attend. The workshop was fun, valuable, and eye-opening in many respects. The seminar instructor mentioned a book that I'd heard of previously but forgotten to check out. The anecdotes the instructor shared from the book ignited my interest to such an extent that I sought it out as soon as I got home. I downloaded a sample, and shortly after reading it, bought the book.

The book is *The Year of Living Danishly: Uncovering the Secrets of the World's Happiest Country* by Helen Russell, a British journalist and writer, now based in Denmark. In this book, Russell reports on her experience of settling in a country with a different mentality and working culture from the one she grew up in. The title of the book says it all: it is about understanding why the Danish people are so happy and well in themselves, even if they have some of the most inclement weather conditions in the world.

I loved the book so much that I checked whether Helen Russell had written any others. Her second book is titled *Leap Year: How Small Steps Can Make a Giant Difference*. The book is as fun and revealing as the first one. However, the chapter with the title "Finance — Got Money On My Mind" rang the loudest bells for me.

This chapter is where I first learned about kaizen and how the philosophy of small steps can improve any area of life, including personal finances. At least, this is what Helen Russell applied it to. She learned about kaizen from Dr. Robert Maurer, Director of Behavioral Sciences for the Family Practice Residency Program at Santa Monica, UCLA Medical Center and a faculty member at the UCLA School of Medicine[*], whom she interviewed for this chapter of the book.

I kept coming back to the concept of kaizen and how, despite being such a seemingly well-proven and oft-used approach, it was, to my knowledge, still largely unheard of. I decided to do a search for kaizen on one of the largest online bookstores. The first book that appeared and seemed to be most purchased and most liked was *One Small Step Can Change Your Life: The Kaizen Way* written by the person Helen Russell had interviewed for her book. Robert Maurer was the one who wrote it, and several other popular books on small steps and kaizen. The other books he has written on the topic are *Mastering Fear: Harnessing Emotion to Achieve Excellence in Work, Health and Relationships* and *The Spirit of Kaizen: Creating Lasting Excellence One Small Step at a Time*.

So I downloaded a sample of *One Small Step Can Change Your Life: The Kaizen Way* and started to read. I immediately couldn't stop. Only the necessity for sleep and family and other commitments helped me to put it down. As I read the book, a realization came, as a big epiphany, that this is what I was doing with my 5 Minute Perseverance Game. Among other things, I was applying kaizen.

3. What is kaizen?

Here is how Wikipedia describes kaizen at the time of writing this book:

"Kaizen (改善) is the Japanese word for 'improvement.' In business, kaizen refers to activities that continuously improve all functions and involve all employees from the CEO to the assembly line workers. It also applies to processes, such as purchasing and logistics, that cross organizational boundaries into the supply chain. It has been applied in healthcare, psychotherapy, life-coaching, government, and banking.

"By improving standardized programmes and processes, kaizen aims to eliminate waste. Kaizen was first practiced in Japanese businesses after World War II, influenced in part by American business and quality-management teachers, and most notably as part of The Toyota Way. It has since spread throughout the world and has been applied to environments outside business and productivity." **

As I read more about kaizen, I discovered Robert Maurer's name appeared frequently when it came to the application of kaizen on a personal level.

In my opinion Robert Maurer's *One Small Step Can Change Your Life: The Kaizen Way* can be considered the master textbook on applying kaizen (including its nowadays well-known features, micro-progress***, micro-resilience****, mini habits*****, atomic habits****** and other similar terms standing for making progress in small steps) on a personal level (whether for work or non-work activities). The book also gives an excellent overview of kaizen's history and areas of application.

I will quote Robert Maurer many times in this chapter, and throughout the book as a whole.

Here is how Robert Maurer summarizes his book *One Small Step Can Change Your Life: The Kaizen Way*:

"The succeeding chapters are devoted to the personal application of kaizen and encompass six different strategies. These strategies include:
- asking small questions to dispel fear and inspire creativity
- thinking small thoughts to develop new skills and habits — without moving a muscle
- taking small actions that guarantee success
- solving small problems, even when you're faced with an overwhelming crisis
- bestowing small rewards to yourself or others to produce the best results
- recognizing the small but crucial moments that everyone else ignores" — Robert Maurer, *One Small Step Can Change Your Life: The Kaizen Way*

That says it all. In the spirit of kaizen, you break anything, either a challenge or a task or whatever you are paying attention to, down into small and effortless steps. And you give each of these small bits your full attention, which is easy if the task is small enough to solve with little effort.

As I learned more about kaizen from Robert Maurer's work and looked at what I was doing with my self-motivational games (and the 5 Minute Perseverance Game in particular), I realized I had been applying kaizen without being aware of it.

Here are the lessons I learned about applying kaizen in the process of turning my life into games:

- I applied the 5 Minute Perseverance Game to myself. I gamified my, not someone else's (which is, of course, impossible), life. So, it was a personal application.
- When given only a short amount of time (five minutes, for example) to address a task, I could only ask myself small questions answerable within those five (or so) minutes.
- The thinking of *"small thoughts"* occurred naturally, as I progressed from the beginning of any game-round. At the start of a month, when I began a project (or a phase of a project) I sometimes still thought *"big thoughts."* But the limited time again came in handy, and every day it got easier and easier to make the next move in the game, and the thoughts about it got smaller and smaller, quieter and quieter, and therefore more and more manageable and pleasant.
- Again the five (or thereabouts) minutes limited the actions that could be taken.

- The brilliance of having only a short period to work in, was in allowing only small problems to be addressed at any one time. (See also the small questions above.)
- The points I gave myself were the small rewards. I discovered that gathering and counting them, as well as the seemingly hard work and challenge to gather as many of the points as possible, brought much more (and immediate) fun than the supposedly big rewards of recognition by someone else.
- Limited time helped me to concentrate on the given moment because I wanted to make each little step work. Otherwise, I wouldn't get the point. With this, I noticed more and more of the small moments, small events, along the way. And the project I was working on then became an enjoyable process, instead of being a vast and unreachable goal, something to be finished with to make me happy.

It is fantastic to discover that something we are doing and having fun with, appears to be based on fundamental and well-tested wisdom. It feels empowering and reassuring.

I am grateful to have discovered kaizen and gamification, and that I was unknowingly applying both to my life, simultaneously. By learning about and practicing these two disciplines, I sharpened the awareness that helped me better understand my mechanical behaviours (which originated from my childhood, and imprints of the cultures I have been exposed to).

Reading more about kaizen, related by Robert Maurer, helped me to resolve challenges that seemed unsolvable with the 5 Minute Perseverance Game. While I made progress with some of my projects and activities as I played this game, I procrastinated about others. Even five minutes on those tasks seemed too hard.

Five minutes wasn't that long, I thought. Why couldn't I persevere in some cases for even that length of time?

Robert Maurer's book brought the clarity I needed. I learned about the natural reason for procrastination: in the structure and basic functions of the human brain.

Apparently, even five minutes can appear too long for some activities, and a few seconds would be just right. It all has to do with how our brains perceive the task at hand. Even a few minutes can appear too immense to accomplish. Here is why.

4. Structure of the human brain

I learned from Robert Maurer that our procrastination might have a natural cause. More precisely, in the nature of how our brains function.

Let's consider the structure of the human brain and how it controls our behavior in some situations.

Our brains consist of three main parts:

- "At the bottom of the brain is the brain stem. It's... called the reptilian brain (and in fact, it does look like an alligator's whole brain). The reptilian brain wakes you up in the morning, sends you off to sleep at night, and reminds your heart to beat.
- "Sitting on top of the brain stem is the midbrain, also known as the mammalian brain... The midbrain regulates the body's internal temperature, houses our emotions, and governs the fight-or-flight response that keeps us alive in the face of danger.
- "The third part of the brain is the cortex... The cortex, which wraps around the rest of the brain, is responsible for the miracle of being human. ... It's where our rational thoughts and creative impulses take place. When we want to make a change, or jump-start the creative process, we need access to the cortex." — Robert Maurer, *One Small Step Can Change Your Life: The Kaizen Way*

So the cortex is responsible for our creativity and rational thoughts, for art, for the books we write, science, music and so on.

But our procrastination and fear of doing or not doing something have their root instead in the midbrain.

"The midbrain is where you'll find a structure called the amygdala. ... The amygdala is crucial to our survival. It controls the fight-or-flight response, an alarm mechanism that we share with all other mammals. It was designed to alert parts of the body for action in the face of immediate danger. One way it accomplishes this is to slow down or to stop other functions such as rational and creative thinking that could interfere with the physical ability to run or fight." — Robert Maurer, *One Small Step Can Change Your Life: The Kaizen Way*

Thanks to this fight-or-flight mechanism, humans, along with other mammals, survive in the face of danger. In this way, we react appropriately and jump out of the way of a fast-approaching car or dodge the suddenly detached license plate falling off the vehicle in front of us on a highway. Or it can help in less dramatic situations, by saving us the additional effort of cleaning or retrieval, had we not caught the wine glass or pen before it fell.

The problem with the amygdala is that its fight-or-flight modus is switched on when we experience any kind of fear, or when we face the need to step out of our comfort zone.

You will know from experience that any new challenge, or opportunity, or desire causes at least some degree of fear. Any creative project is accompanied by fear.

Here is what best-selling author Elizabeth Gilbert writes in her famous book *Big Magic: Creative Living Beyond Fear*:

"It seems to me that my fear and my creativity are basically conjoined twins — as evidenced by the fact that creativity cannot take a single step forward without fear marching right alongside it. Fear and creativity shared a womb, they were born at the same time, and they still share some vital organs. This is why we have to be careful of how we handle our fear — because I've noticed that when people try to kill off their fear, they often end up inadvertently murdering their creativity in the process."

So the fear is there whether we want it or not. And it is ready to jump out and draw our attention as soon as we feel discomfort. However great this discomfort is. The fear grows even stronger when the goals set are not immediately achievable, which is often the case.

As you will have experienced many times, such challenges or goals might be a new job, starting a new hobby, or pursuing and presenting the results of a creative project, meeting someone new, presenting at a conference, and many others.

In all those cases, and I would like to quote Robert Maurer here:

"the amygdala alerts parts of the body to prepare for action — and our access to the cortex, the thinking part of the brain, is restricted, and sometimes shut down." — Robert Maurer, *One Small Step Can Change Your Life: The Kaizen Way*

So, if the task appears to be too big and overwhelming, then we either:
- complain about it, get angry = FIGHT, or
- start doing something else = FLIGHT.

But what can we do about this? Is there something we can do to prevent the creative functions of our brain from shutting down completely? Are there any tools we can use to recognize our fear, bypass it, and create space for creativity, courage, and gratitude for what we are up to?

Yes, there are. These tools include becoming aware of where we are, where our goals are, and what our next step could be. I will address that in the next chapter.

But before we go on, let me emphasize the importance of the awareness of this presence of fear. I started the preface of this book with how I wondered what made successful people successful.

Robert Maurer made an interesting observation in his book *Mastering Fear: Harnessing Emotion to Achieve Excellence in Work, Health and Relationships*, which amounts to successful people having fun with what they are up to:

"Successful people are consistently aware and accepting of their fears. They assume that whenever they are doing something important, fear will show. The bigger the streets they want to cross, metaphorically speaking (for example, creating a loving relationship, dealing with a promotion, starting a new business, or committing to a healthy lifestyle), the more fear will be present."

Further, he insists:

"Fear is good for human beings and it is essential to our well-being!"

and comments:

"Successful people find fear as uncomfortable as anyone else does, however instead of rejecting or avoiding it, they see it as a signal that something important is happening that requires their attention. As children do, they assume that fear is a natural part of life, and they know that whenever they're doing something important, fear will show up. Fear is something to be recognized, embraced, and boldly addressed; and developing an acceptance and awareness of fear is crucial in maintaining success in work, health, and relationships." —

Robert Maurer, *Mastering Fear: Harnessing Emotion to Achieve Excellence in Work, Health and Relationships*

The combination of awareness (that is non-judgmental seeing), kaizen, and gamification, which make up self-gamification, can help you to master fear in a light and enjoyable way.

5. Appreciating small moments

Nothing compares to the feeling of getting the job done. For the day, or in totality. And it is curious that we humans tend to want to make everything big, and to view the significant things as the best: our houses, our cars, our achievements, and even tasks. The harder the job, we think, the greater the satisfaction when we finish it.

However, interestingly enough, when we are happy, we are just happy; without necessarily knowing the reason for it. Often, these happy, blissful moments don't coincide with the job being done, since the finish line for the task or assignment could still be a way off. And conversely, by the time we have achieved the big goal, we might be so exhausted and unhappy that we don't have enough energy to celebrate.

But when we achieve something small, we probably have the energy to celebrate it (by giving oneself a point, praise, a smile), and this boosts us towards taking the next step.

Here is how Robert Maurer describes the effect of kaizen on these small and often ignored events and our lives in general:

"The kaizen approach to life requires a slower pace and an appreciation of small moments. This pleasant technique can lead to creative breakthroughs and strengthened relationships, and give you a daily boost toward excellence." — Robert Maurer, *One Small Step Can Change Your Life: The Kaizen Way*

6. You might have applied kaizen (or other micro-progress techniques) already

Take a look at the large projects you have worked on, and especially those you have finished. How did you make progress in them? Was it always by working in big chunks or were there at least some days when you had to use smaller steps to make progress? Do you remember how you experienced those smaller steps? (Don't worry if you can't remember.)

An example for me was preparing to move from our rented apartment into our first house whilst heavily pregnant. I interspersed packing with making lists and decluttering that I could do while sitting down, and invited my mother for a coffee followed by a joint packing session. In the breaks, I read, wrote or edited my various writing projects, or attended to household chores. This might have been the first time I consciously broke a more substantial project into small steps and was happy about doing each (or at least most) of them. It was about two years before I discovered kaizen.

The following quote by Robert Maurer gives a clue as to how those small steps might feel when they occur:

"These quiet steps bypass our mental alarm system, allowing our creative and intellectual processes to flow without obstruction." — Robert Maurer, *The Spirit of Kaizen: Creating Lasting Excellence One Small Step at a Time*

Use the lines below (or a notebook, if you are reading this on an e-reader) and a pen to recall these large projects, and also what those small steps were (or might have been, if you are not quite sure). Make notes about at least one such project that comes to mind:

_____
_____
_____
_____
_____
_____

References:

* http://www.scienceofexcellence.com/ and http://www.scienceofexcellence.com/one-small-step-can-change-your-life-book.php

** https://en.wikipedia.org/wiki/Kaizen

*** "Micro-Progress and the Magic of Just Getting Started," Tim Herrera, Smarter Living at *The New York Times*, Jan. 22, 2018, https://www.nytimes.com/2018/01/22/smarter-living/micro-progress.html

**** Micro-resilience at https://microresilience.com/

***** Mini-habits by https://stephenguise.com/

****** Atomic habits at https://jamesclear.com/atomic-habits

Chapter 8. The Magic of an Effortless Step

"If you take care of the small things, the big things take care of themselves." — Emily Dickinson

1. Continuing to see ourselves non-judgmentally
Let's continue seeing ourselves and what we are up to non-judgmentally.

In chapter 6 we identified our escape-from and escape-to tasks and realized that they could switch places. Escape-from tasks can become escape-to tasks and vice versa.

We have also seen that as long as we don't give them up completely, both sub-types of escape-from tasks are those we want to complete, independent of whether we think (or say) that we want to do them or not.

We all have many tasks on our to-do lists. To be more efficient we tend to record the end-results of each task on those lists. So, those tasks often end up being as huge as New Year's resolutions. Which could be one of the main reasons for our procrastination, and our escape from them to doing something else.

Do you have something like the below on your to-do list?
- Write a report, an article for a magazine, a blog post, a master or Ph.D. thesis, a non-fiction book,
- Study for an exam,
- Write a novel,
- Learn a language,
- Renovate a house,
- Lose weight (or exercise to lose weight, to become healthier, to get in better shape).

I had most of the above on my to-do list at one point or another.

After practicing self-gamification for some time, I realized that itemising the tasks in this format sounded to my mind as though they had to be completed in one step.

But attempting to accomplish the escape-from tasks on my to-do lists in one go felt as overwhelming as jumping between rooftops without any preparation. No parkour master or stunt-person would ever try something like that in one go.

No wonder I ran away from these tasks!

If a stunt-person concentrated only on that final jump, he or she would never be able to do it. Any stunt requires both physical and mental preparation. One step at a time. And all training involves repetition of the previous level, plus one little step more.

So why do so many of us push ourselves to do the challenging stunts (especially mental ones), either in one go or in just a few giant leaps?

Is it surprising then that we try to escape, either into complaints, or to activities we didn't want or plan to engage in at that moment?

2. What size step to make next

So, what should you do? Robert Maurer and many others who have experienced the magic of making progress with tiny steps recommend making the smallest and most effortless steps possible.

Robert Maurer said another quite revealing, and for me perspective-changing, thing. Here it is:

"Even the small signs that you are resisting the small step are an indication that the step is too big." — Robert Maurer, *One Small Step Can Change Your Life: The Kaizen Way*

Isn't that amazing? Do you see how awareness and kaizen sit brilliantly together?

Together they show that feeling off-balance, overwhelmed, or in resistance to something is not bad. In fact, it is a helpful indicator. It is an indicator that you are trying to jump too far (or too high) to reach what is out of "the limits of [your] own endurance."*

So if you feel overwhelmed by the next task, then first become aware of that. Then identify the smallest step that won't overwhelm you, but will take you in the same direction as what you want or set out to do. Make that step. Appreciate it (we will talk about how to do this, and why it is important, in chapter 14, section 3). And after that, continue with your day. And whenever you feel overwhelmed, simply repeat the process.

Here is how I became aware of the magic of the effortless step.

3. Discovering the magic of a small, effortless step

I mentioned earlier that there were some tasks that I couldn't make progress with, even with my 5 Minute Perseverance Game. Five minutes still felt overwhelming, although I wasn't aware of that then. I simply put off doing them and was angry with myself for being unable to persevere with such simple tasks for even five minutes a day. Then Robert Maurer's simple observation opened my eyes.

So I took the advice to heart and started reducing the time I'd spend on each step from five minutes to two, then to one, and even to a matter of seconds.

Sharing self-gamification with others required more attentive and non-judgmental observation of what I was doing, as well as analysis of my game results. They were quite revealing. The results of my self-motivational games in August 2017 were both surprising and incredibly enlightening.

In that month, I decided to make an attempt to gamify most of my life. Until then I was gamifying various projects and activities, but other areas remained untouched, both by the game and by my attention. So I made a list of all the projects and activities I thought I wanted, liked, or needed to be doing in that month. I came up with twenty-one various projects and activities. Among them were: writing four different books, posting chapters of three of them as blog posts, blogging on other topics, pitching new projects, taking care of my family, household, health, reading books, answering e-mails, and many others.

The rule for each project game was that if I did the minimum amount set for a particular project on any day of that month (this might be to write a sentence or a paragraph, read a page or a chapter in a book, or complete a short task), then I would record a point for that project on that day. I could earn only one point per project per day, giving a maximum of thirty-one points per project in that month (August). The goal was to achieve the minimum in as many of the twenty-one projects and activities each day as possible.

Before taking a closer look at the results, I had the idea that I would have achieved more points for the projects I preferred doing.

I also thought that I never managed to attend to any one project on every single day of the month. So for August, I thought that I would not be able to gather thirty-one points on a project or an activity.

But I did.

There was another surprise too. I hadn't expected to fail to gather even a single point on a project.

But that happened too.

That was exactly what happened with project 10 and activity 16. I gathered zero and thirty-one points correspondingly.

When I looked closer at what these were, I was utterly dumbfounded.

Here they are:
- Project 10: Develop a training course on 5 Minute Perseverance Game (5MPG): outline, slides, text, a little every day (even one sentence would be enough for a point),
- Activity 16: Practicing straight posture: 15 seconds every day.

Practicing straight posture was something I dreaded. I initially tried doing it for a full five minutes a day and failed. I figured I mustn't care about it that much, because I always used to sit and walk around like a question mark. But since I often had it pointed out that I should straighten my posture, including by my pediatrician many years ago, I grudgingly attempted to develop the habit of keeping a straight posture.

After reading Robert Maurer claim that even a few seconds on an activity every day could help to turn it into a habit, I gave it a try without really believing it would work. So my surprise was tremendous when I saw that I had managed to do it on every single day of August 2017.

On the other hand, the project I thought I was very passionate about, number 10, didn't get me a single point. That was, teaching a game I called the 5 Minute Perseverance Game. That "game" was the first framework I used to turn my life into games. At that point I had the basic idea for the course (which was published a year later and the material of which served as the basis for this book), but the concept was yet to crystallize — that only happened several months later, towards the end of 2017.

Now in retrospect, I see that what I was doing then would ultimately contribute to the project. I might not have written down a sentence for the course's outline or created a slide, but I continued playing my games and blogging about my experiences. In doing so I learned more and more about the self-gamification process, and a year later as I worked on the slides and the script of that very course, the steps that had seemed overwhelming in August 2017 were easy and fun to make in May 2018.

Unless I tried to get ahead of myself and concentrated on the finish line. Then the process stalled and I felt powerless again.

But at that time, I was already testing the tools of awareness and making steps as short as a few seconds, and had various game designs to record my progress in points. So as soon as the alarm for being overwhelmed and upset went off, I saw that I had a choice between staying disconcerted and stuck in complaint (and the possibility of fleeing into escape-to activities), or getting curious about how I could use those self-gamification tools.

As I continued using these tools, I saw a drastic change both in my attitude toward the task at hand and the actual progress I made in those initially stalling activities.

I was also delighted to experience how enormous challenges, problems, and questions could be broken down into tiny, digestible, and easily processed components.

4. Preferred versus effortless

This experience showed me the accuracy of what Robert Maurer said about the size of step to take in a project — that if there is even the slightest feeling of being overwhelmed, however small, then the step is still too big.

The activity with the straight posture was anything but preferred by me, but still, I managed to attend to it every day, because standing or sitting up straight and counting slowly from one to fifteen was effortless. Beyond that, halfway through the month, I noticed myself automatically straightening up even after I'd achieved the planned fifteen seconds and a point for that day. That boosted my motivation, and straight posture became one of the first activities I took on in the mornings of the following days.

And the online course on self-gamification remained untouched during August 2017, even if I considered it to be something I very much wanted to do. But preparing the material for the course meant too much effort at that time, so I ran away from it and instead chose to do something else.

Later I observed the same pattern with other activities. The more I felt a step in a project to be effortless — even if I thought that I didn't like the activity very much — the more points I gathered.

Here comes anthropology again. Become aware that you often intuitively choose to do small, effortless things first.

We escape to certain activities because they appear effortless to us. It is much easier to push the button and scroll down in the Facebook app than to walk away from a computer, brush your teeth and get ready for bed. It is much easier to watch YouTube videos than write a sentence for a report.

Or at least this is how we judge them. We think it is easier. It might not be in reality, because the effects of watching and scrolling might not be uplifting or as easy as initially perceived after all. We might just be sticking with the labels we put on those activities, rather than finding out how they really feel in that moment.

And sometimes you might find yourself leaving the watching and scrolling on social media for the things you always thought tedious, such as cleaning or laundry or working out or something else. You might find that the things you used to claim you didn't like doing are now effortless to accomplish, and you instead observe yourself escaping into them. This awareness is priceless!

Do you remember what we discovered in chapter 6 about studying ourselves as anthropologists would? That we also procrastinate over the things we claim we would love to do?

That means we can do anything, whether we *think* we like it or not.

But we have to approach it the kaizen way and break whatever we set out to do in small, effortless steps.

And continue practicing seeing ourselves non-judgmentally, like anthropologists.

Let's take a look at the to-do list we drafted above:
- Write a report, an article for a magazine, a blog post, a master or Ph.D. thesis, a non-fiction book,
- Study for an exam,
- Write a novel,
- Learn a language,
- Renovate a house,
- Lose weight (or exercise to lose weight, to become healthier, to get in better shape).

Here is a suggestion: title your current to-do list "Goals in my Project Games" and create a new list for the next steps.

The clue: these steps should be the smallest and most effortless you could possibly make.

And another tip: try to make the smallest step as specific as possible.

The to-do list above could then look like this:
- Write a paragraph for my report, article, blog post, master or Ph.D. thesis, non-fiction book

(An alternative: choose a topic for the article, blog post, section of the thesis to address next),
- Identify the material that covers the first topic in the list of areas to revise for the exam,
- Choose the genre for the novel or the reader's age,
- Learn one phrase in the language of my choice and try to use it in various situations, either out loud or in my thoughts,
- Choose one room in my house that I would like to renovate first,
- Replace my afternoon snack with a glass of water or unsweetened tea (or do one yoga/stretch exercise before bed or in the morning before taking a shower).

How do these sound to you?

If they still sound too big to accomplish in one go, break them down further. Do so until you are eager to address each of these tasks — and can't wait to do them — not because you want to be finished with them, but because they do not overwhelm you anymore and are easy-breezy and even fun to do.

Let's concentrate on small steps, and enjoy each of them. And even if you are taking those small steps to train for a real stunt or an acrobatic act, then the final feat itself won't be something that gigantic and dramatic, but just another one of these steps that is as easy and fun as all the others were along the way. Or at least much more straightforward than you anticipated at the start of your preparation.

5. When the beginning becomes overwhelming

You might have looked at the last more detailed list I suggested above, and still thought it appeared daunting. Especially when the word "start" is used.

The following items were on my to-do list at various points in time, and sometimes simultaneously:
- Start plotting my next novel,
- Start searching for a job,
- Start writing a report,
- Start networking with specialists in my business niche,
- Start reading an article,
- Start applying for a new passport,
- Start learning to use my new mobile phone,
- Start packing for our holiday.

The phrases above might seem like small steps since they only require that the process is started, not completed. But the word "start" can sound daunting in itself and make the task difficult to approach.

Self-Gamification Happiness Formula

The other issue with these statements is that they are not concrete. The word "start" is vague and doesn't precisely state what should be done.

Here is how you could rethink and reformulate the tasks above:

- Choose a theme/topic/era/setting for my novel,
- Make a list of jobs I would be interested in,
- Find (ask for) or draft the requirements for the report,
- Identify one (or more) local meet-up for my business area,
- Print out the article or download it on my preferred media, or read one paragraph or section,
- Find out where I can apply for a new passport,
- Unpack my new mobile phone, read (one chapter of) the user manual, and charge it,
- Take out the suitcase and put it near the wardrobe, or jot down five items I need to take with me on holiday, or list the documents I need to take when traveling to that country.

If the suggestions above don't seem effortless to do then break them down further, or do something else on the list that does. Accomplishing that task might give you the necessary boost to do the other assignments, or give you an idea of how small the steps should be.

6. What is all this bureaucracy good for?

You might be appalled by my suggestion of how to record your to-do list items. You might argue that by marking them in such detail, the only thing you will be doing is recording all the items and not actually doing them. And you might become even more appalled when you find me adding to this bureaucracy with the recommendation in the next part (part IV) of the book that you design various feedback systems for your self-motivational games and make sure that you record the progress of your projects with points, badges, stars and/or others.

A quick reminder of the goal of this book. It is also a self-help book. So, if you don't need help and your work is progressing well, and you are enjoying what you are doing — in other words, you are on your happy way — then you don't need to write everything down. Don't stop the flow when you are in it.

But if there is no flow, if you stepped off your happy path and feel lost, then you can use these tools to help you. Self-gamification with the three approaches it embraces helps you to return to the flow. And to do so gently and kindly to yourself.

So if you observe that you are continually forcing yourself to move in leaps (especially mental ones) that you can't do, and suffer because of it, then stop.

Next, be your own anthropologist by observing the situation you are in, your state of mind, and what there is to do.

Then, as a designer, adjust your game-design so that you as a player enjoy your project game.

And finally, as an avid player, identify your next, small, and effortless step in the game and take it.

In order to maintain balance, you need to move one small step at a time. This applies both to our physical state (when we're awake) and our mental one.

7. Breaking off a small piece and accumulating the results

Do you remember the following passage about truth that I quoted in chapter 6, section 10?

"When you have chipped away at the edges of your truth and life applies a little pressure, things easily fall apart. But when you operate with integrity, it is far easier to withstand life's pressures." — Ariel and Shya Kane, *Practical Enlightenment*

This analogy of chipping away at something also works the other way around: when achieving something. If you "chip away at the edges" of your project then with only "a little pressure" you will succeed to make more progress than you initially believed possible.

The more I became aware of kaizen and its related techniques and approaches, and the more I practiced the small steps myself, the more I saw I was able to manage many things I thought I couldn't do, or had procrastinated about for a long time. I handled them quickly if I "broke off" a small piece of a huge task and concentrated my attention on that small piece.

After managing that little step I did sometimes glance at the remaining huge piece and get overwhelmed again. But the good feeling I got for succeeding at the small bits easily accumulated over time, and it became more comfortable to concentrate on the little bits and steps.

Each little success was more empowering than I could have expected. Especially if I took a short moment to acknowledge each of those steps. (See more on this in the next part (part IV), and especially in chapter 14, section 3.)

Bringing myself into the current moment of my life, again and again, shed light on why kaizen is so powerful. The results of practicing it and self-gamification as a whole were both immediate and cumulative.

Here is how Ariel and Shya Kane describe these effects of being present on our lives:

"The more you invest in being present, the deeper the experience becomes. And while you can't authentically 'be present' in order to produce positive results, you will find that as a byproduct of being present you are naturally more productive, effective and satisfied." — Ariel and Shya Kane, *Practical Enlightenment*

This natural byproduct of becoming more "productive, effective and satisfied" is the other fantastic thing about slowing down and taking one small and effortless step at a time, in addition to the growing enjoyment of the process. It is normal to assume that by making small steps our progress slows down, but in the end, by making steady progress and not spending too much time looking at the whole thing, we reach the goals faster, and with considerably less effort than we anticipated. This does feel quite magical.

8. Don't judge excuses; they are just an indicator

Let's apply awareness again. Have you noticed yourself searching for reasons as soon as you "caught" yourself procrastinating? I intentionally used "caught," rather than "observed," since the latter denotes non-judgmental seeing.

But when you come up with excuses as to why you have or haven't done something (whether in your mind or out loud), then there is a judgment — unnoticed to you — hovering in your mind.

When we feel overwhelmed we shy away from the task at hand and start looking for excuses, both for what we have or haven't done in the past, and why we are avoiding doing something now. So, like the feeling of being overwhelmed and stressed, the excuses are not good or bad, or even necessary. They are just an indicator, a little light emitting diode going off when something is amiss, and part of our brain wants to draw attention to the fact that action is needed.

One of the reasons for this little lamp going off could be that we are concentrating on the finish line without paying attention to where we are, and what our next step could be. We often think that when we cross that finish line, then we will be happy or satisfied or accomplished, or all of these. In which case we despise the current moment because we're not yet at the finish line.

We forget that each small step can bring massive satisfaction if paid attention and attended to.

In an exchange with a student on the course *Motivate Yourself by Turning Your Life Into Fun Games: Practice Self-Gamification, a Unique Self-Help Approach Uniting Anthropology, Kaizen, and Gamification*, an image was conjured of eating a cake. What fun would there be in jumping to the end of having eaten a piece of your favorite cake, without having savored each little bite? In fact, with all our favorite foods, the first bite is always the best.

What if we thought of the five (or more or less) minutes spent on a project or activity on our list as that first bite?

9. Can a step be too small?

We've talked in depth about the brilliance of small steps or even taking just one tiny step in a project a day. But we often have deadlines for specific assignments (which could also be self-imposed if we wish to learn more or become more prolific in a particular area by a certain date), and small, effortless steps might seem unreasonable. Especially if they are done only once a day.

However, you don't have to do just one of those simple steps a day. You can take several of the small, effortless steps in any one day, doing something else between them.

I do this, for example, with many of my large projects and those that have deadlines. I start with committing to the smallest step for the project and then give myself permission to do something else between the single steps. I often find myself getting more and more into the flow after one or two initial steps, and then not wanting to leave the project for a while.

Sometimes increasing the duration of a step might help too. In September 2018, I realized that I was resisting doing some of my projects for both short and more extended periods. I couldn't record points per completed bit of a project. Like, for example, preparing slides for a presentation: one slide might have taken one minute, another twenty. Giving myself points for the time spent on the project seemed like a good solution.

The first idea I had was to record my points for each minute. No, I thought, that many points would be too tedious to record. Five minutes required conversion of the minutes into points and the uneven number bothered me. Then I had it — ten minutes per point sounded neither too short nor too long. Just right. So I would earn six points per hour, one hundred and forty-four for the whole day (twenty-four hours).

[A small side-note: Enough sleep as well as taking care of my health earned me not only the points but a star too. This was one of the reasons I called this design the "Balance Game" (see chapter 20).]

By recording a point for a specific period of time, I could see how I used my time. I tried it for a week and loved the approach. So I continued by setting the timer for ten minutes, concentrating on a task the best I could, and when the alarm went off, I recorded a point for that project. Then I either continued with the same job or did something else for ten (or another number) minutes and then came back to the project at hand.

You might point out that this little break when the alarm went off could have disturbed the process of performing a task. But actually, it didn't. I realized that sometimes, when the signal of my timer went off, I was lost in thoughts instead of attending to my project, and it brought me back into the moment. So I recorded a point and concentrated again on the project.

10. Other small-step techniques

Many methods have a similar approach to kaizen at their core. Here are some that I discovered after "stumbling upon" kaizen: micro-progress, mini and atomic habits, micro-resilience, and others. I continue to discover more versions of these today. They all have the same idea of making progress in small steps. You can find references to more material on these at the end of the previous chapter (chapter 7).

Kaizen sounded like one of the first of these approaches to be consciously developed and applied, not only by many individuals but by whole corporations, and to even be widespread among people of the same nation. It had its start in the USA at the beginning of World War II and was then applied to rebuild Japan's economy after the war. I discovered that kaizen was very popular on both a corporate and personal level.

Just like with the variety of "being here" techniques (which we discussed in chapter 5, section 5), you should also choose whatever approach works for you here.

As I mentioned in the previous chapter, I discovered that I had been applying kaizen (or a version of it) without having heard the word before, or known about the concept.

But what appealed to me most about kaizen and in the book *One Small Step Can Change Your Life: The Kaizen Way* by Robert Maurer was the hint that if we resisted a step we wanted to take, however small we thought it was, then this step was still too big. Learning about the structure of the human brain and how it behaved when we feared something was a highlight too.

These observations very much resonated with the concept of awareness as defined by Ariel and Shya Kane and with their idea of studying ourselves anthropologically (see chapter 5, sections 1 and 2).

11. Foreshadowing gamification

We've talked a lot about the compatibility of living in the moment and kaizen. But what about gamification? How does that fit with kaizen and awareness?

When it comes to games, I think yes, many of them are broken down into small steps. They may seem to contain challenging steps requiring effort, but usually this increasing "effort" is incremental. And, as in kaizen, if you want to reach a certain level in a game, but can't initially, you repeat the same thing again and again on one level; then, at some point, you find you can reach the next level seemingly effortlessly, sometimes surprising yourself. The repetition of something you can already do, and which seems effortless, allows you to get better and better so that the next level becomes more comfortable to achieve.

In my opinion, anything can be approached with kaizen or other micro-progress approaches and made much easier to achieve. You don't have to, but when you find something a challenge and resist it, then the three techniques together (non-judgmental seeing, identifying and making the next effortless step, and appreciating that step in your self-motivational game feedback system) are a great toolset for getting out of a complicated and seemingly hopeless situation.

Having said that, I would like to address something that might have made you frown earlier. In section 9 above, I suggested that you could make the steps a bit longer. I described how I recorded one point per ten minutes in the self-motivational game design I called the Balance Game (chapter 20).

But didn't I say before that, that five minutes were too much for me in some activities?

I did.

Doesn't increasing the length of a step to ten minutes contradict the breaking down of steps into the bare minimum?

No, it doesn't, if you look at it like a game. I set a timer for ten minutes, but then I get interested in how much "treasure" I can gather in those minutes; for example, how many pieces of clean laundry I can fold, how many words I can write, how many pieces of furniture I can dust, etc. It's like having mini-games or mini-quests within those ten minutes (see also chapter 12, section 4).

You might find it silly, but this approach takes me out of complaint and into the flow. For that, in my opinion, such silliness is worth it.

In most cases, I don't record points for all of this "treasure" — only for those I am resisting most — but I am more and more aware of what I am doing and how I use my time by playing with various types of feedback systems for my self-motivational games.

You will find more on this in the next part (part IV), and in particular chapter 12, section 9.

Before that, we have one more aspect of possible controversy between games and kaizen to talk about.

12. Small steps in kaizen and hard work in games

The reason for this controversy might lie in the typical characteristic of a gamer, who is often willing to work hard in games (chapter 1, section 3). Does kaizen then make sense?

I asked myself the same thing when I read about "hard work" in games for the first time, and saw the truth in it. I decided to test my 5 Minute Perseverance Game for this feature of games. I asked myself, was the 5 Minute Perseverance Game, where I made progress in my projects by working on them for just five minutes a day, an exception to this and all just "a piece of cake"?

Not exactly. We still need to work on our projects. Especially the ones we procrastinate about, those that challenge us so much that we both yearn to do them and at the same time fear the results of. So the work is still "hard" because we fear it, but the five or fewer minutes adjust this overwhelming task to within "the limits of our own endurance"* and unknowingly to us, we start loving the job at hand instead of dreading or even hating it. Thus, even the tasks that we have to do but have the idea we don't want to do, become doable and even enjoyable because we manage to accomplish them. We might find ourselves doing them for a longer period of times, or taking more tasks into the game. And when the game becomes too much, and we push ourselves too far, we can choose to play differently; just like in other games, we can leave one game and seek another that satisfies our interests and "endurance."

So the relativity of a small step (whatever its length) is also its paradox. On the one hand, we still need to make an effort and challenge ourselves to work through the five, more or fewer minutes, or even just a few seconds. We need to motivate ourselves to start and actually take that step. But on the other hand, by delimiting the time we invest into any project during any given day, we can reward ourselves much sooner than if we worked for the whole day, or week, or month on the same task. In other words, we experience the job at hand as more comfortable to manage than we first thought. At the same time, it is as engulfing and engaging as it could ever be.

Now it is time to identify your steps and the "limits of your endurance," the kaizen way.

13. Identify your next steps, the kaizen way
Activity 1:

Take each of your escape-from projects and activities and assess the following question:

What are the big goals behind the tasks on your to-do lists?

Record these goals regardless of how you feel or think about them now; also if you think you used to want to do them but don't any longer and still have to, or that you never wanted to but must because you made a promise. (We will address moving toward goals we do not think of as our own in chapter 12, section 7 and chapter 15, section 2.)

- For example, why do you want to write a book? Is it to become a published author? Is it to share your memories with your family?
- Or why do you want to learn a language? Is it because you recently moved to a country where they speak it? Or is it because you would like to understand the lyrics of your favorite songs in that language?

Your answer (if this is a paperback, then record at least one example here):

_____
_____
_____
_____

Activity 2:

Answer the following question:

What are the smallest, most effortless steps you can take for each *escape-from* task?

- Is it to write a paragraph or a sentence for your work-in-progress? Or is it to write for five minutes on whatever comes to your mind on the given topic?
- Is it to write three sentences with the new word you learned in the language you are learning? Or is it to translate one sentence of your favorite song?

Your answer (if this is a paperback, then record at least one example here):

_____
_____
_____
_____
_____
_____

References:

* *Reality Is Broken: Why Games Make Us Better and How They Can Change the World,* Jane McGonigal (see this quote in the context of chapter 1, section 3)

Chapter 9. The Starting Point and the Next Step

"Every moment is a fresh new beginning, a wonderful inauguration of the great cosmic journey through the universe. We can do whatever we want. We can change reality at any moment." — Russell Brand

1. Each step is a starting point for the next one
In the previous chapter we discussed the magic and importance of small steps. And how we tend to put big, huge items on our to-do lists.

So, if we map the initial state of our lists and thought processes, then the path might look like this:

Us —> Our to-do list item —> Our goal or dream

After discovering the magic of an effortless step, we recognise that the following path is more pleasant and more doable:

Us —> The smallest effortless step —> ... —> Our to-do list item —> ... —> Our goal or dream

Where "..." corresponds to the other smallest, most effortless steps.

I am a passionate writer. So for me, it is straightforward to illustrate these diagrams with what I do almost every day. Thus for a writer, the previous chart will look as follows:

The writer (at her computer) —> Write a paragraph —> ... —> Write a book —> ... —> Become a published author

But here a question arises: will the next step for a writer always be to write a paragraph, when the starting point might be something else, like taking a shower? Many writers have brilliant ideas while taking a shower. So what is the choice? Despair?

No, rather a recognition that the next step is something else that will also contribute to your goal. So if you take a shower, then the next step would be to finish the shower.

The end of the shower will be your new starting point. There you have the option of either continuing your morning routine or taking a small detour to your desk to make notes on your brilliant idea.

You could also play a Role-Playing Game with yourself and ask yourself, as you would a best friend, to remind you later about this brilliant idea. But assure yourself as you would your best friend, that it won't be a problem if he or she (that is yourself) forgets it.

Yes, I again suggest that you be aware, progress in small steps and treat whatever you do as a game.

But here is another diagram that is trickier than having the shower as the starting point:

You (upset, wherever you are) —> (The next step; not identified yet) —> ... —> Your to-do list item —> ... —> Your goal or dream

When we are upset, then the to-do list items and even the smallest steps might seem further away than they do in other moments.

But what does being upset mean, anyway? Oxford Dictionaries say that we are upset when we are "unhappy, disappointed, or worried."*

What could be the reasons for those feelings? Or is there perhaps one source for them? Here is what Robert Maurer says:

"Do all upsets come from fear? We don't know for sure. However, based on the research, I suggest that this is the most useful way of looking at them." — Robert Maurer, *Mastering Fear: Harnessing Emotion to Achieve Excellence in Work, Health and Relationships*

It's a great hint to look at our fears when we're upset. However it is a scary task in itself. What to do then?

Here is what Ariel and Shya Kane say about it:

"It is often challenging to look at how you think and act because it might be embarrassing to see the real truth. But what if you were to take an anthropological approach to how you relate rather than a subjective, judgmental one? If you were a scientist, looking to see how the inner workings of a culture was put together, you would notate what you see — not judge it. If you bring an active interest, an observational approach to how you have been programmed, then you can 'debug' your own personal computer.

"Think of yourself as a highly sophisticated computer with archaic programming. Simple awareness acts like a complimentary upgrade." — Ariel and Shya Kane, *How to Have A Match Made in Heaven: A Transformational Approach to Dating, Relating, and Marriage*

Yes, non-judgmental seeing allows us to become both honest and kind with ourselves.

The path we take while making progress can be immensely intriguing, and if we drop our judgments and expectations, we can discover many surprises along the way.

Let me remind you here of the gift that anthropology, kaizen, and gamification bring together. Being upset is not wrong.

Upset and other "'stress symptoms' ... are not signs of disease. They are our body's gift to us to let us know something important is happening that requires our immediate attention. Without these symptoms we would have perished as a species long ago." — Robert Maurer, *Mastering Fear: Harnessing Emotion to Achieve Excellence in Work, Health and Relationships*

We often fail to appreciate these gifts because they don't fit our preferences for the moments in our lives. It is up to us to decide which moments we extend and which we keep short. Let's remember that each moment is a starting point.

So the next two steps, when your starting point is an upset, could be:

You (Upset) —> Stop —> Take a non-judgmental look at where you are and your fears —> ...

In the next moment after you've had a good look at where you are and the fears you are resisting, will be whatever you choose to do next in your game.

2. When the next step leads you away from your goal

Here is another analogy to reflect the fear we might have of the next step, however small it might be. When you stop and look, you might have the feeling that you are at a crossroads. It is great to have a choice, but what happens if we take the "wrong" road, leading us away from where we were actually heading?

Even if we break down the path to our goals into the smallest of steps, we might shy away from those small steps and do something else entirely.

Or life might get in the way and require us to do something else.

Is that bad?

No, because you have the possibility to get back to where you were heading. Awareness can help you see that each moment is a crossroads. As soon as you detect a stop, take a look and choose the next step.

Sometimes detouring can help you make the best turn on your way to your goals.

Here is what happened as I was working on finalizing this part of the book:

I had a doctor's appointment for both of my children, who had experienced cough and asthma symptoms for quite a while. We went to test them for allergies, among other checks. The prick test revealed that my son was allergic to house dust mites. That called for action. So instead of continuing work on this book for the whole afternoon, as I had originally planned, I spent the time cleaning my son's room meticulously by washing his bed linen, reducing the number of plentiful dust catchers (such as many tens of comic magazines), hunting around the house for plastic boxes that could close hermetically, and putting most of his toys in these boxes. Later I learned that all the dust catchers were not the reason for his allergy, but I am still glad I did all that. Whatever it was that ultimately helped with his dust-mite-allergy and asthma, my son hardly coughs these days. And that is what matters.

Awareness and saying "Yes" to what was requested, along with the experience of playfulness when turning my life into games, and kaizen, helped me to make progress and appreciate each of the small things I cleaned. I noticed how much better the air in my son's room became when I removed old play carpets. All that brought a feeling of satisfaction that overpowered my sense of guilt for not having done it sooner.

I did write a little in these chapters, but only during two ten-minute breaks. These breaks felt like both a reward and progress.

But what surprised me most was what happened the next day, as I was taking my morning shower. I realized how I wanted to structure this part of the book. I saw that I should separate the material addressing the magic of the smallest steps (chapter 8) from the one considering the sequence of steps (this chapter here) and have them in two individual chapters. Before that I had mixed these topics and hadn't felt entirely comfortable with it, despite being unable to put my finger on exactly what it was that bothered me.

So the break I took from writing, also in my thoughts, whilst being preoccupied with the ambition to make my son's room as safe for him to sleep in as possible, helped me achieve the state of mind needed to find the best solution for this part of the book.

Hence, the seeming "curse" of an easy or necessary step that can lead us away from our goals, can actually become the blessing that leads us more quickly or more directly, to what we want, and beyond.

Thus even your escape-to tasks can become the necessary step toward your goals. I continually discover great quotes and thoughts that I add to various chapters of this book while reading the multiple books I enjoy both for leisure and to learn something new. And even when I surf social media at random.

Being an interested and curious scientist is the most brilliant state of mind. The multi-dimensionality of our behavior and thought processes never ceases to amaze me. It's so much fun to look at them non-judgmentally and become aware of the possibilities we have if we stop fighting and fleeing.

After recognizing where we are, where we want to head, whether we are escaping something toward that goal, what that is, and what activities we escape to, without judging all that, we can identify and take the next step that will move us toward our goals.

Awareness and kaizen will help us see that the next step toward our goals and dream is not far away, but exactly where we are right now. And that in most cases, there is nothing else we need to make that step, than what we already have.

3. When you breathe in, don't forget to breathe out

And here is another message to reduce the possible fear of detouring from what you are doing. A step in a project is like taking a breath. You can't take in air for too long. At some point, you need to breathe out. Allow yourself to have those breathing out moments.

When I related this analogy to my husband, he told me about a fun design aspect of the online strategy game he likes playing. After an attack you set and finish, there is a "cool-down" period, in which you are not allowed to attack again, but have to do something else, like building new cities or farming.

So allow yourself to breathe out and cool down. Whether it is a short look out of the window, a brief contemplation of what's been done, standing up and moving around a little, or doing something different. If you observe yourself being afraid to be away from your project for too long, support yourself by using a timer and when it goes off, go back to your projects or activity and take the next "breath" of it.

4. Take a look at where you are and what you can do now

Activity 1:

Where are you in relation to the completion of each task?

- For example, if you want to write a book, where are you in relation to this goal? Do you have a title and an outline, or have you written a few chapters already? If you are learning a language: are you at the beginning, intermediate, or advanced level of the language you chose to learn?
- And to add dimension to this question: where are you now as you read these questions? Are you on a bus or in a darkened bedroom next to your sleeping partner, where you have no pen and notebook to make notes, with your mobile (containing apps for taking notes and learning languages) tucked away so that you won't be

tempted to surf on social media? And how do you feel (upset, relaxed, afraid, happy)?
- Even if you are not at an "odd" place where you can't attend to what you want or need to do in the project, think of those places (shower, on the commute, while making coffee) where you could replace your complaints and worries with creative thoughts about your projects. Agatha Christie was famous not only for her brilliant work but also for claiming that she got her best ideas while doing the dishes. **

Your answers (use the lines below, if this is a paperback):

Here is where I am now in the project:

_____
_____
_____
_____
_____

Here is where I am physically now and how I am feeling right now:

_____
_____
_____
_____
_____
_____

These are the "odd" places and situations often occurring in my daily routine, where replacing the complaints and worries in my head with creative thoughts on my projects could uplift and motivate me:

_____
_____
_____
_____
_____
_____

Activity 2:

What are the next steps in relation to the starting points you recorded above? And what tools could you prepare to take with you to those "odd" places to support your creativity there?

This could be my next smallest and effortless step if I have everything set up to work on my project:

_____
_____
_____
_____
_____
_____

This is what I could do now (Options for the above scenarios: mark this place on the e-reader and make a note there, stand up or open my bag to retrieve a notebook and a pen or my mobile to take notes, or switch off the e-reader, put it away and go to sleep):

_____
_____
_____
_____
_____

I could do the following in those "odd" places where I don't have all the tools needed to make progress with my project; and these are the things I could prepare or use before going to those places. (Examples: put a notepad with a pen in the bathroom, print out the chapter of my thesis I am working on to take and read on the commute, download a free app to plot my novel, put a dictionary in the kitchen to look up the words for kitchen appliances in the language I want to learn, in the small breaks while cooking):

_____
_____
_____
_____
_____
_____

Activity 3:

If you have the means to draw right now, then I invite you to sketch several diagrams placing yourself at varying starting points, your escape-from (to-do-list) tasks and your big dreams and goals in relation to each other (as shown in the examples in section 1 of this chapter above). Use the space below the references or a separate sheet of paper or an app on your tablet to draw these diagrams. Refer to the notes above and also those you took in chapter 8, section 13.

References:
* https://en.oxforddictionaries.com/definition/upset
** https://michaelpnaughton.com/agatha-christie-and-the-mystery-of-mindfulness/

Self-Gamification Happiness Formula

Part IV. Self-Gamification in Design and Practice

Chapter 10. Games, Game Design, Gamification, and Self-Gamification

"Just play. Have fun. Enjoy the game." — Michael Jordan

1. The third addend in the happiness formula

In this part of the book, you will learn about the third and final skill set of self-gamification — that is, the gamification and game design element.

You will learn about it along with awareness and kaizen. Just as was claimed in the third addend of the happiness formula (see chapter 4, section 5): you cannot turn your life into games without being present (as opposed to being deep in complaints), and without making progress in small steps and enjoying each of the small moments of your life.

We will also recall the typical components of a game and consider how you can see, design, and treat your real-life projects and activities as your favorite games.

But first let's look at the definitions of games, game design, and gamification. Subsequently, we will summarize what self-gamification represents.

2. Definitions

A *game* is (in its first three definitions by the Oxford Dictionaries):

1. "An activity that one engages in for amusement or fun."
2. "A complete episode or period of play, ending in a final result."
3. "(informal) A type of activity or business regarded as a game."*

Game design, when it comes to the first two — I would even say all three — definitions of games is a multi-dimensional discipline:

"The design and production of games involves aspects of cognitive psychology, computer science, environmental design, and storytelling, just to name a few. To really understand what games are, you need to see them from all these points of view." — Will Wright in the foreword to *Theory of Fun for Game Design* by Raph Koster

Self-Gamification Happiness Formula

Even though the world of games and game design is complex, there are several main components that are easily understood, and which we discussed in chapter 1, section 6.

These are: goals, rules, feedback system, and voluntary participation. In the next two chapters (chapters 11 and 12), we will discuss how you can see real activities as games and how to design your self-motivational game component-by-component.

But for now, let's recall the purpose of this book. It is to give you a formula that you can use whenever you need help to uplift yourself and make your path, whatever you do while moving forward, brighter.

And since it is often considered that games are created to generate fun and happiness, then it is quite logical to borrow their elements and bring those into real-life situations to make life more fun and joyful too.

This approach is called *gamification*. I have mentioned the most common definition of it already in the preface of this book. But here is another definition of it:

"The use of concepts and elements that make games engaging and enjoyable, in other areas of work or life in general." — Andrzej Marczewski, *Even Ninja Monkeys Like to Play: Unicorn Edition*

This intention of gamification is precisely why I think it complements awareness and kaizen so well in creating a happy way of life. Because it presents the opportunity to use game elements to make our lives more "engaging and enjoyable."

3. Are definitions that important?

Searching for definitions to understand something is natural. But to turn your life into games, you don't need to learn game design and gamification in detail.

I do so myself because this world fascinates me and I am curious about various aspects of it.

As I have learned more about play, games, game design, the theory of fun**, gamification, motivation, behavioral design***, and many others, I have discovered many fascinating facts about games and various areas of their application.

I learned, for example, of the term *serious games*, which are often defined as the following:

"This group includes full games that have been created for reasons other than pure entertainment." — Andrzej Marczewski, *Even Ninja Monkeys Like to Play: Unicorn Edition*

In his both humorous and extremely informative book *Even Ninja Monkeys Like to Play: Unicorn Edition*, Andrzej Marczewski divides serious games

into several types. Here is how he summarizes them:
- "*Teaching Game*: Teaches using real games and gameplay.
- "*Meaningful Game*: Uses gameplay to promote a meaningful message to the player.
- "*Purposeful Game*: Uses games to create direct real-world outcomes." — Andrzej Marczewski, *Even Ninja Monkeys Like to Play: Unicorn Edition*

I was especially fascinated by Purposeful Games and one of its examples, "Genes in Space,"**** which is "a space shooter game that uses gameplay to map genomes to help the fight against cancer in the real world!" — Andrzej Marczewski, *Even Ninja Monkeys Like to Play: Unicorn Edition*

Isn't that fascinating?

When I learned about serious games, I wondered whether the self-motivational games I designed for myself were serious games. I even asked the gamification community on social media, and got many great and enlightening comments in return. Including from Andrzej Marczewski.

My knowledge about games and gamification increased immensely, also of how serious games differ from gamification:
- "Gamification is about taking ideas and elements from games and using them in non-

game contexts." — Andrzej Marczewski, *Even Ninja Monkeys Like to Play: Unicorn Edition*
- Whereas serious games are "full games" and not just the use of some of the game elements.

I had some difficulty understanding serious games***** at first. I guess that came with the notion that these games were not created with the primary intention of making the players happy. I wondered whether, if most people play games because they make them happy, those environments that are made to stir thoughts and emotions (but not the happy ones) are really games as well?

The more I learned about games and gamification, the more I grew fascinated with how philosophical and uncertain both topics were.

I will not relate the whole conversation here, because I might lose you on the way. But I will tell you that many of those who participated in the discussion said that yes, my self-motivational games might be considered serious games. Others said that if I were only adding elements of games into my projects and activities, then that would be gamification.

Now looking at that discussion in retrospect and the fact that I turn my life — my real life and all that it comprises — into games, then it most probably *is* gamification, rather than being a combination of serious games. So the term self-gamification is appropriate.

However, one thing should be said here. Yes, sure, it is correct to say that if you decide to turn your personal or work projects, or your whole life, into games, and bring game elements into these projects and life in general, then this approach *is* gamification. But if naming your projects *games* increases your motivation and "infects" those around you with the same positivity and enthusiasm, then what you are doing *is playing a game*, whatever others might say.

Having made such a discourse on definitions, I think I should stop here because I don't believe you need to dig deep into game and gamification design if you don't want to.

I have mentioned several times already that I turned my life into games long before I heard of the word "gamification" and started reading books on game and gamification design.

And so can you. You don't need to read all the books I refer to before you can start seeing your projects and activities as games. All it takes is curiosity and the question: "How would I design this project to turn it into a fun game?"

You would have come to the same conclusions as me if you had walked in my shoes. Or even if you had a completely different story to me. Jane

McGonigal in her acclaimed books and TED talks, Mitchel Resnick in *Lifelong Kindergarten: Cultivating Creativity through Projects, Passion, Peers, and Play*, Ian Bogost in *Play Anything: The pleasure of limits, the uses of boredom, & the secret of games*, Charlie Hoehn in *Play It Away: A Workaholic's Cure for Anxiety* and others came to the same conclusion that games and play can make life happier, healthier, richer, and more fun.

They developed their recipes on how to do that, and I designed mine.

As you continue reading this book, you will see that I urge you to develop your own recipes. And also to share them.

We will talk about how to design your self-motivational games, and also about fun, in chapters 12 and 13.

But for now let's consider self-gamification, and the gamification part of it — that is bringing the fun and engaging elements of games into our own lives — a bit more.

4. Self-gamification is about making our lives happier

Let's repeat and enhance the definitions of self-gamification we made in chapter 4, section 1:
- *Self-gamification is the art of turning our own lives into games.*

Self-Gamification Happiness Formula

- *Self-gamification is the application of game design elements to our own lives.*
- *Self-gamification is a self-help approach showing us how to be playful and gameful.*
- *In self-gamification, we are both the designers AND the players of our self-motivational games.*

During the discussion I had with the gaming community on serious games and self-gamification, I became aware for the first time of an aspect of self-gamification that I experience several times a day as I practice it. Someone commented that games, in general, are created to generate emotions.

I also discovered this thought by Yu-kai Chou:

"Games have no other purpose than to please the humans playing them. Yes, there are often 'objectives' in games, such as killing a dragon or saving the princess. But those are all excuses to simply keep the player happily entertained inside the system, further engaging them enough to stay committed to the game." — Yu-kai Chou, *Actionable Gamification: Beyond Points, Badges, and Leaderboards*

That's when I saw clearly that,

- *Self-gamification is about creating uplifting emotions for ourselves and keeping ourselves "happily entertained" with whatever comes our way in our lives.*

And here is one more characteristic of self-gamification, which we addressed in chapter 1, sections 2, 3, and 5:
- *If we look at what we want or have to do as a game, then the drama around those activities falls away.*

At this point, I would like to repeat the good news for you. You don't have to study game and gamification design in detail if you don't want to — although you might have a lot of fun and discover valuable information by doing so. You are already the perfect self-motivational game designer for yourself, because, as many compassionate and brilliant people have said, you are the perfect you. "You are enough," as Ariel and Shya Kane, Elizabeth Gilbert and many others often write on social media.

The other reasons for you being your perfect self-motivational game designer are the following:
- You are your own anthropologist.
- You practice kaizen.

You have learned how to look around and see yourself, the world around you, and how you react to it, with interest but without judgment. You don't push yourself towards the end goal as you might have done before, but let your life progress by small but steady steps. You absorb various ideas and apply them incrementally to your life.

Do you remember planning your next steps in earlier chapters, and doing so creatively?

Yes, you have already started designing your self-motivational games! And in this part of the book, we will discuss that a little more.

Let's start with the following.

5. How do your favorite games inspire you?

Think of your favorite games, or those that come to mind first. What elements are the most fun in them?

For example: Are they about sorting different objects into rows? Or about defeating monsters? Is it perhaps a strategical game where you have to build up resources to go on a mission?

A note: If you are a game designer then you might think of the Mechanics-Dynamics-Aesthetics (MDA) framework****** here. But if you don't have anything to do with game design, then consider anything that attracts you to the game or games you are thinking about now.

If this is a paperback, jot your answers below. Otherwise, take a notebook and a pen or your favorite device and app and answer the question above.

_____
_____
_____
_____

Notes and references:

* https://en.oxforddictionaries.com/definition/game
** *Theory of Fun for Game Design* by Raph Koster, https://www.theoryoffun.com/
*** Yu-kai Chou, *Actionable Gamification: Beyond Points, Badges, and Leaderboards*
**** https://www.genesinspace.org/
***** If you also experience difficulties differentiating between games, serious games, gamification, and others, there is an excellent article by Andrzej Marczewski on this topic: https://www.gamified.uk/2019/01/08/introduction-to-gamification-part-2-game-based-solutions/
****** https://en.wikipedia.org/wiki/MDA_framework

Chapter 11. Seeing and Designing What We Do as Games

"Game design isn't just a technological craft. It's a twenty-first-century way of thinking and leading. And gameplay isn't just a pastime. It's a twenty-first-century way of working together to accomplish real change." — Jane McGonigal, *Reality is Broken: Why Games Make Us Better and How They Can Change the World*

1. Seeing what we do as games

We've discussed in chapter 1, section 6, that any project or activity contains or can contain the same components as games. Or at least, it includes the primary ones: goals, rules that the player must follow, feedback (or reporting) system and voluntary participation.

In a discussion about games, I also heard the following statement: each game has a story behind it.

But projects and activities have stories behind them too. Because they have goals. There are wishes and emotions connected to each project and activity. And each dream has its story.

Jane McGonigal, whom I quote many times in this book along with other famous authorities on game and gamification design, seems to agree. She says, "A compelling story makes the goal more enticing." — Jane McGonigal, *Reality is Broken: Why Games Make Us Better and How They Can Change the World*

Recognizing the story behind the goals of your project can be a precious gift, giving you insight into the reasons for it coming into existence. It might encourage the project to become part of your dreams (if it wasn't before), or remind you of the beautiful or brilliant reasons why you started it in the first place. If, however, you don't find the story behind the project goals compelling, but still want to accomplish it, then you can build a compelling story of your own around it. There are no limits to creativity here or anywhere else.

Another component that was pointed out by a follower of self-gamification who, like me, is from outside the game and gamification design world, was the strategy.

After some contemplation, I realized that strategy is two-fold in self-gamification. There is strategy while designing self-motivational games, and also when you consider what moves to make as the player.

Since I am neither a gamer nor gamification designer or scholar, I referred my discussion partner to the expertise of others. But I could say one thing for sure, which is that strategy is a component of both games and any project or activity.

When it comes to the strategy in self-motivational game design, it is partly about setting the goal, and partly about designing the rules. When you play you set up a goal for the next (smallest, most effortless, most efficient) move, then consider how to reach it, while following the rules you developed as a designer.

And as you saw in chapter 10, section 2, even the Oxford Dictionaries mention that various activities and businesses can be informally regarded as games*.

While I was spreading awareness of the benefits of developing various projects and activities into games, I got another fun question. The question was whether flow charts in a project plan could be created and laid out like a board game, and progress be followed by moving figurines along the board.

I immediately answered "Yes" and loved the idea. Of course, you would also need to record progress in another type of feedback system (one you have agreed with your customer or boss), but if this approach will benefit you, your colleagues, and the project, then, by all means, do it.

There are no limits to creativity here either. The trick is to see what you are doing as if it is a game. Mind you, not something to disregard as a waste of time, but something you are eager to be great at, like your favorite game.

We often put too much drama into our projects. But approaching them as a designer would while creating a fun game, can help to simplify and improve the whole process of carrying those projects out, remove the tragedy we might see in them — and often ourselves as their victims, and turn these activities into games that excite and engage us.

Of course, you need to be aware of what is happening while you design your project and all its components. If you notice that the design and its creation (such as making a board game) is taking too much time and has turned into an escape-to activity, then it is time to simplify it and make sure that you also work on the project itself, not only on adjusting its design.

It's worth repeating the following: Starting with seeing the entire thing, ourselves and the world around us non-judgmentally is one key. The next key is to identify the next small, effortless step, also in designing your self-motivational games. And the third is to identify the game design elements for a system that will allow you to appreciate all those small steps in the most fun, simple and effortless way.

Let's touch on the topic of being serious about and excellent in what we do, and whether they mean the same thing, which we addressed earlier in the introduction, section 3, chapter 1, sections 2 and 3 and will discuss again in chapter 15, section 3.

I used to think that it was forbidden to approach anything in a relaxed, gameful way. I thought that if I wasn't being serious, and even dramatic, about what I was up to I wouldn't be (or be seen as) excellent. But since discovering the anthropological approach to living in the moment, and having turned first writing then more projects into games, I realized that I could be both playful and excellent at the same time.

Another brilliant outcome of seeing what you are up to as games, and testing various projects and activities, is that you can more easily identify what is fun for you, what resonates with you, and what excites you.

I also discovered that I learn better, I am more open to new ideas, and that there are many more "Oh wow!" moments in the same day, than there would have been before. Life is so colorful now.

Even though I've been turning my life into games for several years, the more I gamify my life, the more I learn, and the more fun the learning process is — of self-gamification itself and of other new skill sets as well.

If you research more about the application of gamification, you will discover it is widely used for educational purposes. So if it is used in the learning systems designed by others, why not apply it in self-education too?

If you are still skeptical about the possibility of seeing what you do as games, then please answer the following question. You don't need to tell anyone your answer. Have you got one or more of the following items recorded on paper, in an app, or stored in your head:

- To-do lists,
- Weekly, monthly, yearly, plans,
- Project plans,
- Road maps,
- Notes on how you want to accomplish specific tasks,
- Something similar?

I would bet that you have more than one of the above recorded and saved somewhere on scraps of paper, in notebooks, calendars or apps, either set by yourself or by others.

Then I have the following news for you:

These are also all Game Plans.

Thus, even before you started reading this book, you were already a project game designer and player. You just didn't know it and didn't think of it that way.

I used to envy game designers, having the most fun job in the world. I was sorry that I wasn't that interested in games.

After trying various art forms (including singing, playing guitar, painting, making jewelry, and decorations) I discovered that writing was the best one to express myself. So storytelling, both in fiction and nonfiction, was what attracted me most.

Yes, stories were also part of the games, but I wasn't aware of that then. I often heard that writing was hard work. And if I thought of the time it took to write an entire manuscript, it did appear that way.

We often associate the time it takes to finish a project with how difficult it is. Here comes the finish line again.

A.J. Jacobs, the author who often turns his life into an experiment (whom I mentioned in chapter 2), says the following in his book *My Life as an Experiment*:

"It's a strange tic of our brain. Sometimes, the more goal-oriented we are, the *less likely* we are to attain that goal. If you really, really want something, you have to forget how much you want it. Or else you'll be too nervous to get it. But dear Lord, that's a cruel and paradoxical system evolution has devised." — *My Life as an Experiment*, A. J. Jacobs

Gamifying writing, and doing it for a specific work-in-progress for about five minutes a day, was the solution to this dilemma for me when it came to writing (as I related in chapter 3, section 1). It showed me that the writing process wasn't hard at all, as long as I didn't think of it as such, let go of any thoughts of finishing the manuscript, and instead just wrote.

It was then that I realized I didn't have to envy game designers and gamers. I could design and treat anything as if it was a fun game! That was one of the best discoveries ever.

I realized that self-gamification allows me to treat myself as:

- my *best (customer) player*, and at the same time
- my *favorite game designer*, to whom I gladly give my feedback to improve our favorite games.

So my advice is to emulate the games that you like or that make you curious, and bring their elements into your life.

Try them out. Observe how you argue with yourself and attempt to deviate from the rules you set up. Try not to judge the rules before you have let yourself feel what effect is caused by any game designed to increase motivation. But don't judge yourself for judging. It's quite normal for most people, and observing the grudge you might hold against yourself, without judgment, will cause it to resolve itself in an instant.

If you don't judge yourself for having thoughts about seriousness and so on, you might find humor in the whole situation.

More than once I have found myself fretting about whether I chose the best activity for that part of the day. Thoughts such as "I would rather write than take the dishes out of the dishwasher, then I would get more points." I was somehow sure that the dishwasher would earn me fewer points because it was easier than to write a page.

But then I observed the thoughts without judging them, had a good chuckle at the lack of sense in it and came up with a fun idea instead: "I am the Super Mario** now" and simply chose one track in the game instead of another. I realized that I might be earning a different number of points, but I would be faster on the more straightforward track (whichever of the paths I perceived as the easier one).

This idea of being a figurine in a video game made me smile and even hop in the kitchen and finish the chores with a wide grin. After checking the character description on the official website that described Mario as "Cheerful. Inspiring. Jumpy."**, I had to grin even more. Yes, I did become "cheerful" and "jumpy," and also did my best to infect others with good mood and humor; thus, I hoped, inspiring them when I shared this experience with others.

[A side-note: If you have heard about Chore Wars***, then my little one person Role-Playing Game (RPG) might remind you of that. However, this fun family or office RPG is about organizing and delegating chores. In self-gamification, I am concentrating on only one person, myself. In addition, my one-person RPG is meant to be short. I will address Role-Playing Games and my thoughts on them when turning our own lives into games in chapter 12, section 9. As you will see there, there is some drawback in labeling something or someone as an ally or a bad guy for an extended time. Some judgment can be attached to it. But self-gamification puts judgments aside. (See the definition of Role-Playing Games (RPG) in "Glossary and References", chapter 20.)]

I had similar experiences with other chores too. One of my first associations of household chores with games was again the laundry. Once, as I accounted in chapter 2, section 2, when I was folding the clean and dry clothes, I realized that finding matching socks was like playing one of the Match Pairs Memory games****.

I also saw that others draw such associations and bring the humor in what they do too — often unwittingly applying gamification. On a German cooking TV show I saw years ago, a prominent restaurant chef, when challenged to include French fries with the meal, arranged them like Jenga***** bricks and claimed that they were Jenga potatoes.

During the 2018 Christmas holidays, my father-in-law said that he had had to play Tetris****** with the garbage because the trash containers were so full during the holiday season. He described turning the trash bags back and forth so that their shape would fit the small spaces left by the bags of other residents. I had to grin at that because, since practicing self-gamification, I had often also thought of it as playing "trash-Tetris" when I was throwing away our trash bags and trying to make one even layer of bags, even if the trash container wasn't full yet.

You can turn everything into fun, engaging games if you just get inspired by and draw similarities from games that already exist and also new ones that appear on a daily basis.

When you learn to see what you do, want or have to do as games then even your procrastination stops being that and instead will look like an alternative route in the game you play. It will cease looking tragic and wrong, but just a trail you can leave at any time to pursue the path leading to the goal of your game instead.

In the next chapter, we will look more closely at the four main game components, so that you can design your projects and activities to make them both more efficient and more enjoyable.

But before we do that, I would like to urge you to get interested in game design and how different games function. Here's why.

2. Why game design is essential for everyone

I know I said that you don't have to learn game and gamification design in detail if you don't want to. I also claimed that you could start turning your life into games immediately, at least consciously, since unconsciously you have probably already done so on various occasions.

But to turn your life into games you do need to get interested in actual games — and gamified systems — and how they function. Again, be a scientist. This time studying games that come your way and draw your attention. In other words, allow yourself to be an eager game designer, curious about what others do and how this knowledge can contribute to the design of your self-motivational games.

Self-Gamification Happiness Formula

Here are two of the best things about being the designer of your self-motivational games:
- *The software and hardware are always available. You can find them on your shoulders. And the designer is you.*
- *The design process is part of your self-motivational games.*

Let me emphasize again: *The design part is essential.* There is no right or wrong, good or bad design here. But it is critical that *you* do the designing part. Take responsibility for how fun and engaging your games are for yourself as the player. *Don't judge the player, but create the best games for your player, yourself.*

Here is the difference between self-gamification systems designed by you and gamification frameworks developed by others. In self-gamification, you *have to create* your games. You can play other people's games and combine them with yours, but it is your choice how you mix those games with your own. *Only you can design your life.* I believe and hope you wouldn't want it any other way.

By the way, if you are a manager open to gamification and decide, among other things, to gamify the processes at work, then you will design games to motivate your colleagues and co-workers to help them carry out various tasks. But to help others gamify their lives, you need to develop the games for yourself first.

This interest in game design and how others do it can come naturally and without effort. All we need to do is stop suppressing our built-in curiosity. We all tried to "bend" the rules in our favorite games when we were children, and even later. We had that question looming over our heads, "What if we played it another way?"

Sometimes our changes made the games more fun, other times less so.

So, we are natural game-designers and testers. We just might not be aware of it, or we have forgotten.

Right after deciding to write the book *5 Minute Perseverance Game: Play Daily for a Month and Become the Ultimate Procrastination Breaker*, I started reading various books on game design. Books on kaizen and gamification later joined these books.

The first book I read on game design was *The Game Inventor's Guidebook: How to Invent and Sell Board Games, Card Games, Role-playing Games & Everything in Between!*, By Brian Tinsman. In it, I saw the following passage about Richard Garfield, the inventor of the game "Magic: The Gathering":

"For years, Richard had been playing around with ideas for a game that was 'bigger than what came in the box.' Drawing inspiration from a classic science-fiction strategy game called Cosmic Encounter, he envisioned a game that set up rules, then let every card in the game break them in different ways. Further, no player would really know all the powers every card might have — players would constantly be surprised. Only a genius could bridge the gap between imagining such a game and actually designing it. 'I had no idea if such a game could be designed.' Richard recalls, 'But I decided to give it a shot.'"

"Wow," I thought, "Isn't that what a successful manager, a great boss, a brilliant entrepreneur, or an amazing project manager is? A genius who can bridge the gap between having an idea for a product, service, or business, and actually doing it? Even when they aren't sure the idea (either their own or someone else's) will work, giving it a go nonetheless. And aren't our daily lives (at work and at home) full of games with certain rules, along with many surprises that break almost all of them?"

After I realized that, I sat there for a few seconds, open-mouthed. I was in a public place when I had this epiphany, so I hurried to close my mouth and appear nonchalant as soon as I observed what I was doing.

A bit later I understood that the more I considered my work as a strategic game, the more creative and the more engaged I became in the task, and the more interested I became in its success. Truly invested, without the drama of pretended seriousness but with utter concentration and attention for the task at hand. I discovered a (seemingly) new paradox for myself. The more I considered my work as a game and made sure I had fun while attending to my duties, the more diligent and efficient I became. Being excellent became easy.

Here are the reasons I believe everyone should learn how to design their projects and activities as games:

- In the words of Brian Tinsman (from a section title in his book on game design, where he addressed one of the reasons someone would want to develop a game): *"It's Fun."*
- You'll relax, and the task at hand will lose the dramatic scent we are all "perfumed" with when we take our lives and our work too seriously. You'll become increasingly pleasant to work and be with.
- You will have a glimpse into an incredibly fun and — in an inspiring way — strange industry, a magic land of its own.
- You might discover how your favorite games were designed, and in turn learn a little about yourself and why you like them.

Self-Gamification Happiness Formula

- You might also find a connection between your favorite board or computer games and the job you are doing.
- If you are a non-gamer but your spouse, partner, a family member, or best friend is, you might find you stop resenting their passion for games. Instead, you might become interested, start asking questions about their favorite games, absorb what you learn and use the elements of these games in your self-motivational game-design. It happened to me.
- You'll discover new ideas and be inspired to create your own designs for the task at hand or your team.
- There will be less tragedy when something unexpected happens. Instead, you will be immersed in making the best possible next step of the game. In other words, you will be efficiently searching for a solution and realize it without wasting time (or at least spending less of it) on complaints about how your life has not turned out the way you planned or preferred.
- You will enjoy time and project management because you will recognize what these previously annoying and routine tasks are — that they are part of your self-motivational games. And suddenly, you'll have fun attending to them.

- Your newly won playful and gameful attitude will make the people around you smile and infect them with a wish to do the same.

Activity 1:

I am sure with time you will be able to extend the list above. Or maybe you can do it already. If so, and if this is the paperback, use the lines below to make notes on additional reasons that being interested in the game, gamification, and self-motivational game design makes sense, and how that can enrich your life:

_____
_____
_____
_____
_____
_____

Activity 2:

And here is another assignment for you: If you use a calendar, a planner or project book in paper format or have all of your to-do lists under one heading, then open it at the beginning and write your name, followed by the words "Game Book." Feel free to have more than one game book, depending on what you record there. I use three paper planners, two of which are game books

(which I will address several times more, and especially in chapter 12, section 5 and chapter 15, section 17):
- "To-do Game Book," where I record and maintain to-do lists daily (the previous name for it was "Deadlines and Plans Game Book"), and
- "Points and Stars Game Book," where I develop and fill in the feedback system for my self-motivational games.

The second part of this activity is a continuous one. Watch how your attitude changes every time you open your to-do lists and calendars, and how you occasionally (or even regularly) smile, grin, or chuckle as you attend to your projects and commitments.

3. What to do if you stop seeing what you do as a game

Do you experience challenges with seeing and treating your real-life projects as games? That is quite understandable, and please don't judge yourself for that. This judgment might be one of the reasons that people try to turn their lives into games and then stop. But don't judge yourself for judging either.

No one would be able to continuously and always consider real-life projects and activities as games. I don't, even though I've practiced it for quite a while and have no plans to stop.

Like living in the moment, self-gamification is not a one-time pill to fix a problem once and for all, but a lifestyle.

You will often forget to treat what you do as games. You are human. If something touches you, resonates with you, and pulls some sensitive strings, there will be at least a moment when you are thrown off balance.

The trick is to become aware of it, not judge yourself for it, and return to the game.

The more you practice it, the more you will recall the fun and efficiency of turning your life into games, the shorter will those off-balance periods become, and the more creative with your self-motivational game design you will be. The more projects and activities (however small and short) you turn into games, the more often you remind yourself that you could consider and treat what you do as games, the easier and faster it will become to turn something into play, and the less hard you will be on yourself.

With practice — let me remind you, with playful, gameful, and fun practice — you will be able to both excel at what you do and simultaneously see what you do as a game.

References:
* https://en.oxforddictionaries.com/definition/game
** https://mario.nintendo.com/ and https://mario.nintendo.com/characters/
*** http://www.chorewars.com/help.php
**** http://dkmgames.com/memory/pairs.php
***** http://jenga.com/
****** https://tetris.com/play-tetris

Chapter 12. Definition and Design of Self-Motivational Games

"Nobody sets the rules but you. You can design your own life." — Carrie-Anne Moss

1. Two types of projects and activities to gamify
You might have recognized by now that there are two primary types of activities that you can turn into games. And these types cover everything that you want, plan or are up to in your life. These are:
- Concrete projects and activities, and
- The management part of them, including time management.

This enables you to get twice the game-playing fun out of each project. Isn't this awareness brilliant?!

In chapter 3, section 4, I related how I unwittingly turned project management into fun games and suddenly began enjoying it immensely, becoming eager to play with varying the design and developing it further.

Gamification of project and time management has inspired me to play more with the design of each of my projects. The adjustment of to-do lists in general and for each particular project ceased to be a tedious task, but instead a part of my self-motivational game design process.

2. Defining self-motivational games

Even if this is not by the book, I came to call both of these types of games (or gamified activities, to be more precise), and more specifically the concrete projects and their management, *self-motivational games*. And more precisely:

A self-motivational game is a real-life project or activity that you adjust in such a way that it feels like a fun game with which you are eager and happy to engage, both in terms of its design and the playing of it.

3. Types of self-motivational games depending on duration

In chapter 6, sections 1, 2, and 3, we identified escape-from and escape-to tasks; that is the types of tasks dependent on how we treat them with our actions and in our thoughts. At the start of this chapter, I drew your attention to two kinds of activities, depending on whether they are specific projects or the project management task.

There is another classification for your tasks, projects, and activities in self-gamification, which has to do with their duration.

They might cover very short periods, like writing a quick e-mail, or going through the latest post-delivery, to periods lasting hours, days, months, and years.

Project and time management games can also run for those periods of time: minutes (such as jotting down a new to-do or checklist), hourly, daily, monthly, or also yearly.

I do, however, discourage you from having yearly rounds for your self-motivational games. Or if you have them, make sure that you also have sub-rounds of months, weeks, and even days. The reason being that you need to keep your goals in sight and find the balance between smaller and bigger goals and game rounds of different duration. Otherwise you might see yourself giving up your beloved project shortly before the finish line.

You might have heard the story of Florence Chadwick*, an accomplished swimmer who gave up her attempt to cross the channel between Catalina Island and the California coastline in 1952 after fifteen hours in ice-cold water and thick fog. Shortly after leaving the water, she discovered she had been less than a mile from her destination. She told a reporter that she would have made it had she been able to see land. Later she accomplished the swim in a shorter time and very similar weather conditions. But that experience and her explanation remained metaphorical and symbolic for many.

In self-gamification, as the designer and player of your games, you can set the finish line in such a way as to have it in sight and be motivated to reach it.

You could, for example, base the length of a project game round on something other than calendar periods (a week, month, year). Just as in some games a round finishes when a particular event occurs (a specific card appears, for example), you might use the tax year ending, a specific regular meeting occurring, or some other particular set of circumstances.

You need to be aware of these possibilities and play with them, not in spite of but including your current circumstances: where you are right now, what is happening in your life and around you, what you have and haven't got at hand, your physical condition (e.g., tired or not), and also your state of mind.

4. Many games a day

Taking into account the varying duration and design of projects, tasks and activities you have each day, it becomes evident that each day you play more than one game. In fact, you have a whole collection of project *and* management games.

You can't treat all of them the same way since any activity you perform is different. And you are different in each moment. Thus, you can't use the same framework for everything.

And even inside the same project games, you can imagine or invent *mini-games*.

Let's get inspiration from famous games. Being inspired by many of my friends playing Candy Crush Saga**, I decided to watch videos of people playing it to find out how the game functioned. I didn't want to play it but I was curious about its game elements, partly because I was thinking of my project management game as "Project Crush" (see chapter 3, section 4 and chapter 19, section 1). I realized that Candy Crush Saga didn't have only one type of move (sorting candies into rows), but each bigger step or phase of the game also had many *mini-games* in it. There were monsters to feed, treasure chests to open, boosters to collect, bombs to avoid, and much more.

The same will be true of your project and project management. Become aware of all the mini-games and game elements that already exist, and those you can invent to bring the fun factor to what you do. What are the treasure chests in the project, and the bombs to avoid? What about the monsters? Are there candies of the same type that you need to sort out?

5. There will always be more than one design

I discovered something interesting about myself in relation to project management and the means I used for it. I realized I was under the illusion that one approach or system was a magical solution that I could use from the moment I discovered, tested, and liked it, until forever.

As I continued turning my life into games, I learned that one system/approach for recording and planning tasks might be appropriate (and fun) at some times in my life, but not at others. I used apps, monthly calendars, weekly, daily, Microsoft Excel, sticky notes, etc. All of them were of value at one particular time. Sometimes I used several simultaneously.

Right now, I stick with paper planners. In addition to the family calendar, I use three planners for the following: one for appointments, the second for appointments with myself (i.e., to-do lists), and the third is my self-motivational game feedback system with points and bonus stars. The latter two are the tools I currently use for my application of self-gamification (the same books I mentioned by name in chapter 11, section 2, activity 2).

But even using paper I felt I should have had one perfect system to record my tasks as well as the points. At some point though, I realized this is not only impossible but also unreasonable.

Being different in almost every moment is the main reason.

Thus, don't stop experimenting. A design for your motivational games that works well today might not be appropriate a month from now. Don't judge yourself for changing.

Don't judge yourself for trying to find the perfect design, either. It seems to be normal for us humans to try to find one ideal solution for all time.

Approaching my self-motivational game design as a game in itself was of great help, and a great discovery for me. If I enjoy the game I design, I play it. If not, then just like passionate players of strategic games, I make notes for the next moves, which are to change the design for the next round.

I was curious once to hear Alex Rodriguez (nicknamed "A-Rod," an American former professional baseball player) when being interviewed by Ellen DeGeneres, describe why he and Jennifer Lopez ("J Lo") went to a TruFusion bootcamp and liked the new workout approach so much. In other interviews too he has pointed out that doing only one type of fitness is not only boring but also stressful for his body, having had both hip and knee surgery.

Here is the description I found for this new popular workout: "TruFusion is the latest innovation in group fitness offering multiple studios under one roof at an affordable price. With up to 240 group classes weekly in over 65 different styles, TruFusion gyms provide the hottest blend of yoga, kettlebell, Pilates, barre, bootcamp, boxing and cycle classes."***

Over sixty-five different styles of classes? Is it any wonder that this style of workout is so popular? It is quite understandable that it never gets boring to practice it.

So, why do we try to find one single way to manage and carry out our projects and activities? The curious thing I observed is that many of us not only try to find one perfect approach to almost everything, but we also try to "sell" something that works well for us now as an ideal solution for everyone for all time.

Why not instead just enjoy what we do and be curious about how we can modify it, along with the change in our interests and behaviors that occurs all by itself?

Here comes the message of awareness, extended to include what we have established about game design and gamification:

Being a kind and honest designer and player of self-motivational games is the key.

6. Keeping things simple

In the next four sections of this chapter, I will address the four main components of games: goals, rules, feedback system, and voluntary participation.

But before we go into them, here is a valuable lesson I learned from designing self-motivational games: if the apps or designs I use to gamify my life require too much time to use, maintain, develop, or adjust, and I take them too seriously or too precisely (for example when designing the feedback systems and recording my points) then I am escaping other things, including those I want to do. That is why I try to keep these — and the process of adjusting them as my interests also change — as simple and fun as possible.

I want to add another aspect to it. If you were to jump straight into chapter 20 from here and read about my current self-motivational game design, the Balance Game, it might appear complex and sophisticated. However, this complexity and multi-dimensionality grew incrementally. I started by taking a design I already had and making one small adjustment at a time. It all started with the 5 Minute Perseverance Game (chapter 18), then grew into Project ("Crush") Management Game (chapter 19), and finally the Balance Game (chapter 20), maturing gradually as I played it.

Let your self-motivational game designs go through a similar evolution. Start with something simple (we will address this when you practice self-gamification in chapter 15, section 8).

Here is a quick and necessary reminder, before we dive into each of the primary game components and what they mean for self-gamification. When we talked about kaizen (chapters 7, 8, and 9), we built upon awareness. In turn while designing self-motivational games, we will rely on both the anthropological approach to being here and kaizen. This corresponds to the third addend of the self-gamification happiness formula, which we defined in chapter 4, section 5, and where I claimed that we couldn't consider gamification and game design in self-gamification — and in a happy way of life — without awareness and without taking small steps instead of giant ones. We will encounter this truth many times in the following sections.

7. Goals

"The *goal* is the specific outcome that players will work to achieve. ... The goal provides players with a sense of purpose." — Jane McGonigal, *Reality Is Broken: Why Games Make Us Better and How They Can Change the World*

After a text search for the word "goal" in my book about the 5 Minute Perseverance Game, where

I described my first ever self-motivational game design, I found the following:

"The goal is to persevere for 5 minutes a day, for as many days within the given round — which can run for a month for example — as possible."

And this sentence:

"Your goal is to gather as many points as possible along two different scales during each round." — Victoria Ichizli-Bartels, *5 Minute Perseverance Game: Play Daily for a Month and Become the Ultimate Procrastination Breaker*

So, yes, there is a goal in a self-motivational game, as there should be.

Seeing goals is important. Sometimes you start doing something and even force yourself to do it, despite not knowing exactly what the goal is. And when you look at it non-judgmentally, you might identify that they are not your goals at all.

One example might be if you have recently started a business but the income it generates is so low that you think you should give up on it, despite still wanting to continue with your startup. In this example, giving up becomes your goal. Some writers give up writing because of lack of revenue, lack of sales, bad reviews, or other challenges, even though they love writing, it is healing for them, and they might even have a small fan base. But they still give it up (or try to give it up by resisting their wish, but continually thinking of it, and through that torturing themselves) because they think that others expect them to, that they will never "make it" as an author, or that it is the more reasonable thing to do.

Or another example, you want to start a business but instead of researching what you are curious or passionate about you start a business based on what somebody else says is profitable.

This might be one of the most critical aspects of goals. You need to look honestly at them and not try to formulate them in such a way as to avoid judgement from others. When setting goals, be kind, but bold and honest at the same time. Otherwise you will deviate from your truth, and you will again be thrown out of your self-motivational games and the potentially joyful experience.

[A side-note: I am not saying that you shouldn't try what is suggested to you or carry out the assignments you get from your boss or teachers. You won't know what your truth is, and what your favorite life games are if you don't try out various things, wholeheartedly, as if they were your idea. (We talked about this in chapter 6, section 8 and will address it again in chapter 15, section 2.)]

One example of acknowledging my truth was to learn to boldly say that I am a writer when somebody asked me what I did for a living. Or if someone asked me how they could support me, I was afraid to say, "I would love you to buy and read my books or enroll in my online course." Somehow I thought I would be asking too much by doing so, and that I should have been doing more direct consulting instead. But by looking honestly at what I wanted I realized that these resources were not just part of my dream but could also be an asset to my customers, being less expensive and available whenever they needed. So what I really wanted wasn't just right for me, but for my customers too. Maybe that was the real reason I wanted it, but I just hadn't seen it at first?

I'm grateful for the gifts of living in the moment and non-judgmental seeing in helping me to look clearly, kindly, *and* honestly at my wishes and goals.

On the other hand, I think there is a general misconception about goals. I believe many of us consider them static. Set them once and they are written in stone forever. I realized that I used to think that way. But this is not true, and you will hear many startup consultants advise aspiring entrepreneurs and business owners to "review and if necessary reset your business goals at least every half a year."

The same applies to your self-motivational games — that is, to your project and project management games.

Jane McGonigal also wrote the following on goals:

"When we're goal-oriented, we pay more attention to what we're doing." — Jane McGonigal, *SuperBetter: How a Gameful Life Can Make You Stronger, Happier, Braver and More Resilient*

This is true. When we are aware of what we want and where we want to head, then we can adjust the path to the goals we have.

You also need to adjust your goals, especially the number of them (and projects they connect to), based on external factors, like deadlines. Your goals should support external deadlines if there are any. You might find yourself resisting the deadlines in your head and escaping to some other activities and not doing those, which due to the time limit have a higher priority. Observe yourself like an anthropologist, and as a designer, to determine how to motivate yourself to return to the urgent project game.

One of the solutions in the case of an extensive and urgent project is to take a "virtual" sabbatical to complete it. You may not be able to go on a retreat (like some writers do) to finish your project, but when it comes to the number of goals, you could do the following: postpone other projects until the following day, week, or month, and reduce the number of current items to the bare minimum. Take your To-Do Game Book and record the postponed projects in the next month, for example, and delete them from the list you have for today or tomorrow. You might notice yourself breathing a little more freely, and a sense of relief.

The above related to big goals — the number you have, and how to achieve them. But let's not forget the smaller ones. Big goals are important, but small goals are as important, or even more so. Big goals can overwhelm and distract you from playing your project and project management games. But small goals — for example, what you want to achieve today, or in the next hour, on a specific project — are much more appealing and less scary. Is it to write a chapter of your thesis or a scene in your book? To learn one song by heart, or to clean one room in the house?

You could even consider the small, effortless steps, made the kaizen way, as goals. In this case as micro-, nano-, or atomic goals.

Let me bring up the quote by Robert Maurer, with which I started chapter 7:

"Just as a record-setting marathon runner will continue to search out ways to shave another second off his or her best time, you can seek out strategies to constantly sharpen your life's game."
— Robert Maurer, *One Small Step Can Change Your Life: The Kaizen Way*

So, just like an athlete, you can move the goal a little farther as soon as you reach it. Here's what the acclaimed writer (both of mysteries and on the writer's craft), James Scott Bell suggests:

"Write at a pace that is easy for you, and produce words at each session. Next, add up a week's worth of work. That's your starting number. Up that number by 10%. This is your new weekly target. You want to have a word goal that is just a touch beyond your comfort zone." — James Scott Bell, *The Mental Game of Writing: How to Overcome Obstacles, Stay Creative and Productive, and Free Your Mind for Success*

Thus, play with your big and small goals and expand your comfort zone step-by-step.

8. Rules

"The *rules* place limitations on how players can achieve the goal. By removing or limiting the obvious ways of getting to the goal, the rules push players to explore previous uncharted possibility spaces. *They unleash creativity and foster strategic thinking.*" — Jane McGonigal, *Reality Is Broken: Why Games Make Us Better and How They Can Change the World*

Isn't this awareness coming from games amazing? Have you ever complained about the rules set up in a project? I know I did! Before I learned that rules in games promote creativity, and before I started taking an anthropological view of myself and the world around me, I felt that rules were *wrong* and *limited* creativity. But now I realize that they are not. They contribute to the fun factor in games. And if I view my projects as games, then they become fun in my projects too.

If you have difficulty seeing the rules of what you do like those of a game, you could increase the fun factor by adding your own rules. Such as setting a timer as I did in my first self-motivational game framework, 5 Minute Perseverance Game (see chapter 18).

As described in chapter 3, section 2, the rules of the 5 Minute Perseverance Game are straightforward: you have to spend five minutes every day working on the project, for one month. If you manage to accomplish these five minutes in any one day, you get one point. If you work on it for a bit, but less than five minutes, you get half a point. If you work on it for more than five minutes, you still only get one point. The points and half-points you haven't earned go to your procrastinating self (who you are playing against). So yes, there are precise rules for this game, as well as for its possible variants.

I suggest that you take a look at the project you either want or have committed to carrying out, and determine what the rules are: the deadlines, the way you should carry out the task, the format you need to deliver the results in, and so on. And first, become aware that without those you wouldn't have a challenge. In games, the challenges ignite fun and boost motivation. Here is another checkpoint where drawing parallels between real-life projects and games can be utterly supportive. Without those challenges the task at hand might become more straightforward, but it would be boring, and you wouldn't learn anything from it (which is the most valuable asset for us humans).

The more I read about games and gamification, the more I encounter golf being used as an example of how rules contribute to the engagement and fun factor of the whole process:

"As a golfer, you have a clear goal: to get a ball in a series of very small holes, with fewer tries than anyone else. If you weren't playing a game, you'd achieve this goal the most efficient way possible: you'd walk right up to each hole and drop the ball in with your hand. What makes golf a game is that you willingly agree to stand really far away from each hole and swing at the ball with a club. Golf is engaging exactly because you, along with all the other players, have agreed to make the work more challenging than it has any reasonable right to be."

— Jane McGonigal, *Reality Is Broken: Why Games Make Us Better and How They Can Change the World*

So those limits to your project or activity, put there either by yourself or someone else, are some of the factors that make your project a game.

A question: what do designers do with the rules they are keen about, if they don't contribute to the excitement and engagement of the game's players?

They improve the rules.

So instead of complaining about all the things we need to do in the project, we can choose to see how to improve the rules, so that the players of that project game, who are ourselves, enjoy the process more.

There are no constraints to creativity here, and as we discussed in chapter 11, section 1, the easiest way to identify great and fun rules is to get inspired by other games. Do you remember how my chat partner had the idea of using figurines on a board to track the progress of a project? So the rule would be to include the movement of the figurine on the board after each small step in the project. It could be considered silly and unnecessary, but with the element of fun it adds, it will increase motivation and promote further progress in the project.

So think of games that come to your mind and consider how you could use their elements in your project games. Don't judge the ideas that appear.

Self-Gamification Happiness Formula

Here's a scenario of a quick game that came to my mind as I was writing this chapter. Imagine you have an e-mail you need to write, which you have procrastinated about for some time. Every time you think of this e-mail you cringe or at least frown, feeling deeply uneasy. So you notice your discomfort and pick up this book in the hopes of getting an idea of what to do. Then you read the paragraphs above. And suddenly you have this image of Super Mario in your head (as I had in chapter 11, section 1). How could you use that image? You could add a rule for this mini-game, to stand up and hop around your computer chair three times before you sit down and write the e-mail.

What would this achieve?

You will probably chuckle at the silliness of the idea. But the grin will reverse the frown you had when previously thinking about writing the e-mail. And the smile still lingering on your face might also positively affect the language with which you'll formulate the e-mail. You might also observe yourself being more present and aware of the topic you need to address, and you will do so creatively.

You don't have to develop rules too far ahead. If you need immediate help with something, then apply self-gamification, that is, to get interested in what is happening and how you are feeling, see what ideas come from your awareness of games, and identify how you could use them right now in your project, for its next smallest and effortless step. Thus, *the power of awareness and kaizen will be enhanced with the power of fun that comes from game design.*

Remember you are the designer and have all the freedom you need.

But remember to use the rules and elements of your favorite games as an inspiration or idea for a recipe, not as a prescription. And don't stop observing yourself non-judgmentally. If you notice yourself escaping by designing sophisticated (even if very fun) rules for your project games, then you know that you stopped playing the game you initially wanted to play and started playing another.

As with everything else, the following applies: the more straightforward the rules, the better.

Before we move on to the next section in this chapter, I would like to share a lesson I learned from my son, when he was developing his own card games. Once, as he introduced his new game to me, he gave me an unbeatable card. He wanted to do me a favor and to make the game more fun for me. He assumed that if I kept on winning, then I would have more fun. We played the game with that unbeatable card, but it became clear to both of us very quickly that each component in a game (in this case the playing cards) had to have a weak side for the game to remain engaging for all of its players.

[A side-note: Sarah Le-Fevre, an expert in games-based learning design and delivery, and Lego Serious Play facilitator, who read a previous version of this book, pointed out that the "Jokulhaups" card in the game "Magic: The Gathering" was banned from tournament play for this very reason, for being invincible. The card bears the following text: "Destroy all artifacts, creatures, and lands. They can't be regenerated."****]

Even for the winning player, the lack of dynamic in a game is both boring and tiresome in the end. Every game needs tension and unexpected moments.

The same applies when you adjust the rules of your project and project management games. If you have an activity that beats them all, in other words, to which you often escape, limit the number of points or even give yourself negative points or loss of virtual life or similar. But be careful with those negative points. You might start using them to punish yourself. And the self-motivational games are not there for punishment. You create them to uplift yourself.

I will mention negative points again, and also Role-Playing Games, where you can identify your allies, villains, power-ups and so on, in the second half of the next section.

9. Feedback system

"The *feedback system* tells players how close they are to achieving the goal. It can take the forms of points, levels, a score, or a progress bar." — Jane McGonigal, *Reality Is Broken: Why Games Make Us Better and How They Can Change the World*

Let's look at the simple design of the 5 Minute Perseverance Game again. In contrast to regular games, it has two feedback systems. One in the form of points (described above) and one in the shape of progress in the project or projects you take into the game. If you chose a writing project, then the second scale would be word counts, if your activity is to learn to play a musical instrument it would be the number of songs or pieces of music you have come to perform. And so on.

So, in the 5 Minute Perseverance Game, you can see how close you are to the goal by checking how many points you have collected in each monthly game round. The maximum score is between twenty-eight and thirty-one, depending on which month of the year it is. When you look at the word count for a writing game, you might view the word count from the previous month as the line you want to cross before the current game round ends.

I think this example is quite revealing. In the same way that the rules of a project, when seen as game rules, can become less annoying or dramatic, so too can the reports you have to prepare, the Microsoft Excel sheets to fill out, or the road maps to update, when viewed as the feedback system in a game. You might well notice that your interest in fully engaging with them grows.

And then you can add game elements, like color codes, stars, and so on, to various types of entries in your Microsoft Excel sheets, or even sound effects to your PowerPoint presentation that contains the road map. But, of course, only if it doesn't bother your project partners or customers (or take any of you out of your project game), but instead benefits all of you through improving your mood and making the game more engaging and exciting.

You might also create a different feedback system in which to record the points and stars, for example, as I currently do in a separate weekly calendar for the Balance Game (chapter 20).

Here are a few thoughts and lessons learned on separate "game-only" feedback systems (those with points, badges, gems, stars, and so on), which I urge you to test for yourself before deciding whether to deviate from what I discovered or not. This is again just my experience, and not an instruction.

I find it more comfortable to keep my Point and Stars Game Book, where I record my score, separate from my To-Do Game Book, where I document my to-do items.

Crossing out the completed items might seem like feedback in itself, but in a to-do list, you don't record everything you do during the day. An unexpected call from a colleague asking for a favor, to which you attend immediately, would earn a point (or more) in your point gathering feedback system, where you can see what you have accomplished in various projects, or during the day.

That is why I now see the to-do lists as separate feedback systems, very different to the one where you gather points. In a way then, you play two games in parallel. In the first game, the goal is to reduce the number of items on your to-do list. Whereas in the other one you have a blank field for each project to begin with, and the goal is to gather as many available points as possible.

Seeing my to-do lists, reports, Microsoft Excel sheets, road maps, and the additional feedback system I developed for myself, as a multi-dimensional game (or even several games played at once), was the key for me. This multi-dimensionality added to the fun factor of each of my project games.

Furthermore, there are various media you can use for your "game-only" feedback system.

As I mentioned in section 2 above, I prefer paper at the moment. I did use Microsoft Excel to record the results when my project management game rounds were a month long.

To find the perfect tool for your "game-only" feedback system, the one where you record the score in your own Points and Stars Game Book (with your own title), look at your preferences or what you use right now as reporting tools for your projects. This might give you a clue as to what to use. Here are the options that I see for how you can record your score:

- In writing on paper,
- Digitally,
- Mentally,
- A combination of the above.

Here is what I mean by mental recording for your score. Sometimes you might not have your record system with you, for example when doing dishes or being outside. So instead you can appreciate your point with a wide grin, patting yourself on your shoulder or a fist pump with a cheerful "Yes!", as we mentioned in chapter 4, section 4.

Don't worry too much about recording your points precisely. Remember that although points, badges, and leaderboards provide a fun and effective reporting system, their primary role is to increase the fun you experience (such as, for example, the warm fuzziness you feel), not to keep an exact account.

Then there is the question of how many points to give yourself, and even negative points when you didn't manage to do something or did something incorrectly.

Let's start with the number of points. You might have heard me recommend simplicity several times in this book, including in section 6 above, and you will read it again in chapter 15, section 8. But in the Project ("Crush") Management Game (chapter 19), I discovered that the more points I assigned for completing a project and the greater the difference in scores for each project and activity game, the more unpredictable the score was for the day, which made the whole "competition with myself" much more fun. Being kind and honest to myself, as well as keeping the humor and fun present throughout the whole process, let me keep the game in balance without overdoing it, or to notice when I was putting too much pressure on myself.

Now, let's address the negative points. Some games might have penalty points or loss of "lives" in their games. I have considered this element, but so far haven't used it. The reason being that negative points require judgment and finding fault with your actions. If a negative score adds to your fun, then go ahead and incorporate it in your feedback system design. The clue here is to observe how you feel about it non-judgmentally, and to determine whether the whole process still feels like a fun game.

For me, negative points felt like a form of punishment, which isn't a motivator for me; thus, I haven't applied them to my designs.

I have a similar feeling toward defining allies and villains in a Role-Playing Game (RPG) as a design for my self-motivational games. Jane McGonigal uses such an approach in the game she developed for herself while dealing with the consequences of a severe concussion, as described in her book *SuperBetter: How a Gameful Life Can Make You Stronger, Happier, Braver and More Resilient*. If you would like to recall what that was about, then refer to chapter 2, section 3. (See the definition of Role-Playing Games (RPG) in "Glossary and References", chapter 20.)

I recently realized that I could use the SuperBetter approach when it came to navigating my food sensitivities. I would need a hero name then. I decided that "Victoria, the Stormy Food Sensitivity Sea Navigator" was long but to the point. The bad guys would be all the foods to which

I am strongly sensitive. These are products containing gluten, ingredients rich in carbonhydrides and/or fruit sugar (fructose), also nuts, seeds, milk products, any products containing sorbitol, xylitol, and other sugar alcohols, which "can block the already malfunctioning transport system in the intestines of people affected by fructose malabsorption."***** The power-ups would be eating the meals that I can tolerate and have nutrients, drinking enough water, getting enough sleep, yoga and working out, and other activities that promote my well-being. My allies are family and friends, as well as the cafes and restaurants that serve the food from my power-up list.

But I think you and I need to be careful when considering and appointing our allies and villains. Let's try to see if we add any judgment when assigning these roles to various aspects of our lives. The villains are, in fact, very helpful because they indicate that we shouldn't go their way and instead choose another path. This was one of the reasons I didn't name myself a "Slayer" but a "Navigator" in my "food sensitivities game."

[A side-note: This last sentence wasn't meant as a judgment of the hero name Jane McGonigal chose for herself when dealing with a concussion. On the contrary, "Jane, the Concussion Slayer" was appropriate for her in relation to the "bad guys" she had to deal with, such as bright light, and crowded, noisy places. At some point, she "slew" them and they ceased to pose a challenge to her. In my case, my food intolerances aren't likely to disappear any time soon. They cause more problems if I try to ignore them and am not careful enough with what I eat. Thus "Victoria, the Stormy Food Sensitivity Sea Navigator," is more appropriate for my situation, because if I keep watch of that stormy sea of food sensitivities and intolerances and navigate it skillfully, then I will not drown but win the race. Another possible reason for Jane McGonigal having fun "slaying," whereas I do not, was suggested by Sarah Le-Fevre, whom I mentioned in a side-note above. She guessed that, being an avid gamer (unlike me), Jane McGonigal might have happy memories of lots of "slaying."]

Fighting something is resisting it, which can emphasize the things you declare as villains so that they become bigger and more dramatic. So, if you select a Role-Playing Game approach to your self-motivational game design, try assigning these roles to different things once in a while. If you have "defeated" some of the villains, don't keep them "alive" by still having them on your game plans and thinking you need to fight them. See if these former villains in fact turned into allies or power-ups, and indicate so. Then turn your attention to the new "characters" in the game. There is always something (or someone) new.

On the other hand, I do find limiting points for escape-to tasks a brilliant tool to help me return to my escape-from activities. I shared with you in chapter 6, section 5, how limiting points to a maximum of one per day for doing laundry, motivated me to come back to writing and other activities I feared and procrastinated about, so that I could earn more points.

When it comes to the number of points, or sizes or colors of stars and badges as various rewards, just follow what I call the "fun-detecting antenna." See what feels fun and right for you. Apply the first idea that comes to mind and then adjust it from round to round. In the very first round of the Project ("Crush") Management Game framework (described in chapter 19), I used to give myself two bonus points for attending to all projects/tasks I planned for the day, and later I increased that number to ten bonus points, making that bonus more substantial than the bonus points for the completion of every single task. And both numbers (two and ten bonus points) had their reasons at the time. In the monthly round with two bonus points, there were several projects with tight deadlines, while in the later game rounds there were fewer externally set deadlines and I wanted to praise myself more for managing all the projects that I wanted to pursue.

The number of points, sizes, and colors of stars, badges or other indicators of your success in the game can also be seen as rewards, the topic of which I will address in chapter 14.

In this chapter, we still have several other things to consider. One of them is the final major component of games. Here it comes.

10. Voluntary participation

"Finally, *voluntary participation* requires that everyone who is playing the game knowingly and willingly accepts the goal, the rules, and the feedback. Knowingness *establishes common ground* for multiple people to play together. And the freedom to enter or leave the game at will ensures that intentionally stressful and challenging work is experienced as *safe* and *pleasurable* activity." — Jane McGonigal, *Reality Is Broken: Why Games Make Us Better and How They Can Change the World*

Voluntary participation is closely connected to goals, rules, and the way the feedback system is designed. So, if you see these three components as part of your game and do everything as a designer and player to keep them fun and efficient, then voluntary participation in your projects will become effortless.

In self-gamification, voluntary participation is three-fold. It includes the will:
- *to see your projects as games,*
- *to design and never stop developing these games* (that includes the will to learn from other game and gamification designers; also those who practice self-gamification), and
- *to play*, in other words, actively engage in your self-motivational, that is your project and project management games.

These three components of voluntary participation are essential for you to keep turning your life into games if you wish to do so.

Some of my friends gamified some of their projects using the 5 Minute Perseverance Game and then stopped turning their lives into games, at least intentionally. That is not a problem at all and ceasing to practice self-gamification doesn't mean a loss of something, or that your life will take a turn for the worse.

I mentioned in chapter 3, section 1, that after turning my writing into a game for the first time, I forgot about it but still felt its positive effects. I suspect that I turned bits of my writing process into a game without recording the points. After all, I did have a feedback system in the form of word count, and chapters reviewed and edited.

Equally for you, if you stop recording points, it doesn't have to mean you will lose the fun you experienced in the projects. Even today, in some of my trickier projects, I use the feedback system to get my work flowing and as soon as it does, I stop recording the points and just enjoy the work on the project. I call this quick and fun framework the "Project Booster." You can read more about it in chapter 19, section 7.

So don't judge yourself if you notice that you aren't following the plans for your games to the letter. You still have all three components of voluntary participation if you actively engage in what you are doing and have fun.

But if you notice yourself resisting and being "thrown out" of your game, then you can use the self-gamification tools in your always available toolset to address the fear, resentment, anger, or anything else that hinders you in your games, boldly, honestly, and kindly.

There is a clear benefit to turning our lives into games, which is also the reason I keep playing. The resisting thoughts and urge to procrastinate (including things we think we really want to do) will never stop appearing. They might occur more rarely as we discover fun in whatever we do, but there will always be a moment when our creative minds come up with some fretting ideas. In this case, self-gamification can help you turn the projects you fret about into self-motivational games, in other words, real-life projects or activities that you love to engage in, both the design and the playing of.

When I got the feedback from friends who applied the 5 Minute Perseverance Game (or some version of it), I realized something. Not only do self-motivational games like those described in part V require voluntary participation, but playing them *facilitates* voluntary participation in our lives' projects. It also helps us to experience the work on our projects as a *"safe* and *pleasurable* activity."

11. Why are unnecessary obstacles beneficial, both for games and for real-life projects?

In her, often quoted, book *Reality Is Broken: Why Games Make Us Better and How They Can Change the World,* Jane McGonigal claims that the following is "the single most convincing and useful definition of a game ever devised":

"Playing a game is the voluntary attempt to overcome unnecessary obstacles." — Bernard Suits, quoted by Jane McGonigal in *Reality Is Broken: Why Games Make Us Better and How They Can Change the World*

But apart from the fun factor and consequences that it might bring with it, are these unnecessary obstacles really beneficial for real-life projects?

I believe so. What follows below in this section is an edited and enhanced excerpt from a blog post I titled "The 'Unnecessary' Obstacle of the 5 Minute Perseverance Game and Why it Turns an Overwhelming Task into Doable"****** and shared in June 2017.

(The beginning of the updated excerpt)

In the 5 Minute Perseverance Game, there is only one unnecessary obstacle. And this is that you are not allowed to work on your project and finish it in one go. You must work on the project for a maximum of five minutes on any given day and then stop until the next day. Without this obstacle you might try to finish the task in one day, or over a couple of days.

The latter approach might seem straightforward, but it can be much more stressful. The seemingly unnecessary obstacle of limiting your work on a given project only for short periods can work miracles.

First, it takes the pressure off a significant and overwhelming task. "I can do five minutes," is the most common response I get when I introduce the game to someone who has never heard of it or similar games before. So the game makes hard and overwhelming tasks doable.

Furthermore, the 5 Minute Perseverance Game provides continuity and brings well-being (by reducing stress). Projects cease to be goals, or something to be over and done with, and instead become paths to follow, which is much more enjoyable.

If happiness is also a path then you can make sure to always follow it, or if it is an accessory, to take it with you wherever you go. But if it is a goal, you never know when you have reached it. Turning projects into fun and exciting processes enriches life, and we start to enjoy what is happening along the way, amazed by the many adventures we have during one single day.

I re-discovered this while preparing a presentation for a large conference. I realized how much I wanted this presentation to be excellent and how scared I was that it wouldn't be. So I called on the 5 Minute Perseverance Game for help. As soon as I had the instructions from the organizers, I took the making of the presentation into the game and started working on it for about five minutes a day, completing one or two slides at a time.

What I hoped for had happened. I stopped being concerned and worrying how the presentation would turn out, and instead was glad to create those few slides each day. I had fun trying out various things like playing with the layout design, searching for illustrations, and adding suitable text.

The breaks between the short daily sessions when I worked on the slides, helped me identify and improve the weak points, and recognize the valuable contributions of the reviewers of the slides, as well as letting my defensive thoughts (which appeared after first reading the e-mails with comments and suggested changes) fade into the background.

The main lesson learned here is that the seemingly unnecessary obstacle of limiting the time available to work on a project becomes necessary to make the project doable and fun, and to achieve a better outcome than expected.

(The end of the updated excerpt)

12. Game design tips for escape-from and escape-to tasks

Before I invite you to create one of the first designs for your project games, in particular those you escape from, I would like to share a few self-motivational game design tips for *escape-from* and *escape-to* tasks, which summarize and add to the game components discussed above.

Please keep in mind that these are suggestions based on the lessons I've learned. They are by no means instructions or things that must be done.

In chapter 6, sections 1, 2, and 3, we identified two types of tasks, each with two sub-types of their own, depending on how we treat them and think of them.

These are:

Escape-from tasks:
- *Things we want to pursue, but claim not to have time for,*
- *Tasks we say we have to do but think we don't want to.*

Escape-to tasks:
- *Obvious,*
- *Productive.*

Let's start with several suggestions on game design for *things you want to pursue, but claim not to have time for.*

Give yourself:
- A little time (even five minutes a day) to work on the project.
- Points if you do actual work on the project. Thinking about, planning, or researching the project doesn't count. I don't mean a short search online for a word, phrase, or fact and then returning to your project. That counts, of course. What doesn't count is stopping work on the project for a more extended period and, for example, reading on the topic for hours. The planning and researching parts could be games of their own.

- More points (bonus points for example) for doing it before escape-to tasks.
- More bonus points if you complete a task and deliver something to your boss, customer, editor, agent, a project partner, family member, or a friend.
- The chance to attend to these projects first thing in the morning, but limit the time. The sense of achievement will give you a boost of energy in whatever you do next.

Don't underestimate the influence that recording your progress in your feedback system will have on your state of mind. Remember that with each point you give yourself, you learn to better appreciate each step along the way. I find this part critical to the success of turning one's life into games (and to a happy way of life in general). Hence, I will emphasize it several times throughout this book (see especially chapter 14, section 3).

Let's continue with suggestions on game design for *tasks you say you have to do but claim not to want to*.

For these tasks:

- Give yourself points for each tiny little step. Have you read and understood a paragraph in your textbook for an exam? Then jot a point in a notebook for that task. Have you dusted a room in your house? There's another point for you.

- Observe yourself being more and more willing to do the task, and starting to have fun as you gather more and more points for the activity (see also the Project Booster in section 10 above, in chapter 19, section 7, and in chapter 20, section 5).
- You could give yourself bonus points for doing it before escape-to tasks.
- Don't forget to collect bonus points if you finish a task and deliver something.

And finally, here are ideas for the *activities you escape to* (applicable to both *obvious* and *productive* escape-to tasks), so that you can enjoy doing them without feeling guilty about it:

- Enjoy them as long as you are having fun doing them.
- Observe the moment when you stop being present and start feeling guilty about attending to them.
- Thoughts of escape-from tasks indicate that you actually want to do them, and not the escape-to activity you are currently in. Recognize that, stop the escape-to activity, give yourself a point and move on to the task that "calls you."
- Observe all of that and don't judge yourself for it. But if you do, observe that too, without judging yourself for judging.

- Limit the number of points you give yourself for that activity when you plan the next round of your project game. The ambition to do better in the game will motivate you to avoid the escape-to tasks and do the escape-from activities instead.

If you still have difficulty stopping your escape-to activity (as I sometimes do with watching random videos on YouTube) and switching to your escape-from projects, even after all the tips above and regardless of how loud the escape-from tasks might be "calling your name," take an honest and kind look at the fears you have toward what you are procrastinating over. These could be fear of not doing a good job, or what people will say when you deliver your work, fear of success and not being able to justify it. See that, don't judge it, and then ask yourself, what power-up could help you gain the courage and strength to answer the "call." It could be a glass (or a gulp, a sip) of water, brewing a cup of coffee or making yourself a tea, standing up and walking away from your computer and doing a little chore, a few yoga exercises, meditating, or something else.

Remember not to judge the escape-to activities. In fact, you can consciously use them to take a break from the project that stagnates and contemplate it with a little distance.

Sometimes this contemplation occurs on its own in our subconsciousness. That is what I think happened to me in the story I related in chapter 9, section 2, when I took a break from writing this book to thoroughly clean my son's room.

But conscious contemplation away from your desk or other workplace can also be recharging and beneficial to your project. Do you remember the anecdote in chapter 9, section 4, activity 1 about Agatha Christie resolving and developing the plots for her books while doing the dishes?

13. Design your self-motivational games

Now it is your turn. It is time for you to create your own frameworks. Yes, more than one. Remember you are both the designer and the player who tests and plays your games.

Before you get to planning, take a look at the notes you made previously, especially those at the end of chapters 6, 8, 9, and 10.

I haven't included any lines below because the inevitably limited space would not be enough for your requirements. What I mean by "framework" is the actual design, both of your specific project games, and your project and time management games (see below). You might use any number of calendars, diaries, notebooks or planners in paper format (as I do right now), or several files or apps (including digital calendars and timers), or a combination of these for various aspects of your designs. You will need the space and means to record both the goals and rules, and the feedback systems where you will record your scores.

Design these elements for:

- *Specific project games:* I suggest that to begin with you select one of each of the two sub-types of escape-from projects/activities you listed at the end of chapter 6. You can see my designs for a single project in chapter 18 and in chapter 19, section 7.
- *Project and time management games:* These should include both the "game-only" feedback systems (addressed in section 9 above) and the reporting systems that are required in your work and personal life, to include your calendars and to-do lists. Take into account both escape-from and escape-to activities when you design your management games. You can use the tips from section 12 above as a starting point. The frameworks I have applied to project and time management to date can be found in chapters 19 and 20.

Create your own game and game framework plans by defining their:

- *Goals* — what you want to achieve in each game,

- *Rules* — what limitations you put on how you are going to accomplish that goal,
- *Feedback system* — how you are going to reward the player, that is yourself (or your active and procrastinating selves), or players, if you are also helping others to turn their lives into games (read more on this in chapter 16), for each step, each milestone (quest) and at the end of the round.

P.S. Don't forget to give each of your games a name. It could be a project name plus the word "game" at the end. You can also be playful and use something that will help you to see your project or activity in a different light. You can use this name just for yourself, or even with your colleagues and friends if you decide to share self-gamification with others (more on this in chapter 16). You can adjust the name as you develop your self-motivational game designs. I have modified the names of two of my three game designs during the process of designing and playing them (see chapters 19 and 20).

P.P.S. You will need these game designs to practice self-gamification, which we will address in chapter 15. You also need to be aware that you will most likely adjust your self-motivational game designs as you continue reading this book and practicing self-gamification.

References:
* https://en.wikipedia.org/wiki/Florence_Chadwick
** https://king.com/game/candycrush
*** https://www.franchisegator.com/franchises/trufusion/
**** https://www.cardkingdom.com/mtg/5th-edition/jokulhaups
***** https://www.food-intolerance-network.com/food-intolerances/fructose-malabsorption-intolerance/basic-facts-dietary-fructose-intolerance.html
******
https://www.victoriaichizlibartels.com/unnecessary-obstacle-5-minute-perseverance-game-make-overwhelming-task-doable/

Chapter 13. Fun in Self-Gamification

"We have come to realize if we are not having fun, we are moving in the wrong direction." — Ariel and Shya Kane

1. Why is there a fear of fun?
I suspect that the word "fun" is the most frequently used one in this book. It first occurs in the subtitle, and is also in the first sentence of the preface. I also intend to finish this book with a sentence that contains this word.

I love using this word. And I assumed that most other people did too. Hence my surprise to discover that there was some reluctance amongst the game and gamification design community to talk about fun. Gamification and game designers talk more about "engagement" than fun.

Curiously enough, the following is one of the very few, if not the only, definitions of gamification I have found in an acclaimed work in this field to include the word "fun":

Self-Gamification Happiness Formula

"*Gamification* is the craft of deriving fun and engaging elements found typically in games and thoughtfully applying them to real-world or productive activities." — Yu-kai Chou, *Actionable Gamification: Beyond Points, Badges, and Leaderboards*

I am very interested in an anthropological approach to gamification. Many people will tell you that they play games primarily to have fun. Because games make them happy.

So if games are about fun, then in my opinion gamification cannot be about anything else.

So I asked the gamification specialists, why fun was so rarely mentioned by professionals in gamification design. I also told them that I wondered why there was a tendency to separate fun from engagement and motivation? There seemed to be some resistance towards fun. Was it because fun was "prejudiced" as not being *serious enough*?

The answer was that fun is utterly subjective. Certain people might find something fun, which others would not. We all enjoy various things and experience fun differently.

I agreed that what was fun for me might not be fun for someone else. I also could see that what we find fun is not only subjective to various persons but even to the same person in different circumstances. You might enjoy playing a game one day and not so much on another.

But, I wondered, didn't that apply to engagement too? For example, I could be fully engaged and enjoying something that another person (or me at another time) might struggle with. The same applies to motivation, passion, curiosity, etc. I don't believe we can say that fun is relative while these others are absolute.

2. What is fun?

This conversation helped me see that the objects we find fun, motivating, engaging, or interesting are the matter of subjective taste. But not, in my opinion, the term itself. *Fun* is *fun*. Everyone knows how fun feels for them. We might not be able to express this feeling in words, just as we can't exactly describe how love and happiness feel, but we know how they feel for us. If you ask a person if something is fun for them right now, they will know the answer, whether they reveal it to you or not.

But let's see how dictionaries define fun.

Fun according to Oxford Dictionaries is:
- "Enjoyment, amusement, or light-hearted pleasure.
- "A source of fun.
- "Playfulness or good humor.

- "Behavior or an activity that is intended purely for amusement and should not be interpreted as having any serious or malicious purpose."*

Looking at these definitions, I understand that it might be hard to grasp what fun is.

I imagine that the controversy about fun, especially when it came to games, was what moved Raph Koster to write his famous book *Theory of Fun for Game Design*.

Here are just a few enlightening quotes about fun from this book:

"Fun is light, energetic, playful and...well...fun." — Will Wright in the foreword

"Fun is all about our brains feeling good — the release of endorphins into our system."

"Fun is the act of mastering a problem mentally."

"Fun is primarily about practicing and learning, not about exercising mastery."

"Fun is contextual."

"Having fun is a key evolutionary advantage right next to opposable thumbs in terms of importance. Without that little chemical twist in our brains that makes us enjoy learning new things, we might be more like the sharks and ants of the world."

"Fun is about learning in a context where there is no pressure from consequence, and that is why games matter."

"Fun is another word for learning."

"'Fun is the emotional response to learning.' – Chris Crawford, March 2004. Also, Biederman and Vessel's research shows that curiosity itself is inherently pleasurable." — Raph Koster, *Theory of Fun for Game Design*

This connection of fun with curiosity resonated with me. My struggle to consider engagement the primary measure of a game's success (rather than how happy it makes the player) was due to the fact that you can be engaged in a game without actually having fun, or being curious about it.

Some people play games *not* because they enjoy them or are curious about what new things they can learn, but because they mean to escape the other things they want or need to do. Playing games (or any other escape-to activity) seems easier, than, for example, writing a book. And they might have the idea that games are more fun to engage with than anything else. But when they play the games to escape something else they don't enjoy them, and become even more frustrated, though still unable to stop playing.

So, in this case, having fun (along with being curious) would be a more accurate parameter in determining whether a game or a gamified environment brings value to the player or not. Because, if the people enjoy what they are doing, then they will also be successful at it. Being aware of whether they are having fun or not can help them to become more successful.

Fun equals full, wholehearted, and rewarding engagement.

3. Fun is what reduces drama in real life

As a child, I was fascinated with Mary Poppins and how she related to children. She wasn't very serious. At least not "seriously serious." Although she appeared to be *serious* about the necessity for fun.

Like many other children who were born around the 1970s in the Soviet Union, I learned about Mary Poppins from a Soviet 1983 two-part musical film titled *Mary Poppins, Goodbye***.

Only much later as an adult did I hear her "concept" and song, "A Spoonful of Sugar."

And only as I am writing this book and continuing to research the topics of games, gamification, kaizen, awareness, and fun, have I discovered this verse:

"In ev'ry job that must be done
There is an element of fun
You find the fun and snap!

The job's a game."
— From Mary Poppins' Song "A Spoonful of Sugar"

Mary Poppins' song was again a discovery of profound wisdom, somehow forgotten as we live our lives.

I love how in the process of turning my life into games, sharing this possibility with others in my online course and in this book, I rediscover these beautiful pearls of wisdom and make myself and others aware of them.

So, what makes the drama fall away?

When we find and experience fun in what we do, the drama and heaviness we previously attached to the task disappear.

4. Fun is the compass *and* the measurement for self-gamification

Ariel and Shya Kane, and many who have been inspired by their work and discovered the magic of living in the moment, claim that:

"Fun really is the way to access enlightenment."
— from a short story "Fear Not, Just Dance" by Simon in *Being Here...Too: Short Stories of Modern Day Enlightenment* by Ariel and Shya Kane

Emulating this statement, I would dare to say:

Fun is an access point to self-gamification, that is to truly and repeatedly turning our lives into exciting and engaging games.

To take this even further, I am convinced that fun is the only *compass* you can use to turn your life or parts of it into exciting games.

But it is also the ultimate measuring tool for success in your self-motivational game design. The amount of fun you feel can be a valuable tool when designing and prototyping your games. And your life in general. This brings us back to the beginning of the book, when we discussed how successful people have fun in what they do and it shows.

I still wonder why fun is often forgotten and underestimated, although it is truly one of the prerequisites and indicators for success. Both having and not having fun, show.

Is it because we are in too much of a hurry to have fun, and don't notice when we experience it?

Here awareness and kaizen can help us again. Let's pause, see where and how we are, identify the next little step that we recognize as fun, and take that step.

But what if you can't identify that fun step? Then, as we became aware in chapter 8, section 2, you are resisting something. It is just an indicator of your resistance and fear of the task at hand. Instead of being curious, you are having a discussion in your head about why this task and the whole project don't make sense. So, if you can't come up with an idea to bring the fun factor into a task, then you're merely saying "No" to that task. Which, as we established in chapter 6, section 4, is neither good nor bad. It simply is.

Here is one of my favorite quotes about observing ourselves (it is the same one I started chapter 5 with):

"Self-discovery isn't meant to be painful. If it is, then you're working on yourself, lost in the story of your life, or simply resisting what is." — *Ariel and Shya Kane, Practical Enlightenment*

As soon as you non-judgmentally see that you are resisting and saying "No" to the task at hand, as well as experiencing fear towards it, you will become aware of a threefold choice, to either:
- continue resisting (often along with complaining),
- let the task go, along with the guilt of not doing it, or
- think of a game and other fun elements you know and like and see how they could help you become excited about doing it.

Let's take the example of cleaning. Many of us consider — or learned to consider — cleaning to be anything but fun. But if you look at it as a game and find ways to make the activity fun, it can become tremendously so. For example, you could put on music before wiping the floor, and make specific movements for each type of cleaning.

You could "play" with the sequence of steps in your routines. I discovered once that I usually started cleaning our house in my daughter's room. There wasn't a specific reason, or at least not one I can recall now. So every time I notice myself marching automatically (and immersed in various thoughts) into my daughter's room with the vacuum cleaner, I turn around and ask myself, "What room do I want to clean first today?" Funnily enough, there is always an answer, and I discover a little spark of curiosity and delight in cleaning a specific room first. Sometimes it is my daughter's room, and other times it is not. But the choice becomes deliberate and fun.

Here is another example, and one of my favorites as a writer.

About a year after turning writing into a game for the first time, I read an article by Rachel Aaron called "How I Went From Writing 2,000 Words a Day to 10,000 Words a Day."*** This article addressed her productivity as a writer. [A side-note: Later she turned this material into a book for writers.] One of the three criteria that best enhanced her productivity and increased her word count was that twin of fun, enthusiasm.

Here is what Rachel Aaron wrote in the section of her article (and the book based on it) titled "Side 3: Enthusiasm":

"The days when I broke 10k were the days when I was writing scenes I'd been dying to write since I planned the book. They were the candy bar scenes, the ones I wrote all that other stuff to get to. By contrast, my slow days (days when I was struggling to break 5k) corresponded to the scenes I wasn't that crazy about.

"This was a duh moment for me, but it also brought up a troubling new problem. If I had scenes that were so boring I didn't want to write them, then there was no way anyone would want to read them. This was my novel, after all. If I didn't love it, no one would.

"This discovery turned out to be a fantastic one for my writing. I trashed and rewrote several otherwise perfectly good scenes, and the effect on the novel was amazing. Plus, my daily word count numbers shot up again because I was always excited about my work. Double bonus!" — Rachel Aaron, *2k to 10k: Writing Faster, Writing Better, and Writing More of What You Love*

I uncovered this effect of fun in everything I do. The more fun I have with the activity, the more productive I become, and the happier I am with the outcome. The more creative I am in bringing joy to whatever I do, the more I feel in control of my life, and the happier I feel.

Yes, we are designers and players of our games. Let's remember that fun is always at our disposal, we just need to take it out and apply it.

5. How does having fun show?

When I teach and share self-gamification, I often invite my listeners to think of their role models, and ask them to answer the questions I asked you in chapter 2, section 7. One of the respondents mentioned that someone inspired her, but she wasn't sure how much fun this person had, because he often appeared so serious. After some contemplation, I sent her the following comment:

(The beginning of the comment)

For a long time I thought that only those who smiled broadly were happy and having fun. Smiles and laughter were for me strongly connected with fun, joy, and happiness. I thought that fun and happiness did not exist without smiles and laughter.

Until I was inspired to look at those who love reading books. They might be frowning due to the tension in the book, but at the same time still be having fun and feeling happy. The same is true for those who play board, video, or other games. They might not be smiling the entire time, and at times even appear to be working hard to reach the next level, but if you ask them if they're having fun, they will answer in the affirmative.

Being fully engaged and having fun might not always show externally, but they are still there on the inside. I am convinced that people who are passionate about what they do are most certainly having fun. It is made evident by the fire in their eyes when you ask them about the topic of their passion.

(The end of the comment)

6. When does the fun start?

You can't enjoy a game until you start playing it. So if you are seeking to detect fun in an activity, you better start doing it. You can't find out if you'll enjoy a book until you actually read it. You can't have fun in a self-motivational game until you jot down your ideas and test them out.

And here is another thing: talking about having fun is not the same as having it. And thinking that something should be fun is not the same as experiencing it. Again, only by playing a game will you determine whether it is fun for you in this moment or not. There is a difference between thinking something would be fun, either because others do it or because it used to be fun, and actually experiencing it and being fully engaged in an activity in the current moment.

I agree here with Raph Koster, fun is about learning and curiosity. And these can't occur before or after the moment, but only in the moment of now.

7. An almost impossible assignment

Even if it is hard to describe what fun is and how it feels, I would like to ask you to give it a try, and make a few notes on what fun means to you, and which activities you remember experiencing as fun and in which circumstances.

Use the lines below if this is a paperback:

_____
_____
_____
_____
_____
_____

References:

* https://en.oxforddictionaries.com/definition/fun
** "Mary Poppins, Goodbye (Russian: Мэри Поппинс, до свидания!; translit. Meri Poppins, do svidaniya) is a Soviet 1983 two-part musical miniseries (part 1 Lady Perfection, part 2 Week ends on Wednesday), directed by Leonid Kvinikhidze. It is loosely based on the Mary Poppins stories by P. L. Travers. The TV series was ordered by the Gosteleradio of USSR and produced by Mosfilm. The official television premiere was on January

8, 1984."
https://en.wikipedia.org/wiki/Mary_Poppins,_Goodbye
*** http://www.sfwa.org/2011/12/guest-post-how-i-went-from-writing-2000-words-a-day-to-10000-words-a-day/

Chapter 14. Let's Talk About Rewards

"Rewards are one of the key components of a successful game activity; if there isn't a quantifiable advantage to doing something, the brain will often discard it out of hand." — Raph Koster, *Theory of Fun for Game Design*

1. What is a reward?

Many consider success the reward for what they do in life. And if fun is a measuring tool for success, then you could see it not only as a prerequisite and a tool for your self-gamification, but also as its reward.

Let's talk a bit more about rewards. It's always fun to get rewards. Isn't it?

Yes, but it depends on what the reward is. So what should it be?

According to Oxford Dictionaries, a *reward* is:

"A thing given in recognition of service, effort, or achievement."*

I don't believe any person on earth is without yearning (or hasn't in the past) for rewards — either material things or in the form of moral recognition and appreciation — for their efforts, both in real life and in games.

2. Why are points enough?

When I share with others the fact that I turn my life into games, people often ask me how I reward myself. When I tell them about the simple scoring system I use, they ask me "Is that all?"

The first time I was asked this question and looked confused in reply, my friend clarified and gave a few examples of what she does: such as eating a small piece of chocolate, or buying herself something upon completion of a big task.

I've heard and read of similar scenarios many times. In "Chapter Six: Bestow Small Rewards," of his book *One Small Step Can Change Your Life: The Kaizen Way*, Robert Maurer gives many examples of small rewards and experiences used by people who apply kaizen on a personal level.

After getting the question, "Why are points enough for you?", I stopped and contemplated. Why were they? Why didn't I see the occasional espresso I make for myself during the day as a reward for project work?

A direct answer was the fact that I considered this, and other similar "rewards," as activities in themselves, for which I'd give myself additional points. I didn't see them as indulgences as I had before turning my life into games. Instead, I saw them as games in themselves.

After more thought, I realized something else. Were I to reward myself with material things that cost money (like a trip to the Bahamas or the cinema), I would no longer regard my projects as a game I was playing for fun, but as something challenging that required effort.

The trick was to see what I was doing as a fun game, not something to prove I was worthwhile. If I thought the points were no longer enough and I needed a bigger reward, I would be adding drama to the task at hand, and it would stop being a game.

I realized that when we agree to play a board or online game, we don't usually expect a material reward.

I am consciously omitting gambling here, since the stress factor excludes such games from the definitions used in this book and for self-gamification, and makes them another type of game altogether**.

So, when we agree to play a board game, for example, with our children or our partner or a friend, all we want to do is to score more or less than they do, depending on the aim of the game.

This helped me realize why points are enough for me as a reward — because I experience my day as if it was a game. It doesn't mean that I don't concentrate on the task at hand, but I increasingly lose the desire to just "get things done" and to think poorly of the assignments I have to address. Enjoyment starts to prevail and with that — as an unintended side effect — the rate at which I complete tasks goes up.

There are still moments of resentment, complaint and even anger that something isn't going as I'd like. But these are brief and become a part of my games. Passionate gamers might also get upset if they don't manage a level or if the game doesn't go the way they want. I witness this often with the gamers in my family. But I also observe how they leave those resentments aside and go back to their games. This is also an excellent approach to have in your self-motivational games.

Let's recall the condition of voluntary participation, which was necessary for our self-motivational games to be experienced as such (discussed, along with the other components of games and how they are used in self-gamification, in chapter 12, section 10). For such a game to be successful you must be willing to see what you do as a game, design the game, its rules, test the game, play it, follow the rules you have outlined, and through it all, be *willing to have fun*.

Self-Gamification Happiness Formula

Please note, I don't mean that you should expect to have fun. It is easy to take suggestions from others and test out whether they are fun for us, with the intention of proving it one way or the other. But what makes a game or any activity enjoyable is first and foremost the willingness to have fun.

So if you want to create a point or other non-material reward and feedback system for your game, then you will manage it with less than a pinch of effort and a delicious cocktail of curiosity, creativity, and fun.

3. Points help us to appreciate what we do

One of the most prominent authorities in gamification, with whom I had the honor of talking to online, Yu-kai Chou, often emphasizes — including in the title of his acclaimed book — that gamification is "beyond points, badges, and leaderboards." — Yu-kai Chou, *Actionable Gamification: Beyond Points, Badges, and Leaderboards*

Many gamification experts agree with him.

I do too. Very much. Which is one of the reasons I started this book with awareness, then went on to kaizen, gamification, and only now am talking about rewards and points.

You probably sense a "but" here.

Here it comes. Allocating points (or badges, stars, leaderboards and any other means of recording your score in a game), not the amount, but the process of recording them, is crucial in self-gamification, and I dare say in gamification as well.

Here's why.

When you pause to give yourself points in your self-motivational games, you take a moment to appreciate what you've achieved.

Have you noticed that you are the last person you usually expect to appreciate what you do? Most of us hope for others to praise us before we allow ourselves to acknowledge all the effort we put into various projects and tasks; be it at work or at home. But if we take little steps and appreciate each of them, we will be less dependent on external praise, and blame others less for not praising us enough. We will appreciate life the mindful and kaizen way, moment by moment.

That is where self-gamification comes full circle. Using game design elements and recording scores in our games helps us to melt procrastination and lets us become more aware of what we do during the day.

The point system helped me to overcome my procrastination when I thought a task was too hard to do, and to avoid spending too long on other duties that were "cozy" to be with, while the more pressing projects waited their turn. Limiting available points to just one per project per day was a brilliant way of keeping a balance between preferred and less-favored projects.

By the way, as mentioned briefly in section 2 above, I discovered that buying something for oneself could be part of a well-being game. I noticed that when I included shopping in my self-motivational games and did it intentionally (i.e. making it one of the tasks for the day and giving myself points for shopping), I enjoyed the process more. Besides that, I started experiencing the purchase of those things I thought I had to buy but didn't like buying (for example groceries, or essential toiletries like shower gel), as a treat. I began to be more aware of and grateful for the simple things in life, and to take less and less for granted.

Another positive byproduct was that I started buying fewer things I didn't need. I realized that the things I needed were also the things I wanted. And those I thought I wanted but didn't need were on the list (often in my head) because I had heard someone say, or read somewhere, that they were good for me, or because I wanted them in the past and therefore thought I still had to want them. But I didn't really want them now. Self-gamification, including non-judgmental seeing, helped me to become aware of this and to be more deliberate and intentional with my shopping.

The same goes for having a cup of espresso or tea. I consider it a treat (and part of my well-being games) and give myself points for having it. Having reached the points I wanted on that day for a specific activity, I move on to the next game, which could be a household chore or something else.

Recording points for various types of activities also made me aware that I was taking care of my family, my friends, and my health, when I had thought I was doing none of it. Keeping score also helped me to see where I wanted to do more and to invest more time.

Bonus points made me proud of completing a task and delivering what I had promised to a customer, a partner in a project, a friend, or myself. A star showed me that I had reached one or more of the goals I had set for the day. And when I gathered all the stars I wanted to collect, I smiled like a winner for that day, which I was. Which I am today, too. And so are you.

So create a well-being game or a shopping game for yourself and record points there in a certain way: limiting points for some tasks (like browsing through a department store or perfumery) and increasing them for others (like saving money on certain products). A reminder: you don't have to record all these points. Now you have the idea in your head, you might start observing yourself recalling it and smiling during your shopping trip, as soon as the thought of bonus points pops up in your mind.

Turning various activities into games and treating them like video or board games (including a lack of material rewards) can help you both take the drama out of these activities, and be more intentional about performing them.

Here is an inspiring story about a writer who struggled with writer's block, and how a fellow writer from her writers' group suggested rewards in the form of stars:

"Always mindful of our goal to be published, B.J. initiated her star program, offering stars to anyone who sent out a manuscript. I thought it was corny. After all, I wasn't five. But my way wasn't working. The truth was that the stars jumpstarted me. And I have to admit, I liked seeing them under my name. They were tangible proof that I was writing and submitting." — Tsgoyna Tanzman, "Turning Blocks into Stepping Stones," a contribution to *Inspiration for Writers: 101 Motivational Stories for Writers — Budding or Bestselling — from Books to Blogs* in the series "Chicken Soup for the Soul" by Jack Canfield, Mark Victor Hansen, Amy Newmark, and Susan M. Heim

4. Give yourself a point and move on

So the points are important. But not so much as to dwell on them.

If you notice yourself discussing in your mind whether you deserve a point for something or not, then you are procrastinating about the next step, taking the whole thing too seriously, or both. Meaning you have stopped having fun and the whole "thing" ceases to be a game.

The whole point of self-gamification is to have fun with what you do. So just give yourself that point and move on.

Shortly before having this epiphany, I was procrastinating over cleaning our house, and had to talk myself into cleaning one room after another. I asked myself whether I could give myself points for each cleaned room, and if so, how many. As soon as I asked myself this question, which sounded non-judgmental to me, I realized that eight points sounded great and would be motivating for me. Three of them as follows: one for dusting and tidying, one for vacuum cleaning, and one for the fact that I was moving and doing a kind of household workout. And the remaining five points were bonus points for finishing cleaning one of the rooms in our house. So I developed a scoring system for cleaning one room after another, which made it fun.

On other days I applied a different scoring system or started with the living room first, for example, rather than one of the children's rooms as I usually did. I told a little story connected to the latter in chapter 13, section 4.

The clue was to see that if I, as the player, was not satisfied with the situation (i.e. with the game I was playing), then not judging myself for being unhappy with it, but quickly tweaking the design instead, would make the activity fun again. Performing the task and then taking a moment to appreciate what I have managed, by giving myself points for the game, as well as possibly for its successful design too, renders the design of self-motivational games a self-motivational game in itself. I can also continue to play the game design game by making notes on how to further improve the design of the project game.

So, record the points in a daily, weekly, or monthly progress sheet and observe how your score changes over time. But don't take the score too seriously. Appreciate it for a moment (smile, do a little dance, or whatever else comes to mind) and move on to the next activity.

Again observe yourself anthropologically (that is non-judgmentally) during the whole process.

Another possibility for when you see yourself fretting about the points in your project game (especially if you have only turned one project or activity, as I did at the beginning, into a game), is to gamify more of your projects and activities. So after recording the points for one project, turn the next project into a game.

5. Should the rewards always be "virtual"?

So we saw the benefit of sticking to non-material rewards like points, badges and stars etc, or those that don't cost much, such as little semi-precious stones or star-stickers to mark your points or bonus points.

It is essential that the weight of the reward doesn't add drama or effort to the project. The rewards are supposed to support us in seeing what we do as games.

But should the rewards always be "on paper" or "virtual," that is only in the form of points, badges, and stars?

Yes and no. Here is what I mean by it.

Do record the points, badges, and stars. But you can also give yourself other rewards every once in a while. Surprise yourself, but remember not to fret too much about it. And don't make them too expensive. Appreciate everything you get or give yourself. I was inspired to read about the following practices in Japan:

Self-Gamification Happiness Formula

"In Japan, the value of the average reward is $ 3.88 (as opposed to the American average of $ 458.00). For the best suggestion of the year, Toyota gives a reward called the Presidential Award, bestowed upon the recipient at a formal ceremony. This coveted reward isn't a fancy watch, a new car, or a shopping spree. It's a fountain pen. And it's such an effective reward that Toyota chairman Eiji Toyoda boasts, 'Our workers provide 1.5 million suggestions a year and 95 percent of them are put to practical use.'

"Japanese executives love small rewards not because they're stingy (although kaizen does encourage us to value cost savings), but because they utilize a basic tenet of human nature: The larger the external rewards, the greater the risk of inhibiting or stunting the native drive for excellence." — Robert Maurer, *One Small Step Can Change Your Life: The Kaizen Way*

I discovered that also about myself and people with whom I interact. Small rewards and gifts are more comfortable to both give and receive. As I just added Robert Maurer's quote to this manuscript, I recalled how, many years ago, my colleagues and members of the team I was leading, appreciated the little gifts I gave them either as a thank you or on festive occasions. These personal gifts were in most cases a postcard with a few words of gratitude or congratulations. Sometimes I added an inspiring quote. When my contract with that organization ended, my colleagues mentioned these postcards as something they cherished.

There are also other types of reward. One of my favorites these days is a change in activity. For example, I work most of the day at my computer, so standing up and doing housework for ten minutes with music playing in the background feels like a reward. Because I am moving and doing something useful, it is accompanied by a good mood. Or even just taking my work to another room can work wonders. I love editing my writing on paper while sitting on our sofa in the living room with my feet up. This work, which I used to despise, now feels like a holiday or a weekend activity. These are just some examples of my experience of the famous saying: "A change is as good as a rest."

If you are learning a new skill just for fun, as Elizabeth Gilbert did at the beginning of her *Eat, Pray, Love* adventure by learning Italian, then you can consider acquiring this skill set as a reward.

It is always helpful to look for the fun factor in whatever you are doing in a given moment, rather than imagine what else you "should" or could do instead.

One more note on material rewards, because I often get questions on them. You can also receive a material reward or go out to dinner, to the movies, or similar.

But here is a reminder again. Don't give these to yourself regularly, or for every finished project. Have them spontaneously. Otherwise you will start expecting them, and there will be too much weight added to what you do. You don't usually expect big prizes when playing a board or computer game. You may have a bet running with your friends and bet something small. But you won't do that regularly, or at least not too seriously.

Thus keep those material rewards as small and as irregular as possible, and don't take them too seriously. And treat all the material rewards or those that cost something (like a trip to the cinema) as your well-being and experience games, which you choose to do consciously, boldly (without a guilty thought, "I shouldn't do it, but I will anyway."). Treat them as your power-ups and gather points for contributing to your happy state of mind. You can also add some rules when you can go and gather such a power up. For example, you could roll a dice at the end of a month, and if you get a five, for example, then you can treat yourself with something special but not expensive like a new book, having a coffee and cake at your favorite cafe, or something else.

6. Take a closer look at your rewards
Activity 1:

I invite you to consider the small but precious rewards in your life. Please answer the following questions:

Have you given or received a small gift that produced immense joy in the other person or yourself? What was that gift?

Another example for me: I used to do little drawings of my son's Lego figurines and put them under his plate at mealtimes. He loved discovering them. A year or two passed, and he asked me to do it again. I did, and he liked that very much too. It's fantastic to see that even if my children ask for new toys, they treasure these little signs of attention and effort as much or even more.

Use the lines below (or a notebook, if you are reading this on an e-reader) and a pen to jot down these memories worth rekindling:

_____
_____
_____
_____
_____
_____

Activity 2:
And now please answer the following question:

Self-Gamification Happiness Formula

Do you need to adjust your feedback system?

Take a look at the notes you made on the feedback system and rules for your self-motivational games, and see if you need to make any adjustments after what you learned in this chapter. Use the same notebooks, calendars, diaries, planners, files, or apps you started using after doing the exercise in chapter 12, section 13.

Notes and references:
* https://en.oxforddictionaries.com/definition/reward
** Go to *SuperBetter: How a Gameful Life Can Make You Stronger, Happier, Braver and More Resilient* by Jane McGonigal on pp. 84-87 to find out more about differences between beneficial and harmful addiction effects of games, as well as origins of harmful addictions in general.

Chapter 15. Practicing Self-Gamification

"I learned that when you play golf you're actually supposed to play golf. It's a game. You play it. You don't think it. It's before and after a round that you do your thinking, your analysis, your practicing."
— James Scott Bell, *The Mental Game of Writing: How to Overcome Obstacles, Stay Creative and Productive, and Free Your Mind for Success*

1. Don't wait — start playing right away

We have already touched on the topic of practicing self-gamification many times in this book, especially in the preceding chapters. For example, many of the self-motivational game design tips provided in chapter 12, section 12 for escape-from and escape-to tasks have as much to do with practicing self-gamification (in other words, playing your project and project management games), as with developing them. And that makes sense because whenever you design your games, you play. And whenever you play, you design. Since you are both the designer and player of your self-motivational games.

In this chapter, I would like to summarize (and therefore, sometimes repeat) and add to the lessons I have learned and continue to learn while practicing self-gamification, that is while turning my life into fun games. As you will discover, these lessons and the tips resulting from them are many, and they are multi-dimensional. This fact has made this chapter the longest in the whole book. But many of the sections are short, so you can process the information shared here in small, digestible portions, between which you can take a break should you wish.

The first message is, don't overthink turning whatever you do into games — test out the ideas in the book, and add your own. In other words, start playing right away, if you haven't already. You may have done so without even realizing it, but now you can do it deliberately and intentionally, should you put your mind to it.

I fell in love with the quote at the beginning of this chapter as soon as I read it. It is utterly revealing and eye-opening. We often tend to analyze the game while playing, which is not entirely possible. You can't do both. Do you remember the second of the three simple ideas by

Ariel and Shya Kane, which we considered in chapter 5, section 4?

"No two things can occupy the same you at the same time." — Ariel and Shya Kane, *Practical Enlightenment*

Thus, when you analyze (including judgments and complaints) your game, you aren't playing it. And as we discussed in chapter 13, section 6, a game is not fun unless you play it. You can enjoy watching someone play it but not for long. In chapter 12, section 4, I told you that I watched videos of people playing Candy Crush Saga. I didn't want to play it. I just wanted to see how the game functioned. If I remember correctly, I watched only two videos and not even in their entirety. As soon as I had the information I was after, I wasn't interested in watching other people play anymore. I wanted to return to my self-motivational games and see how I could implement what I had seen into my project and project management games, and play them.

You have to experience a game or a project to truly enjoy it. In other words, if you want to "play" your projects like games, then start right away.

If you have difficulties in starting your game, then go back to chapter 8, section 5, and chapter 9, section 1. They will give you ideas on how to proceed.

Yes, the best way to start a game is to play it. Not to think about playing it. But remember that planning a project *is* a part of your game or another game altogether. You can choose how you see that. But if you design your game (i.e. plan your project), then actively and actually do that, don't just daydream about your game (project).

So if the next appropriate step is to take out your art materials for the next painting session with friends, then take a big box and put what you need in it. Or put in it what you have to hand and jot down that the next step will be to make a list of everything that is missing. And if you have time now, you can jot that list down right away. By the way, making such a list later can be beneficial as well, because you might recall objects you need that you didn't think of when you dug out what you already have.

And as soon as you make those first preparation steps, pull out your notebook or open the file where you record or draw your points, stars, gems, and badges and record your score. Smile about your achievement and move on.

Thus again to start seeing, playing, designing, treating a project or activity as a game, these three approaches can empower you:

1. *An anthropological approach to living in the moment:* That is, observe non-judgmentally

your state of mind, your bodily responses, the circumstances you are in, the dynamics of the world around you and the thought-processes connected to all that, and recall that they can't be any different than they are; and neither can you.
2. *Kaizen:* Meaning the identification and taking of the smallest, most effortless step you can do right where you are with the means available to you.
3. *Gamification:* And finally remind yourself that this could be a game, that games bring fun and can help you reduce the drama of it all. As soon as you manage that, reward yourself with a point or a badge (in writing or mentally).

A reminder: you might recall that you wanted to play a game when you observe yourself non-judgmentally. The three techniques that self-gamification brings together complement each other tremendously, but their synergy always starts with awareness.

2. You can't discover which games are not for you without playing them

You might agree with the above statements that you need to play a game (actually working on a project or carrying out an activity) to enjoy it. But what about those goals or suggestions that you didn't come up with, which were recommended by others? The same rule applies here. You won't know if that game (project or activity) is for you unless you test it. Don't just assume based on your own or someone else's prejudices.

However, don't judge yourself for judging either. We all often compare what we hear to what we know and label it either as true or false. The nods and the shakes of our heads when we listen to someone show this clearly.

Ariel and Shya Kane unveiled a new possibility here. They say that there is another possibility of listening. And they call it "True Listening." Here is what they say:

"True Listening is actively listening to another with the intention of hearing what is being said from the other's point of view."

and,

"This act of listening is enough to pull you into the moment. However, you have an incredibly facile mind. You can race ahead in your thoughts and finish another person's sentence before he or she gets to the point. Or you can take exception to a word he or she uses and stop listening altogether. If you pay attention, you will see that there are many times when you have an internal commentary on what is being said rather than just listening. If you can train yourself to hear what is being said, from the speaker's point of view, it takes you outside of time and into the current moment." — Ariel and Shya Kane, *Working on Yourself Doesn't Work: The 3 Simple Ideas That Will Instantaneously Transform Your Life*

Thus, truly listen, without judgment. You might discover something entirely new and fresh even in the things that have been said to you before.

And trust your gut and "inner vision." If a suggestion comes and looms in your head (possibly through resistance to an outside influence — boss, partner, friend — or your thought processes) but curiosity draws you to it over and over again, wondering how it would be to give it a try, then go ahead and give it a try. One, two, five or more minutes a day, but do it.

That happened to me with the book you are reading. I used to think a lot about crowdfunding*. I heard about its advantages and drawbacks, and I found myself checking crowdfunding projects for books more and more. I backed some of them and purchased the products of campaigns that had already ended. I wanted to try this process for my books, but was afraid of the reportedly enormous effort involved.

So I went to a crowdfunding event, downloaded many book samples about crowdfunding and started reading them, but I still resisted giving it a try. At some point, the wish grew so big that I decided to turn this project into a game. First, I chose to make a game out of the campaign's planning and preparation stage. I read about the platforms featuring book crowdfunding projects and selected one that resonated the most. As to the book project, I chose the one you are reading now for various reasons. One was that book crowdfunding campaigns can be useful in helping to identify the content readers would like to see included. And at that time, I wasn't sure how to structure the book, or precisely what the content and style should be.

The preparation for the crowdfunding campaign was a fun game, in which I made progress step-by-step, all in the spirit of self-gamification. I sent the material to my editor for polishing, designed the preliminary cover for the book, and made a video to present the project.

And then I stopped. There was nothing left to do. It was time to launch the campaign. My resistance, rooted in the fear of what the campaign would or wouldn't bring, led me to more polishing of the content, preparation of post-launch material (which was cut, reworked, and discarded many times), and, most of all, day-dreaming of how the launch would turn out.

No, I wasn't in the game anymore. I wasn't enjoying the process of my project game. Instead, I was thinking about it.

Noticing that without judging it was again the saving grace.

I asked myself, "It is a game. So, what's next?"

The answer was simple. If it was a game, then I just needed to start playing it. I read the rules; now it was time to test playing it. So, I went to the dashboard of the crowdfunding platform I had chosen and decided to set a starting date for the campaign. I still feared that I wasn't ready enough, but I wanted to commit to a particular day. Yes, I thought, I should set a starting date for my game of the first of the next month.

But, as often happens in life — and life loves playing games with us — I couldn't set a date to start the crowdfunding game in the future. There wasn't a button "Launch the campaign on March 1st, 2018." There was just the button "Launch." I looked at it and thought, I could make a note in my calendar to press that button on March 1st.

But I wanted to have fun then, in that moment. I wanted badly to play the game.

So I pressed the "Launch" button and immediately had ideas for next steps, and became active and excited.

I didn't reach the goal of that crowdfunding campaign and discovered that the crowdfunding "game" was not for me. At least at that time and to the present day. But the experience described above remained clear and valuable in my memories.

I realized that whatever the outcome of our games — and we often play games to have fun and without fear of losing, if they are considered as leisure — we make the "effort" to take those steps and to become better at the game, without drama.

So seeing a task or a project we are up to — either one we initiated or an assignment from someone else — as a game can help us to take the drama out of our lives and make the whole process exciting and fun.

The fear shrinks in games. It's just a game after all. The drama and resistance to trying something others have recommended or assigned to us reduces considerably, and we can try out many new things without resenting the fact that we didn't come up with those ideas in the first place.

3. One more note on being serious

We already talked about being serious in the introduction, section 3, chapter 1, sections 2 and 3, and chapter 11, section 1.

A disclosure: As a non-gamer, I used to be too serious about games. As a child, I didn't think of them as games. They were just what I was doing and immensely important to me. As an adult, I thought I didn't like them and considered them something requested of me in order to socialize with others. But that turned out not to be true. I might have had these thoughts before the games, but when I played them, and shortly afterwards, I felt joy.

Discovering my resistance toward games was a gift. Because this let me see that my seriousness was a lifestyle choice, not something caused by nature.

Games and game design taught me many things. Of course, we need to prepare our game field and learn the rules, but at some point, we need to start playing to test it. Otherwise, we will be *thinking of playing* the game instead of actually playing it. Many will agree with this, also non-gamers like me.

But why then in real life don't we start playing (that is, living), rather than just thinking about life so much?

Seeing what is in front of us as a game can help us to actually start playing and living.

One of my children's favorite games is when I pretend to be extremely serious and tell them not to laugh or smile. This usually results in fits of laughter combined with their vain attempts to straighten their faces and not to smile or laugh. My solemn praises of their attempts to be serious make them explode with laughter, at which I playfully scowl and tell them not to laugh. That only makes them laugh even harder. We all end up laughing so hard we cry.

But even deliberate attempts to be serious about something, when observed non-judgmentally, can be very funny to ourselves.

So let's not be too serious about our intention to either start or do something, and just start doing. I realize now that the crowdfunding campaign I described in section 2 above could be considered me just thinking about writing this book, but it wasn't. I was taking concrete steps and producing content, bits of which were included in this book. And this current stage in my "writing-the-book-on-self-gamification" game, where I write the final chapters of it, does feel like an advanced level in a game.

4. "You can't edit a blank page." — Nora Roberts
I was thrilled to discover recently that one of my all-time favorite pearls of wisdom for writers originates from my all-time favorite fiction writer.

This wisdom has supported me in many projects, and not only in writing. Also in self-gamification. Sometimes I had the idea that my game rules were not good enough and I wouldn't be successful in either designing them or in playing the games they defined (in other words, in pursuing my projects). Often before trying the idea out.

Seeing the whole process non-judgmentally, making progress in small steps, and seeing it as a game, let me see that such an attitude is ingrained in most of us. Yes, it again has to do with fear. Fear of failure *and* fear of success. The latter possibly being the fear that success will somehow fall undeservedly into our laps and we won't be able to justify it. People will see that we don't deserve it and our "fundamental" failure and unworthiness will become public.

Seeing these fears and then acting upon them, which resulted in day-dreams of both failure and success and escaping to other activities that I assumed were more reasonable and easier than doing what I wanted, helped me recognize that it was all a means of running away from the discomfort of creativity. The awareness I gained from this realization (see chapter 6, section 5) and also realizing that fear grows along with the yearning to accomplish something (chapter 7, section 4) helped me to return to my games and to resolve other stagnating activities.

In section 2 above, I told you the story of my crowdfunding campaign for the book you are reading, and that the planning of it along with preparing material for the launch was beneficial for writing this book.

But sometimes, planning and mind-mapping can turn out into a solution to save us from "playing and enjoying the game" and from creating something we very much want to create.

I had a big epiphany on this whilst leading an international working group (Business Rules Working Group, BRWG) to establish a relationship between over five hundred decision points for an international technical standard, which organizations we represented or worked for (as consultancy service providers) were implementing into their projects and programs. We spent many meetings creating many maps without completing any of them or achieving anything worth showing.

In the meantime, I became a professional writer and learned the truth I quoted above, "You can't edit an empty page." (See the other story connected to this wisdom in chapter 3, section 2.) Then just before another online meeting of our working group, it hit me. That was what we were trying to do with these five hundred decisions. We were editing an empty page! We spent hours and hours of meetings arguing about which decision points were more important than others, and how we should group them. We were trying to find a perfect solution, each of us coming from various organizations with various contexts from all over the world. We failed to see that all of the views in the group were perfect. And that we were spending time editing something that didn't exist yet.

So, after some contemplation, I sat down and asked myself how *I*, with my background and experience, would arrange those 500+ decision points in a sequence if I personally were a project implementing it. I took several decision points to consider each day and place somewhere in a sequential chain. These were my small and effortless steps. After each step in this project, which often consisted of considering five decision points (sometimes more, sometimes less, depending on their complexity) every day, I collected a point. This project, which I took on out of curiosity, resulted in a series of blog posts (which I shared with the community and the working group), and two books, which were bought and used by many projects applying the international specification S1000D**.

My books serve as one of the possible mappings of relationships between those decision points, which their readers can now "edit" and use as is most appropriate for their own projects and organizations. I shared the lessons I learned while working on these books with the working group and we came up with further concrete solutions for modification and improvement of the S1000D concepts, and guidance to facilitate its implementation.

5. When to apply self-gamification

As you can see from the examples above, self-gamification and the approaches it embraces gave me the tools to solve challenges in creative and sometimes wholly unexpected ways, helping me reach my goals and beyond.

The experiences above also confirm that the best time to practice self-gamification, and indeed anything else we really want to do, is now. And to do it again and again. At least when we need a hand in uplifting our mood and motivating ourselves.

As you probably know yourself, there are many times in a day when you might experience discomfort or upset. These can be big or small.

Even if we think we haven't had significant challenges for some time, we often have little upsets that we ignore and resist, which can gather into a bigger one that eventually explodes. Then we think we don't know how it happened or why. Awareness, kaizen, and gamification are brilliant in helping you to become aware of each or at least most of those little upsets, compensate or bypass them by making small steps toward your goals, and appreciate those steps in your game feedback system.

6. All games are supposed to become boring at some point

I recently discovered a new paradox of games, which upon closer look makes complete sense.

Games are perfect for learning something new, but they are also supposed to become dull with time. At least if you are not incorporating new elements into them regularly.

In chapter 12, section 5, we discussed our hunger for new things and experiences, as well as our reluctance to stay with the same activity over and over again, or in other words, to play the same game over and over again.

Recently I discovered the following statement by Raph Koster:

"The destiny of games is to become boring, not to be fun. Those of us who want games to be fun are fighting a losing battle against the human brain because fun is a process and routine is its destination."* — Raph Koster, *Theory of Fun for Game Design*

This awareness is fantastic, isn't it? Both the understanding that there are many perfect ways to do the same thing, and the realization that games or gamified systems are not a one-off solution for all our troubles and a one-time pill to regain our happiness. They are the stepping stones on our way to identifying what is fun and joyful for us in any given moment.

The same applies to our self-motivational games, that is to our project and project management games. They don't have to and can't always be fun for us. In various situations, different things are exciting.

Here is what Raph Koster adds to the statement above in an endnote of his acclaimed book *Theory of Fun for Game Design*:

"The destiny of games: Many games, of course, seem to become more fun as you learn more about them. This has a lot to do with the nature of the challenge presented in those games; they tend to present problems of a certain complexity level that reveals more subtleties the deeper in you go." — Raph Koster, *Theory of Fun for Game Design*

This additional statement might seem like a caveat to the previous one, but it's not. Some games and projects are multidimensional and have a deeper, changing nature. Real-life projects often have this changing nature. We usually resist it, but seeing and treating them as games can show us how fun they can actually be.

But if you have learned everything you can from your project game (or even if you haven't but have the definite feeling that you have), then you can either add fun elements to its design to keep you engaged until the end (if you want to finish it), or leave that game and go on to another.

I once asked my then seven-year-old son why he liked Minecraft*** so much. His first answer was that it's an "infinitely generated" world where there is always something new, and new rules appear with each new landscape. Because of these new rules, which you have to read when you enter the new world, you must behave differently, to at least some extent, than before.

I asked, "do these new rules mean you learn something new all the time?"

His answer was "Yes."

You can add new types of treasures, adventures, and rules to your real-life project games. So, when you see anything that comes your way as a game, you have the possibility of learning something, having fun, and being captivated, then, as soon as you notice you are no longer enjoying the game, either adjust its design with new fun elements or switch to another game.

We will talk about switching to other games in the following section.

But let me emphasize the central message of this book again. You are both the designer and the player of your self-motivational games, for the entire time that you are turning your life into games.

It is your responsibility to make and keep your games fun.

Thus never stop improving your games.

7. You can always switch to another game and then come back

I love writing this book. Especially now, having reached the advanced level of this game, which is writing the later chapters of the book, where the whole concept comes together. But even today I realize there are times when I need to take a break from this game and do something else. Today these were to attend to my four-year-old daughter's needs, who has had to stay home from kindergarten with a cold.

Just like when playing fun games, we might be reluctant to do these other things when we are in the flow and enjoying what we are doing. This fight, and thoughts like "I don't want to do that, I'd rather stay where I am and continue doing my favorite thing" takes you — probably against your expectations — out of your game.

Seeing that without judgment is priceless.

All those various activities in your life, both expected and unexpected, can be both separate self-motivational games, and a part of your day-long self-motivational game. So if something unexpected comes up, or you notice yourself growing tired of the activity at hand, then switch to another game. As I mentioned in chapter 9, section 3, this other game might be taking a break, looking out of the window, moving around or doing something completely different.

You can always come back to your (at this point in your life) favorite game. Observe how recharging these smaller games can be, whether they are intentionally planned or come unexpectedly (such as my daughter entering my little home office and asking me to readjust her hairpin).

When switching from one project to another, should you not know what to do next, the following question can help: "Which project or activity game do I want to play now?"

8. Start simple

I have a question for you. On a scale of one to ten (ten being the biggest, and one the smallest), how would you grade your curiosity and enthusiasm for turning your projects and activities into games? If this is a paperback, record your score here:

_____

If it is less than five, then put this book aside and continue with your day.

But I suspect that if you got this far in the book, it is at least five and probably even higher. In which case, go ahead and turn your life into games. But start simple. Take one project of each type and subtype for escape-from tasks. Play the five minute perseverance game with them (see chapter 18 for details).

For longer-term goals, make rounds of at least a week but ideally a month. You need to gain experience with these games before modifying the design or extending the approach to others.

Be playful with shorter tasks too. For example, when you clean-up in the kitchen, imagine you are a Super Mario or Princess Peach**** on a secret mission to save your pans and spoons from the evil fat-monsters. Whatever is fun, think of it.

When these games become boring, as we discussed in section 6 of this chapter, then either add new game elements to your project games (if they are not completed yet) or extend your self-motivational and gameful approach to other projects as well (see the last paragraph of chapter 14, section 4). Or both.

On the other hand, if you notice that the design for your self-motivational games and especially the feedback systems become too sophisticated, then as we mentioned in chapter 12, section 6, you might be escaping other projects you want to pursue but are scared of.

9. Number of projects to turn into games

Some time ago, when I was turning only parts of my life into games, I discovered another quirky idea my brain had produced: that I had to limit the number of projects I gamified. But then I realized that I didn't have to do so and could consider which projects were relevant for me that particular month.

With time I realized that I could and wanted to turn my whole life into games and try various designs to the management part of it. The games described in part V will show you the evolution of my self-motivational game designs from single projects (5 Minute Perseverance Game; chapter 18), to project areas (Project ("Crush") Management Game; chapter 19), to whole life (Balance Game; chapter 20).

10. Turning work and studies into games

In the process of turning my life into games, I once wondered whether there were any projects or types of activities that were unsuited to it.

Initially, I didn't have an answer to this. Later my answers changed over time.

I used to think that consulting and teaching projects were too important to be treated as games.

But interestingly enough the point system helped me to stop the commentary in my head when I had to perform some tricky or lengthy tasks.

For example, I once had to analyze a long document and provide a written report on it. Another time I feared implementing the self-edits for one of my book projects. In both cases, giving a point for each tiny bit of the task done (a section or paragraph analyzed or edited) did the trick, and at some point I forgot to record the score anymore. The work continued smoothly and it became a fun task. On top of that, describing the approach to my customer (they asked about the funny marks on a scrap of paper next to my computer) was an excellent ice breaker and made for brilliant small talk. My excitement (and possibly also quirkiness) brought smiles, and we could dive into the documents I had analyzed with ease.

The same applies to studying, especially when we are learning by ourselves. I used to think of studies as hard work. Do I believe that now? No.

But this is still a widespread belief.

That is why I felt compelled to answer the following question on Quora: "Is hard work really necessary for studying?"*****

This was my answer:

(The beginning of the answer)

No. If you treat studying as a fun game and adjust your studying approach so that it appeals to you as a "player," then it won't feel like hard work anymore. Remember, you are both the designer and the player of your self-motivational games. Concentrating on the smallest steps can also help you make your studies both effortless and fun. Here's how to proceed:
1. Observe yourself non-judgmentally and discover what exactly you are resisting in your studying process or the material you have to go through. What overwhelms you there? Be as specific but as non-judgmental in your observations as possible. You are your own anthropologist.
2. Identify the smallest step or piece of material you can learn that would cause no effort. Take that little step.
3. Appreciate this little step by giving yourself a point (a badge or something similar) in your game's feedback system.

Repeat 2 and 3. If you find yourself resisting again, go back to 1.

(The end of the answer)

11. Turning family life and time with friends into games

OK, you might say. Those experiences have to do with work and studies. But what about your personal life and your family?

When first asked whether I was turning my personal and family life into games, my immediate answer was "No." I thought my time with my family and friends was too "sacred" to be gamified. That it was unethical to turn it into games.

But when I gave it a try, I realized that I didn't "play" the game to earn points when it came to playing with my children or spending time with my husband, extended family, or friends. I discovered that I didn't need to. These came naturally, and I enjoyed those times. But self-gamification helped me to take that time without self-reproach, and to do away with thoughts that I could better spend my time doing something else.

It also helped me to become aware that I did take time for my family and to appreciate those moments.

Here is what I wrote in a blog post titled "Closing May Round and Starting June Round of the 5 Minute Perseverance Game" on June 5, 2017, about lessons learned in this area of my life:

(The beginning of the excerpt)

Meeting and communicating with family and friends.

I am happy about this one for two reasons. First, it reminded me to answer emails I had forgotten about in the busyness of everyday life. And secondly, I often wouldn't notice that I had spent time with family and friends. I was simply there with them, enjoying them and my time with them.

Only on two days of this month did I not record a point for this activity. I suspect that I simply forgot to do so. The discovery, when looking at my day and counting the points, that I took care of my loved ones and devoted time to them without watching the clock, brought me much joy. This activity is one of the sweetest ones, and it showed me that my loved ones are not being neglected while I follow my passion for work and personal projects.

[A side-note: even though this project was placed almost last in the list of eleven projects, it still got nearly all possible points and earned more than any of the other projects in this round. Wherever it stands, the fact that I am drawn to do something here shows that my heart's wishes are much stronger than my Fear Of Missing Out (FOMO)****** or fear of doing something wrong.]

(The end of the excerpt)

12. Taking care of family and personal (official) matters

Do you remember the story from chapter 3, section 3 about how I turned the process of applying for a new passport for my son into a game?

We all have many of these tasks to accomplish regularly. These are perfect candidates for being turned into games.

The main result when I turn these, as I call them, administrative activities, into games is being able to bypass my traditional annoyance with them. These activities include registering my children for one or other event or activity (like dancing or swimming), paying for these and other bills, communicating with doctors, accompanying my children and mother to health checks, organizing meetings with friends, and setting meeting dates for the local writers' club on Facebook. Turning these into games helped me to become less and less upset at having to do all of them, and I hardly ever sigh about these things anymore.

Even if thoughts pop into my head like "Oh, there is always something to do," there is the knowledge, "I only need to spend a few minutes on it and a step toward the goal is done. And I get the point."

Besides which, I discovered that I even look forward to doing these tasks because if I just follow the instructions provided (without evaluating and complaining about them), they are often straightforward to do. So the points are earned easily. Yes, the most significant results here are the removal of drama, fun factor in doing something simple and straightforward, and pleasure at witnessing visible progress in those necessary things (without having to put much effort in).

13. Turning health and well-being into well-being games

Self-gamification is perfect for developing healthy habits. Although, the word "habit" is probably a bit misleading.

The primary definition of the word "habit" by Oxford dictionaries is:

"A settled or regular tendency or practice, especially one that is hard to give up."*******

From experience I can tell you that a healthy habit is easy to give up. Especially if we resist and resent it.

Let's take having enough sleep, for example. I often found myself resisting going to bed at a reasonable time because I thought I didn't want the day to end. There were so many fun (or even not so fun but still necessary) things to do! I also feared what the next day might bring. I am sure there were other good reasons my mind came up with then too, which I don't remember now. The fact is, I went to bed too late, while still having to get up early in the mornings. I did that every night for many years, with just the occasional long sleep in-between (due to exhaustion).

I tried giving myself points for enough sleep, and it did work for some time. But gathering one point for so many hours of sleep wasn't that appealing to my insatiable mind. And as soon as I took the activity off my game plans in the hope that it would happen all by itself, I started getting less and less sleep again.

The same happened with the straight posture activity, about which I told you in chapter 8, section 3. Soon after I stopped treating it as a game and earning my points each day, I found myself with back bent and shoulders hunched more and more often. Tensions in both my back and shoulder muscles returned, and my husband started straightening my back with his lovely hugs again, more and more often.

As much as I loved my husband hugging me, I didn't like the fact that my healthy back straightening habit had disappeared.

Another example was with work-out and daily movement. I tried jogging once a week and had a lot of fun going on weekly runs with my children. We managed this for a couple of weeks before the weather changed, or so I claimed, and we stopped. My children continued getting exercise at school, kindergarten and through the sports they were practicing. But I didn't.

And I resented it and labeled myself as hopeless in this area of my life. But then, after overdoing things, I had two incredibly painful diaphragm spasms in the space of one week, between Christmas and New Year's Eve 2018. It was a wake-up call. I knew I had to come up with some game "hack" to keep up this healthy habit.

I had to do it not just for my body as a whole, but in particular my eyes, in which I have a condition that gives me slight double vision (and makes playing video games uncomfortable and tiring). But even doing the necessary exercises for just a few seconds or minutes a day wouldn't last for long if I trusted they were already habits that would be done regardless.

What to do?

The solution was to put enough sleep, straight posture, and both work-outs (for eyes and body) into my daily games. Now if I sleep for more than seven hours a day I get one star, and I get another if I do both workouts and practice straight posture every day.

I must tell you that I am very diligent in earning my stars now. I am quite proud of rarely sleeping less than seven hours a night, and now love the yoga and work-out sessions I previously thought I hated, and look forward to practicing them every day.

Having learned from experience, I will keep them as daily games, even if at some point they seem hard to give up. (You can read more on my current self-motivational game design in chapter 20.)

Thus, self-gamification can help you to make healthy habits intentional and can support you in keeping them up, as well as appreciating everything you do for your well-being. By gathering points and stars for what you want to keep up, you will strengthen what you want to cultivate in yourself and stop worrying about what you don't like about yourself, without noticeable effort.

14. Voluntary work and hobbies

This category of work often encompasses those tasks that we say we want to do but don't have time for. Or they can become our escape-to tasks. Self-gamification can help you become creative at breaking your tasks into small bits and appreciating each of them if the work stalls. Or it can help you to become aware that you are using this work as an escape-to activity, in which case stop at some intentional point, appreciate what you have managed with a point, badge, gem or star, and move on to other projects and activities.

15. Household
I used to — and sometimes still do — have thoughts about household chores being something I have to do, but don't want to (except, possibly, for doing laundry).

Thanks to turning household chores into games, the work became much smoother with time and with fewer complaints, especially the duties I thought of as tedious and annoying, like cleaning and tidying a house with two small children.

Another great thing that has been mentioned several times already, was "one point only" for my escape-to activities like laundry, which helped me to limit these activities and attend to other tasks.

16. One big project game
While writing this book and developing the Balance Game (see chapter 20), I realized that ambition and drive could add to the balance in my life, rather than contradicting it.

This book and self-gamification as an approach often preoccupy my creative thought processes, but I had the idea that I should spread my attention and efforts concurrently over several large projects that I would like to accomplish this year (including working on other books). Even when making almost daily progress in many of these and gaining points for them, I somehow didn't feel like I was having fun. Then I realized that I had the ambition to write the book you are reading now, first. I wanted to see it come together and become a completed product. So that was the game I wanted to excel in now, and I wanted to try the others later.

In the Balance Game (described in chapter 20), I use weekends and holidays to recharge, and I collect stars when I manage not to work too much on projects and activities at these times. But I now make an exception for this one "ambition project." I allow myself to be creative in this project in my free time and weekends too. Mobile, scraps of paper, and the computer are all used as soon as creative thoughts appear. Awareness, kaizen, and gamification help me to enjoy this project as well as anything else that calls for my attention on the weekends. This "ambition project" turned out to be a great game to play whenever I have a break between enjoying time with my husband and children, visiting family members and friends, or doing household chores or other things around the house, and I take a little time for myself. I discovered that being creative in a project I am passionate about is one of the best things I can do for myself. (See more on how I handle these "ambition projects" in chapter 20, section 5.)

Seeing and enabling myself to respond to this big wish was an enlightening and self-empowering discovery. Ambitions, nowadays often prejudiced as bringing us nothing but stress and depression, can actually contribute to the balance and happiness in our lives. Gamers usually have one game that preoccupies their minds and where they feel most creative. They might play other games too, but they come back again and again to one. For my son, it is currently Roblox******** and its many games and simulators.

[A side-note: As I am self-editing this book, my son's preferred game is Minecraft again (I mentioned the reasons for his love for it initially in section 6 above). He said that he had regained his passion for the game thanks to the many updates in it since he had last played. The same can happen with real-life projects. The project games we thought had stopped being of interest to us might catch our attention and become exciting again after some time. The project might be the same as it was, but you received an "upgrade" from all the experiences you had since then (see the quote by Ariel and Shya Kane about awareness acting "like a complimentary upgrade" in chapter 9, section 1).]

You might need such a project too. If you look at what you have in your to-do list (wherever it is recorded: on paper, digitally or in your head), you will recognize this "ambition project" by identifying which of them appears to be both the most attractive and the scariest. It is basically the one, about which, while daydreaming, you have both illusions and nightmares.

Yes, as I write this book, this project is both the most yearned for and the scariest. I want this book to be both valuable and fun to read. So, I now allow myself the ambition of finishing writing my book on self-gamification soon (Spring 2019) and also enjoy each step on the path to that finish line. I record the points (one per ten minutes of writing) in the little field marked with "SG" (stands for Self-Gamification) in my Points and Stars Game Book, which is the weekly planner where I record my points and bonus stars. (I introduced this and another game book I use in chapter 11, section 2, activity 2, and mentioned it in chapter 12, section 9. You can also read more on this in chapter 20.)

17. Turning to-do lists into gameful feedback systems

We discussed project management games many times in Chapter 12 (sections 1, 3, 4, 5, 7, 8, 9, and 10) and will also address this specific type of activity throughout chapter 19.

But let me address to-do lists here, specifically. Many of us don't enjoy recording them and find the task of regularly updating them tedious and annoying.

Self-gamification came to help me here as well. As I started seeing the updating of my to-do lists as a game, I became creative in how to handle them. I came up with the idea of calling my daily paper planner, where I record my to-do lists, a "To-Do Game Book" and began to enjoy the task more and more. I discovered again and again that the question, "If this task was a game, how would I approach/design it so that it becomes fun?" was extremely helpful.

In the course of designing my to-do lists, I tried many approaches: writing on scraps of paper, sticky notes, or in a notebook; several online and standalone tools; and even an electronic pocket organizer. I discovered that each time I found a method, and it seemed to work, I hoped that it would work forever. I became aware that I was putting too much pressure on sticking with the same method forever. But this is like trying to play just one game over and over and nothing else. Just as in exercising, many people discover that it's too monotonous to stick to only one type to stay healthy. We jog, play ball games, go for a swim, do yoga and so on. Trying various kinds of sports helps us to keep having fun while staying healthy (we touched on this topic briefly in chapter 12, section 5.)

As mentioned briefly above in this section as well as in chapter 12, section 5, I currently record my to-do tasks in a daily paper planner. So, I use three paper pocket planners (calendars): one for my appointments, one for recording the points of my project games, and one for daily to-do lists. In the latter, I plan on which day and week I want to address what, and with that have an overview of what I have scheduled to do for that week or month. I also try to see non-judgmentally how I feel about the tasks. Am I comfortable with them today or not? Why did I plan to do them: because it is a step towards my dream goals, or just to conform to some kind of stereotype? And again, this helps only when I see all of that honestly *and* non-judgmentally, as an anthropologist would do.

My recommendation is to test various approaches and observe what is right for you at any given time in your life. Both for to-do lists and project management.

And continue practicing to see your projects as games, and yourself as their player. If you think of some of the board or card games, where each move consists of many steps, you might recognize that the sequences of these steps are like entries on a to-do list. That means that you can — if you set your mind to it — see your to-do lists as game-plans too. And bring fun into them. You just need to figure out how. It is always worth approaching it in a non-judgmental, one-little-step-at-a-time, and gameful way.

18. How self-gamification helps increase concentration on each step

Multitasking was "in" several years ago. And since it didn't work for many people, concentrating on one task, or in other words, unitasking, is more and more appreciated and emphasized today.

I found the following revealing statement about multitasking:

"Multitasking is the wrong word. Our brains can't handle more than one higher cognitive function at a time. We may think we're multitasking, but we're actually switchtasking. Toggling between one task and another. First the phone, then the e-mail, then the phone, back to the e-mail. And each time you switch, there's a few milliseconds of startup cost. The neurons need time to rev up." — A. J. Jacobs, *My Life as an Experiment*

So unitasking, or in other words concentrating on doing one thing at any given moment, is more beneficial, both for our well-being and progress of the project at hand.

I must admit that I used to confuse unitasking with doing just one thing for the entire day, or at least most of it. This misconception led me into upsets and being annoyed at any kind of interruption, including from "inside" (hunger, thirst, needing to go to the bathroom, and so on) and from outside (phone calls, urgent e-mails, knocks on the door).

Then came the day when I became aware of this behavior on my part. So I started a game with myself to name all the roles, jobs and/or activities I was taking on and practicing that day. Here are some of the things I jotted down that day (please, don't take them too seriously or literally):

- Day-care provider for my then six-month-old daughter,
- Entertainer for my children,
- "Santa-Claus" for International Children's Day (I recorded this list on June 1st, 2015),
- Cook for my family,
- Cleaning personnel,
- Moving specialist (unpacker) with interior design skills learned on the fly (it was less than a month since we had moved into our house),
- Writer,
- Editor of technical content,
- Job seeker (it was before I started my business),

- Homeowner showing the building company specialist which small quirks in our then new house needed correction,
- Travel manager assistant (for my family),
- Laundry master,
- Knowledge manager (in our new home, where to find what),
- Etc.

Some of the roles, jobs, and activities were played, done, and finished. But most of them were started, interrupted by another one (often by the very first one in the list above), and then started again.

If I smiled at this "chaos" and approached it playfully and with humor, then it became productive. If I complained, the space around me darkened, in spite of the bright sunny day outside.

Fortunately, the complaints were often replaced by wonder at all the surprises life had in store for me, and how my plans for several hours up front were always overthrown.

So, during one of the washing/cleaning activities, I think it was while drying Emma's bottles, I tried to imagine a pattern that would symbolize my day. Braids came immediately to mind. I considered the alternative of mosaic but realized that some of the activities were not granular and continued after being interrupted, and if I took care of and time for them then the "hair" inside was smooth and "obedient" and braided nicely into a clean arc.

You might ask what this kind of symbol is good for. Well, it helped me to visualize my day, and seeing it as a braid made it pretty, rather than the ugly and miserable way I would have experienced such "chaos" in the past.

In the past, I often considered only one activity to be worthy and important, so that I subsequently thought: "I didn't manage anything today!" But when I listed the items above on that sunny day of June 1st, 2015, the only thing I had to say was "Wow. Not bad at all!"

I am sure most of us juggle tens of activities in our job, family and many other areas. We complain that we don't make any progress in what is supposedly our preferred occupation.

But isn't one step forward fun in itself?! Every step is a step forward because we can learn from any of our experiences, even when being tired and irritated. But only if we disengage from those feelings and consider them in a non-judgmental way.

Then we are free to choose the next step and concentrate on it without any pressure of achievement or fear of what others might say.

[A side-note: I had the epiphanies described in this section on June 1, 2015. It was about a year before I started consciously turning my life into fun games and recording points for various projects. Observe yourself, how you sometimes do something out of curiosity, as you would in a game. Such ideas might start with the following words in your thoughts, "Let's try this." or "What if I/we try it that way?" If so, you are already approaching your life as a game designer and player.]

19. You can't complain and play your self-motivational games at the same time

I learned this wisdom before I started turning my life into games. Maybe even before I ever tried to deliberately turn any activity into a game. The wisdom comes from the many resources Ariel and Shya Kane provide on the topics of awareness, and living in the moment. One of my favorite videos made by the Kanes is "Transformational Tips For The Workplace."*********

In this video, Ariel and Shya Kane formulated three brilliant and to the point tips on how to work efficiently and have success at work. If you watch it, make sure to watch the whole video. It's less than three minutes long. You will be utterly inspired. The transformational tip for workplace #2 is called "Close Your Complaint Department":

"You should recognize that if you are complaining, that's the only thing you can be doing. Work, complain, choose one. That goes back to that Second Principle again. [Author's addition: 'No two things can occupy the same you at the same time.' — Ariel and Shya Kane] You can only do one thing at a time. If you're complaining, that's your moment. You don't get any work accomplished." — Ariel and Shya Kane, *Transformational Tips For The Workplace**********

Here's what to do when you have turned your life into games, and you observe that your starting point — where you are right now — is a complaint, which is a form of an upset (we discussed upsets as starting points in chapter 9, section 1): stop, become aware that you are complaining, and then choose whether you want to complain further or take the next step in the project game you were playing until you opened "Your Complaint Department."

20. Don't stop playing

As mentioned many times already one way or another, if you want to turn your whole life into games, or at least many aspects of it and not just one project, you need to practice.

Play, design, and play again. Then go back to adjusting your designs and testing them again. In other words, you "level up" in your game of being a self-motivational game designer.

Of course, as in any other game you can — in your mind's eye — lose (or "die") any time. But you can also start a new round and win ("rise") again. And again.

Here's what to do when you think you have lost in your self-motivational games:

Practice, practice, practice, and always start with awareness.

If you would like to refresh your memory about the three approaches that can help you hone the three skill sets, then go to the chapters introducing them (chapter 5 for awareness, chapter 7 for kaizen, and chapter 10 for gamification), as well as Recommended Reading at the end of the book.

When you practice, succeeding becomes a constant byproduct. With time, your goal might turn out to be to become more skilled in your life's game and all the project and activity games within it, including relaxing, being with your family, being present and concentrating, or concrete projects, either technical or artistic.

The thing I love most about self-gamification is that I never have to finish practicing it and playing my self-motivational games. I can try out various projects at different times of the year, during different life circumstances, and with altering states of mind.

These endless possibilities have never been as visible to me as they are now, when I experience my life as a bundle of fun and exciting games.

21. Don't forget to record your points, but don't be too serious about them

You won't be able to avoid thinking about and daydreaming of your project game instead of actually playing it. Don't judge yourself for it, but bring yourself back to where you are. And feel free to appreciate it as soon as you observe yourself coming back to the present moment and noticing how you move from one little point in your life to another. Even the mental, "One more point for me!" might draw the corners of your mouth and eyes into a smile.

I noticed that I was more diligent about recording the points and bonus points some months (or weeks and days) than others. At those times, when I rarely forgot to record points, it felt as if I had slowed down a little. Before looking at the score, I imagined I would have achieved less because I took time to record all those points. Even if these were only seconds, they did accumulate into minutes, didn't they? But when I looked at both the score and what I had managed in the project, I discovered that I actually completed much more than when I hurried through and forgot to record the points.

The paradox here was also that, although recording points is technically an additional task in itself, it didn't feel like I had worked any harder. I had actually had more fun than in those activities for which I didn't record the points. Here we go again: the success of the game, the feeling of satisfaction as well as the success of the projects, resulted from allowing myself to appreciate every moment of the game and give me time to have fun playing it.

Appreciating what you do with points and also having breaks between the steps (taking a detour to another project or activity game, for example) will let you both recognize what you have done so far, and give your ideas space to ripen, so that the next small step will occur with less effort, more fun, and more creativity.

However, let's remember *not* to be too serious about recording the score. As I did in chapter 14, section 4, I would like to urge you again not to dwell too much on your score. Don't judge yourself if you forgot to record a point. Your feedback system is supposed to increase your fun, not be an exact record and punish you if you don't manage to do something or to record everything meticulously.

Self-Gamification Happiness Formula

Here is a lesson I learned in the September 2017 round of the Project ("Crush") Management Game. At some point into the game I realized that I hadn't recorded all of the scores immediately after accomplishing a task or attending to a project, and when later trying to recall how many points I should have earned, I couldn't remember. At first I found it frustrating. But then I reminded myself that in video games you didn't manage to gather all the treasures available out there either. Some of them needed to be left behind if I wanted to move forward and keep going. I loved this realization because it also showed that sometimes when I didn't record my score, it was because I was in the flow and enjoying the projects I was working on. So the points I didn't log were the treasures I didn't retrieve along the way. But while forgetting those, I gathered others. And I got the best rewards of all — a smile on my face, the warm feeling of achieving and completing something, and the joy of having moved forward.

The ease I felt in myself, as well as honing my creativity and gameful attitude, helped me to come up with a design where I wouldn't forget how many points I had made in any particular day, because there were only one hundred and forty-four available (see chapter 20).

22. There are many perfect ways to design the same game

I mentioned this briefly in section 6 of this chapter and also indirectly in chapter 12, section 5. But I would now like to draw your attention more explicitly to this particular lesson.

There is no bad design in self-gamification.

Or at least only you can say, *and* in retrospect, what suited you and what didn't.

I discovered this truth myself many times with writing, and also from a story Elizabeth Gilbert (author of the famous memoir *Eat, Pray, Love*) told of having to cut a ten-page short story by thirty percent:

"The new version was neither better nor worse than the old version; it was just profoundly different." — Elizabeth Gilbert, *Big Magic: Creative Living Beyond Fear*

So are your designs, when you rework them, "profoundly different."

Another wisdom in this direction comes from physics.

It is the *uncertainty principle*:

"The Uncertainty principle is also called the Heisenberg uncertainty principle. Werner Heisenberg stumbled on a *secret of the universe* [emphasized by the author]: No thing has a definite position, a definite trajectory, or a definite momentum. Trying to pin a thing down to one definite position will make its momentum less well pinned down, and vice-versa."**********

So to "pin down" for sure what your design (or your project) feels like and whether you should make changes or not, take time testing it. Be your game designer's (reminder: that is yourself) most engaged player. Play it for the length of the round you set up, make notes and suggestions for improvements, and then implement these before starting the next round of your games.

23. Expect to never stop learning and discovering

I recently read a quote by Sandra Bullock, where she urges to "always be the student." It applies to life in general, and to self-gamification. I often experience epiphanies and recognise new things several times a day. Or I rediscover those I had earlier, in a new context. There is always a new context, even if we try to tell ourselves otherwise.

I discovered that when I observe the flow of my project and project management games non-judgmentally, along with those changing contexts and circumstances (one of which is my mood), my thought processes no longer bother me the way they used to. Instead, seeing them without reproach helps me to investigate different strategies for my self-motivational games in varying conditions, and adjust them accordingly.

So what do I think now after playing this game every day for several years? I believe that my experience and creativity will continue evolving from round to round, from one project game to another, from one move I make in each of those games to another, from one moment of my life to another.

Here is a brilliant quote illustrating the dynamics of practicing a gameful and playful style of life:

"Creativity grows out of a certain type of hard work, combining curious exploration with playful experimentation and systematic investigation. New ideas and insights might seem like they come in a flash, but they usually happen after many cycles of imagining, creating, playing, sharing, and reflecting." — Mitchel Resnick, *Lifelong Kindergarten: Cultivating Creativity through Projects, Passion, Peers, and Play*

24. Immediate and continuous effects

A quick reminder to be here, where you are right now, in this moment of your life fully, with will, and attention. Because when you do, then each moment will feel amazing and crisp. All these new moments will also accumulate and will facilitate your practice and experience of life as a fantastic, always changing and exciting collection of your favorite games.

Here, I recommend re-reading chapter 8, section 7 and chapter 12, section 4.

25. When you are feeling down, ask yourself, "Would you like to play a game with what you want or have to do?"

I noticed that being creative with the self-motivational game design and testing that design can pull me out of a situation where I feel down, desperate, and overwhelmed. It is like helping children when they are sad or angry by asking, "Would you like to play a game?", or suggesting a gameful approach to help them accomplish a chore.

Why don't we apply this approach to ourselves?

So, when you are feeling down, ask yourself, "Would you like to play a game with what you want or have to do?"

26. Less drama, more joy at crossing the finish line

Become aware of how far you've come in each project, how many steps you have taken, and how much is left. You can play with measuring how far you are from the finish line, experimenting with the scales for your score (the maximum number of points or stars you can earn). This estimation can help you relax and enjoy crossing the finish line. I will also address this more in the next chapter (chapter 16, section 2), where I will relate how my husband and I helped our son to turn the assignment he got from school (and resented), into fun games.

27. Don't judge others; they are their perfect designers and players too

Sometimes, when we have success in our life, we might be tempted to judge others who complain about their lives. But remember that you can't design their games, because your "shoes" won't necessarily fit them. Only they can develop their own self-motivational games and make their own experiences.

And also remember that when you judge others, you are complaining too. (I had to chuckle when I observed myself complaining about other people's and also my own complaints, for the first time.) And when you are complaining, you aren't playing your games. So instead of analyzing what others do or don't do while turning (or not turning) their lives into games, concentrate on playing your games and having fun with them. This is the best way to share self-gamification. More on this in the next chapter (chapter 16).

28. Remember your tools for success
Being in danger of repeating myself, I would like to list here the three factors determining your success, in addition to your compass and measuring tool for success, which is fun. These are:
- *How present you are* —> Awareness and anthropology,
- *How often you permit yourself to do the smallest steps, instead of hurrying forward* —> Kaizen,
- *Whether you are willing to design and play* —> Gamification.

29. The simplest flow chart
And these three tools (or factors) result in three recurring steps to take:
1. Observe yourself non-judgmentally to determine where and how you are in this moment. This is your current starting point toward your goals, dreams, or items on your to-do list:
   - While doing so be simultaneously kind and honest. That is the key to being a successful anthropologist for yourself.
   - Don't worry if you observe yourself judging. Just start seeing yourself, the world around you, and your thought processes non-judgmentally again. Thus, if you discover that you treat yourself with reproach, repeat step 1.

- Otherwise, go to step 2.
2. Identify the next smallest and most effortless step. Then:
   - Take it. Go to step 3.
   - If you notice yourself attempting a big jump after jump and experience "muscle aches," go to step 1.
3. Appreciate having taken the step by giving yourself a point, a badge, a gem, a star or other unit in your motivational game design. And then:
   - Finish this cycle for the step you just took by moving on to the next step in your project or project management game (step 2).
   - If you feel lost, go to step 1.

30. Did I forget anything?

As I warned you at the beginning of this chapter, it is the longest in the whole book. The second longest is chapter 12, which defines self-motivational games and their design. Upon closer inspection, you might see the reason. Self-gamification concerns turning our whole lives into games. And our lives have an infinite number of aspects to them.

I tried to cover as much as I could of what I learned when turning my life into games. Because of this, I repeated some of these truths, both in this chapter and the rest of the book. I hope these repetitions didn't bother you and instead helped you make connections between the various skill sets you learned about in this book.

Considering various aspects of practicing self-gamification has reminded me of the process of looking at each side of a cut and polished diamond. Each of the sides shines in multiple, colorful ways, depending on how you tilt it and how the light falls on it. Without the other sides and angles of the diamond and without its transparency, the surface we look at would be smooth and dull. I see and experience self-gamification in a similar way. It has many additional angles and features that shine through when we consider any one of them.

But if you notice an aspect that I haven't covered anywhere in the book, then you can contact me through the channels indicated on my website (see "About the author"), and I will take them into account, along with the new lessons I will gather in the future, for the next edition of the book.

In the next chapter (as I mentioned above), I will address how you can share self-gamification. And why you should.

31. Short and long term activities
I have two activities for you in this chapter.
Activity 1:

How do you see the need to turn your life into games now?

Repeat the test you carried out in chapter 5, section 4, and see how your view of yourself has changed after reading more of this book and starting to practice self-gamification. Are you viewing yourself more kindly now than you did then? How do you feel about yourself and the world around you now?

Below is the question I posed then — with slightly adjusted text for this chapter — along with the space for your notes. Please don't look at your records at the end of chapter 5 before you answer the question here.

How do you feel when you try to look at yourself non-judgmentally? Take a few minutes or even put a timer on for let's say three minutes and try to look at the things you do and don't do non-judgmentally. Look at how you feel when you try to consider that:

1. Are you completely comfortable with what you see?
2. Or did you judge yourself for procrastinating over what you want or have to do, and for doing something else instead, which doesn't bring you further towards your goals?

Use the lines below (or a notebook, if you are reading this on an e-reader) and a pen to record your thoughts and feelings when trying to observe yourself non-judgmentally. Record the first things that come to your mind.

_____
_____
_____
_____
_____
_____

Now take a look at your notes in chapter 5 and compare (but without reproach!) your answers now and then. How do your statements from now and then sound and differ:
1. Do you sound more comfortable with what you see today than before?
2. Or do you still observe yourself judging your procrastination? How did these judgmental statements sound now and then? Were they stronger or weaker, more or less dramatic?

Use the lines below (or a notebook, if you are reading this on an e-reader) and a pen to record the differences you noticed between the thoughts and feelings you had here and in chapter 5.

Remember, whatever the result, don't judge yourself for it. It can be surprising, exciting, and revealing when studied non-judgmentally and with interest.

_____
_____
_____
_____
_____
_____

Activity 2:
Practice and enjoy self-gamification.
Duration:
Depends on the period set for a move or a game-round (e.g., a few seconds, several minutes, an hour, or a day, a week, a month).
Pre-requisites:
1. The game plans and rules you developed in chapter 12, section 13, and the adjustments you made in chapter 14, section 6, activity 2.
2. Any of the physical or digital objects you need for your game feedback system (for example, little stones, beads, paper stars, stickers, a notebook or a planner, and a pen, a file, or one or more apps that you purchased or developed for this purpose).
3. Any tools you need to carry out your project games (for example, a canvas, brushes, colors and anything you need for your painting).

Guidelines:

Self-Gamification Happiness Formula

There are no specific guidelines except the game rules you developed in chapter 12, section 13, and chapter 14, section 6, activity 2 when you designed your self-motivational games.

And the reminder to:
- Observe yourself non-judgmentally, as an anthropologist would,
- Devour and concentrate on each move in your games,
- Appreciate every small step you take by recording the points or other entities in your feedback system,
- Have fun.

Glossary and references:
* Crowdfunding is "the practice of funding a project or venture by raising money from a large number of people who each contribute a relatively small amount, typically via the Internet." — https://en.oxforddictionaries.com/definition/crowdfunding
** www.s1000d.org
*** https://www.minecraft.net/
**** https://mario.nintendo.com/characters/
***** https://www.quora.com/Is-hard-work-really-necessary-for-studying/answer/Victoria-Ichizli-Bartels
****** FOMO (Fear Of Missing Out) is "anxiety that an exciting or interesting event may currently be happening

elsewhere, often aroused by posts seen on social media."
— https://en.oxforddictionaries.com/definition/fomo
******* https://en.oxforddictionaries.com/definition/habit
   ******** https://www.roblox.com/
       ****

https://www.youtube.com/watch?v=7aL0WsOoY3Y
   ****

https://simple.wikipedia.org/wiki/Uncertainty_principle

Chapter 16. Sharing Self-Gamification

"Each person's 'ordinary' is another's 'extraordinary'. Being one's self and sharing that with others is simply a gift." — Ariel and Shya Kane, Practical Enlightenment

1. The best way to share self-gamification is to practice and enjoy it

"According to the UN, by 2050, the number of over 60's is expected to double – however, when examining the cause of this, scientists are beginning to realize that diet and exercise are not the only factors. A person's social life may be playing a more important role than anyone initially thought." — longevitylive.com*

Social life doesn't exist without the sharing and exchange of thoughts, ideas, feelings, compassion and understanding, among others.

But the best way to share something we find positive and useful is to live by example. Judgment repels and destroys social life. Compassion and demonstrating hope make it stronger.

In chapter 15, section 27, I encouraged you to concentrate on your games and enjoy them.

I would like to emphasize the same here. Turn self-motivation and self-gamification into a habit, and with that, you will inspire others to do the same.

You can't motivate others without being motivated yourself. The same applies to successful management, leadership, awareness, living in the moment, anthropological (non-judgmental) seeing, kaizen, and (I would dare to say) gamification. You might be a gamification designer, but if you don't apply it to your own life, you will have enormous challenges in demonstrating its benefits to others.

Yes, the best way to share self-gamification is to practice it. People will notice, start asking, and become infected by your good mood and positive drive.

That is what happened to me. In the beginning, I hadn't thought about teaching self-gamification. I hadn't even thought of a term for what I was doing, let alone what it was that kept me doing it. I was just playing my games, experimenting and having fun. The reduction of the drama in my life, in spite of the challenges I had, and the increases in my productivity and optimism aroused genuine curiosity in those I encountered.

Their questions about how I was doing what I wanted and needed to do, which seemed to them to happen effortlessly for me, led me to contemplate and ask myself several questions. These questions prompted me to find out what it was, and how and why my behavior and attitude were different to what they had been when I was considerably less happy, much more desperate, and at times even miserable.

I am immensely grateful to all those questions at the beginning — when I shared the writing game for the first time (see chapter 3, section 2) — and also for those I get now as I teach self-gamification. They make me more and more aware of its potential, and as an eager experimental scientist I revel in testing and examining all its effects on me, and learning about the experiences of those I share it with.

Yes, having fun shows and is the best way of sharing what we enjoy.

Especially when doing so with adults.

When it comes to children, however, I learned that you might need to get creative to motivate them and show them the benefits of turning life into games. But this creativity can teach you many valuable lessons for inspiring and motivating adults too (especially reluctant adults, if you are a manager of them), and generate ideas for modifying your own self-motivational game design that will engage you even more in what you do.

2. What helping my son to turn a hated assignment into fun games taught me

You might have heard that children in Finland don't get homework from school. I was quite surprised when I heard about it for the first time**.

Even more surprised was I to learn that the school my son attends in Aalborg, Denmark, changed their approach to become 99% homework-free. Their method is to motivate children to finish all of their assignments at school. If they haven't accomplished them by the end of the week, they can take the textbooks and tasks home for the weekend. Parents then decide whether the children should do it that weekend or not. In the case of travel or otherwise busy weekends, the parents do not need to overload their children by making them do the assignments.

Such a system was both surprising and pleasant for all of us in the family. We didn't have to fret and sit up until late at night for Niklas to complete his homework. Instead, he could relax, read, play inside and outside, do sports, watch movies and videos, or play on the iPad.

But at some point, a day came when Niklas brought an unfinished assignment home. An additional challenge to admitting that he hadn't managed to complete what was asked of him, was the fact that he resented the exercise deeply. He thought it was absolutely and entirely BORING.

On top of that, it was for one of his favorite subjects, math. The exercise consisted of doing a large number of sums. That in itself wasn't a problem. The problem was that the resulting numbers were attributed different colors. And he had to color in an A4-sized illustration accordingly, to find out what the picture was of.

Coloring was for small kids, and not for a big seven-year-old school-boy, right?

My attempt to remind Niklas that he loved drawing didn't bear any fruit because he immediately dismissed it by telling me that he enjoyed drawing something new of his own, not coloring in something predefined by others.

I could see myself in this reasoning and showed him my understanding. But there was no other choice: he had to do the task.

But how? I called on self-gamification for help. I shared the 5 Minute Perseverance Game with him, and my simple scoring system. "Let's record a little line, or a check-mark or a cross, or any shape you like on a piece of paper for each segment you finish coloring," I said.

Niklas' eyes sparkled, and he agreed. He chose the check-mark sign to record his score for each point. But soon this wasn't fun enough, and the recording of the score soon bored him too.

Intuitively and without much thinking, I suggested that I take an assignment I had to do but which I thought I didn't like, sat alongside him and recorded a point for each piece I had to accomplish. In the end, we could see who was faster and had gathered the highest score.

Now that was interesting! Niklas had some competition in me. He did spend some time checking out how my score was progressing and got a little nervous when it grew, and I started to gain on him (he was leading initially since I started gathering points later than he did). But this approach did help him forget most of the resistance and complaints that had initially prevented him from making any progress at all (once the gathering of points had become dull).

Two hours' work on this assignment, including all the complaints and discussions, was taking its toll by the time Niklas had finished coloring forty out of the fifty segments (which I later counted out of curiosity). He started to moan again.

Then my husband — caught up with our gameful spirit — proposed a new little game to Niklas. Michael suggested that Niklas took an abacus — of which we have a few in our house, some of them integrated into fun books for children — and moved a bead to the left as soon as he managed to color one segment. In such a way he would see how many remained and that the number was decreasing with each he did.

Niklas was washed by a new wave of motivation, and he smiled brightly at this new possibility, and especially with the realization that he was close to the finish line.

And finally, Niklas had a surprise for us that he kept secret until he had finished the assignment. He had invented a game of his own. Or rather a feedback system of his own. He had made a drawing of a house which he drew line-by-line as he progressed with his coloring assignment segment-by-segment.

The results were terrific, in terms of both short and long term benefits for all of us.

The immediate results were a great atmosphere, the pride that the assignment was done, that he had managed to work for almost three hours in a row, and had fun for at least some of it.

Once the carrying out of the assignment became less stressful, Niklas had the chance to look at the reasons for the situation he was in non-judgmentally. He realized that if he talked less during school hours and hadn't resisted the assignment so much, he would have managed to do all the work at school.

Since then (and this was over a year ago), Niklas has managed to finish most of his assignments at school. After that fateful day there have only been a few occasions when he has had homework to do. Even when he has had to bring homework with him on a Friday, such as after an illness at the beginning of that week or the occasional distraction and inattention, he has resisted the tasks much less and completed them much more quickly, and with barely any involvement from my husband or myself.

That day, when he turned his assignments into games for the first time, contributed to teaching him to take responsibility for his actions, without any feelings of guilt.

As I contemplated the main factors in Niklas' success at gamifying his homework, I came up with the following conclusions:
1. He needed the will to play and see the homework as a game. And he was intrigued by that possibility.
2. He needed a co-player and a competition to compare his score to someone else's. My work and my willingness to face a similar challenge to him served this purpose well.

3. He needed to see the finish line. Each game requires a definition of the finish line, of a goal, and to be able to see how far it is from where the player stands (see chapter 12, section 3). It might be defined by a time limit, reaching a specific score, or exhausting resources. His father's suggestion with the abacus helped Niklas to see the finish line and how much effort he needed to invest to reach it.
4. He needed to be in control and plan his own moves. He also needed to be creative and be the designer of his own game. Designing his game and coming up with his own solution, in addition to those suggested by us, was an essential factor. Creating his own games (and its components) was a critical component and condition for my son to practice self-gamification.

These four factors resulted in success and in a win-win situation for all players (my husband and I were players in this too through our active involvement and interest).

I also believe that this memorable experience was only made possible by the thread that ran through all of it — namely, concentration on the *fun factor*. We were on the look out for tools and solutions that would make the task at hand fun.

This is what we do when we want to play games: we are looking for fun. And it is simply a gift if we apply the same approach to everything in our lives.

With our help and his own will to play, Niklas managed to concentrate on the possibility of having fun, rather than on his complaints and dismay at having to do something he didn't want to.

3. Why it makes sense to share self-gamification

This fantastic experience of helping change my son's attitude to school (without really intending to), motivated me to share self-gamification even more.

Now whenever someone wonders what they can do to make what they want or have to do possible, I say, "Turn your life into fun games."

Since I used to experience similar feelings myself, I understand the desire to complain and blame their "failures" on themselves, other people, or circumstances. Then I share my stories and epiphanies with them and say that something else is possible. That only *they* can take charge if they want to be in control of their lives. I am also eager to show that this taking charge doesn't have to be hard. It can be done in playful and gameful ways.

Through each of these conversations I have discovered something new and exciting about self-gamification. This book and the online course

Motivate Yourself by Turning Your Life Into Fun Games: Practice Self-Gamification, a Unique Self-Help Approach Uniting Anthropology, Kaizen, and Gamification would not have existed in their current forms, had I not shared this approach and the techniques it brings together with others.

The biggest reward I get from sharing, however, is witnessing the lives of those around me transform, to become more vibrant and more joyful.

I told one of the stories of sharing self-gamification in chapter 3, section 2.

Another story that is dear to me is of a friend who started practicing self-gamification and told me shortly afterwards that it had changed her life. She had opened up to her extended family and began undertaking more with them. I loved seeing her smile broadly while recounting how the attempt of her sister-in-law and herself to make home-made ice-cream had turned into a big disaster. A hugely fun and joyful disaster.

But most of all, this gameful approach to her entire life took away some of the very understandable drama caused by the chronic disease she has to deal with every day. One of the first significant victories in her self-motivational games was completing a story (which corresponds to a novelette in length), after struggling for many years to move her multiple story ideas beyond the plotting of a couple of scenes. Her condition poses many challenges to her wish to write, and it was quite understandable that she gave up so many times.

I will never forget the tears of pride and joy shining in her eyes as she read her story to us at one of our local writers' club meetings. And my stunned feeling of utter surprise when she told us that this was the first story she had completed in years, despite having been a passionate and published author before her condition became more critical.

Here is another reason why it is worth sharing self-gamification: you will often find yourself being inspired in return. This happens to me more and more as I continue practicing and sharing the possibility of turning our lives into games. For example, a friend might say a variation of the following, "Your approach has helped me. I could see that I was a bit too serious about what I was doing. Imagining it was just a game helped me relax and even have fun with what I had to do." This feedback often comes when I, myself, am being a little too serious about what I want or have to do. And in that moment I am inspired to switch my fun-detecting antenna back on and have fun with whatever I am up to.

And this leads to another aspect of sharing, which is asking others for advice and inspiration in your self-motivational game design. I ask my husband and children what they think about elements of my self-motivational game designs, or ask them about their experiences as gamers in various situations, or why they enjoy one or other games they play. These conversations bring joy to all involved, because I am sincere in my interest in their experience, and they help me to enrich my experience as a "self-gamer."

I recently discovered in Robert Maurer's book *Mastering Fear: Harnessing Emotion to Achieve Excellence in Work, Health and Relationships*, many brilliant thoughts and quotes that support the reasons and examples of sharing self-gamification related above. Here are just three of them:

"We are meant to reach to another for support. We are suggesting that the Law of Success, the fork in the road to success is to be aware of and accepting of fear and be willing when afraid, to reach to another for support."

"Growing up and living in an enriched, caring environment gives a person the freedom and opportunity to practice asking for help and the opportunity to learn to compete or collaborate selectively, whichever might be called for in a given situation. These skills are essential in our adult lives, where collaboration is most often the key to success."

"What Darwin wrote was: 'In the long history of humankind (and animal kind too) those who learned to collaborate and improvise most effectively have prevailed.'" — Robert Maurer, *Mastering Fear: Harnessing Emotion to Achieve Excellence in Work, Health and Relationships*

4. Sharing self-gamification in the workplace

Kindness and fun were previously emphasized little in work environments. I am glad that this is changing. Self-gamification, for yourself, your colleagues or employees, can help you to increase the awareness, necessity, and presence of both.

When you share self-gamification at work always start with yourself first. Turn your projects into games. Make sure that elements you add do not hinder your work, i.e. don't become your escape-to activities, but add to the fun and flow in your work.

When you take the next step and show others how you turn your work into games, which might be in the form of a meeting, a presentation at a conference, or a casual chat with a colleague, then I suggest doing the following. Start by summarizing what the approach is about (and the three techniques it brings together) and illustrating the benefits of self-gamification using your own example, i.e. how it has changed your work (and maybe also personal) life.

5. Sharing self-gamification at home and with friends

I discovered that the best way to share self-gamification at home and with my loved ones (both extended family and friends) is to do so case-by-case.

My advice is: be completely and totally present with them; in other words, give them your full attention. Get interested in the people you are with, and then when the moment comes, you will know how to help them. You might find yourself suggesting creative, gameful solutions in those moments, without forcing the outcome.

Teaching and lecturing tend to be resisted at home and in circles of friends. I am talking from experience, both of giving and receiving such advice. I learned that when I tell someone something I have rehearsed beforehand, I am putting the attention on myself. But showing interest in someone, and a desire to help (as well as praise), are about the other person.

So be there for them, get interested in what they say or do, and express what you feel when they ask for it.

As in any area of self-gamification, and life, use kindness, honesty, compassion, and fun as your compasses.

6. Don't be afraid to share

As with self-gamification designs, there are no wrong ways to share self-gamification. The above tips were just ideas, and you don't have to follow them. Find your own ways of sharing.

There are many perfect ways to do so, even for the same person. Mine vary from time to time. Sometimes I share it on social media, sometimes in person, and as I write this book also through writing. Also the method and the words I use to formulate what I have to share, differs from one situation to another.

As long as you practice its three components — (1) seeing and treating yourself and those around you non-judgmentally and with compassion, (2) letting yourself and others progress in small, effortless and appropriate for you and them steps, and (3) appreciating each, however tiny, effort in a fun, gameful way — you can be sure that you will share the best of it.

Before I end this chapter, I would like to draw your attention to the quote I shared at the beginning of it. It is another favorite of mine by Ariel and Shya Kane and is a gift.

What you have to share is also a gift.

7. Why are you turning your life (or parts of it) into games?

Now that you have applied self-gamification to various areas of your life (or your whole life), I would like you to consider again why you think turning our lives into games makes sense, as you did in chapter 1, section 7. But this time I would like you to think about the recent effects of self-gamification on what you do or don't do. How has it changed your work and private life, your thought processes, mood, attitude, and well-being?

Answering this question will help you to become aware of why you enjoy turning your life into games and why you might feel compelled to share self-gamification with others.

It will also help you to formulate clearly your perception of self-gamification and the gifts it brings while sharing it.

Please do this exercise here first, before checking how you answered in chapter 1.

Use the lines below (or a notebook, if you are reading this on an e-reader) and a pen to record your reasons and other related thoughts:

_____
_____
_____
_____

Now take a look at the notes you made in chapter 1 and compare (but without reproach!) your answers now and then. How do your statements from now and then sound and differ? What new insights have you gained since then?

Use the lines below (or a notebook, if you are reading this on an e-reader) and a pen to record the differences you notice between your reasons for turning your life into games then and now.

Remember, whatever the results, don't judge yourself for them. They can be surprising, exciting, and revealing when studied non-judgmentally and with interest.

_____
_____
_____
_____
_____
_____

References:
* https://www.longevitylive.com/anti-aging-beauty/social-life-longevity/
** https://www.youtube.com/watch?v=4-DcjwzF9yc

Part V. Self-Gamification Framework Examples

Chapter 17. Introduction to Optimist Writer's Self-Gamification Frameworks

"Adapt what is useful, reject what is useless, and add what is specifically your own." — Bruce Lee

1. A non-gamer's simple self-gamification frameworks

Despite having deliberately turned my life into fun games for several years now, and having enormous pleasure doing so, I am still a non-gamer in the classical sense.

I am also not a game or gamification designer. I do have some experience with writing conversion scripts in XSLT*, and I tried my hand at the older programming languages Fortran and Pascal** many years ago. But that is as far as my programming skills go, and I have even less experience with actual game design (video or otherwise).

I must admit, this recently changed slightly when I assisted my eight-year-old son in learning Scratch*** — a simple, but powerful programming language — to program his first video games. But that was only on two occasions, and for a short time, and since then he has practiced programming without me at his side. So right now, the most I can claim is having less than an hour's experience of being an assistant amateur video game programmer.

As I learn more about game and gamification design (on the theoretical side, through reading), I often encounter the term "framework." After searching for a definition, I found a discussion considering the difference between game frameworks and engines. ****

The following answer, by long-time self-taught game programmer Patrick Hughes was illuminating for me:

"You can build an engine on a framework, but you would never build a framework on an engine. One is the skeleton that determines architecture and program flow; the other is the muscle that does the work."****

So, yes, my self-motivational game designs are exactly that: they are frameworks upon which you can build your own "engines," your own designs.

And like the legendary Bruce Lee once said (see the quote at the beginning of this chapter), use what you think is useful for you, forget what doesn't resonate with you, and add your own touches.

For me, the designs are also "engines," since I use them as described. But they are not static. I continue adjusting them and mixing in elements from the games I encounter, new skills I learn, and new experiences I have. I left some parts of them behind and don't play them anymore.

It's fantastic to be aware that if at some point the current self-motivational game designs stop being balanced, fun and helpful for me, then I can redesign them. It is such a brilliant way of life to be both the designer and the player. (Sorry for repeating that again.)

I often use the pronoun "you" when describing the rules for my frameworks. By "you," I still mean mainly myself as a player, since these are my self-motivational games.

I invite you to test them as described in this part of the book. But the most important thing to remember is that at least with time you need to adjust these frameworks to your tastes, and preferences. You are the designer *and* player of your games. (There I go again.)

2. This part of the book is different
And two more notes before I share the details of my designs with you.

This part of the book does not contain any exercises. Because the designs shared here are intended as ideas and inspiration.

It doesn't contain many lessons learned about the designs either because they have been shared throughout the book. But if there was anything to add to them, then I wrote those additional thoughts in the section with the title "Notes on the current use of this design" of the following three chapters, as well as in other parts of these chapters, where applicable. I have also tried to connect these additional lessons learned to the lessons related in other parts of this book, by adding references to corresponding chapters and sections.

3. A special note on the feedback systems
The feedback systems described in the following chapters are the ones I have developed for these frameworks. These are my "game-only" feedback systems. This specific type of feedback system and means of recording progress was introduced to you in chapter 12, section 9. You tried your hand at

developing "game-only" feedback system(s) for your self-motivational games in chapter 12, section 13, and perhaps adjusted them in chapter 14, section 6, activity 2.

Your project's specific feedback system, which I mention below as well, would be something different. It might be word count for a writing project, the number of words in a language you learn, or the number of Chinese/Japanese characters, if you learn how to write in Chinese or Japanese, and so on. You will need to record these separately if you would like to keep track of them.

Remember that recording the progress in your project and activity games, whichever feedback system you use, is part of the game.

References:
* https://www.w3schools.com/xml/xsl_intro.asp
**
https://en.wikipedia.org/wiki/Timeline_of_programming_languages
*** https://scratch.mit.edu/
****
https://gamedev.stackexchange.com/questions/31772/what-is-the-difference-between-a-game-framework-and-a-game-engine

Chapter 18. 5 Minute Perseverance Game

"Perseverance is not a long race; it is many short races one after the other." — Walter Elliot

1. About the Game
As mentioned several times before, I developed this self-motivational game framework and wrote about it before I had heard about gamification and kaizen, but after having discovered and practiced living in the moment for a couple of years. The little book I devoted to this game is structured like the description of a board game and has the title *5 Minute Perseverance Game: Play Daily for a Month and Become the Ultimate Procrastination Breaker**.

2. Goal
The goal is to collect as many points as possible for the project or activity of your choice and along two different scales during each round (see section 4 below). Or at least more points than your procrastinating self, which will try to do the same (that is to get as many points as possible).

3. Rules
- Prepare everything you need to work on your project.
- Work on your project and persevere for five minutes every day, for one month. You have to be doing actual work on the project (such as, for example, writing a book). Thinking about and researching for the project doesn't count. A small caveat to that: short searches online for a word, phrase, or fact, and then returning to your project, counts, of course. What doesn't count is stopping work on the project for a more extended period and, for instance, reading on the topic for hours. The research part could be a game on its own.
- Use a timer to keep track of the time.
- Record your progress for each day and at the end of the monthly round. You can also record the sum for each week. Any points you didn't earn go to your procrastinating self.

4. Feedback system
Point system. You earn:
- One point if you manage to work on your project for five minutes.
- Half a point if you do something for the project but don't manage to do it for five minutes.

- Zero points if you don't manage any concrete work on the given project.
- The maximum number of points you can earn per project is equal to the number of days in a month (minimum twenty-eight, maximum thirty-one).

Your project's reporting system:
- Word count, number of rooms cleaned, number of songs practiced on guitar, pages or percentage read in a book, etc. (see also chapter 12, section 9, and chapter 17, section 3).

5. Tactical Variants

Number of projects

You can take more than one project into the game, or, you could say, have several 5 Minute Perseverance Games running in parallel.

Duration of one move/step

You can vary the length of the step to make it shorter or longer. The step can be as short as one second (although you won't be able to measure half a point then), but avoid making it too long. I wouldn't recommend steps longer than what is defined by the widely known Pomodoro** technique of twenty-five minutes. You are ultimately the one to choose how long or *what* the step should be. Some tasks might have logical "time-chunks," or other chunks, associated with them. For example, one step in a knitting project perseverance game might be "knitting one row," however long it might take, while for toothbrushing it would be the generally recommended 2 minutes, twice a day.

Length of a game round

I recommend rounds of one month for the 5 Minute Perseverance Game, especially when you start practicing self-gamification. Weekly rounds are also possible, or you can have both weekly and monthly (or a bit longer) rounds and see how your score changes over the year along with seasons, holidays, commitments, etc. Daily rounds make less sense since you can only collect a maximum of one point per project, per day. I don't recommend yearly rounds either, because you need to have the finish line in sight (see more on this in chapter 12, section 3).

6. Notes on the current use of this design

I often set the timer to ten minutes nowadays, since this is the period that earns me a point in the Balance Game (see chapter 20).

But I do sometimes set the timer to shorter periods, without recording points.

For example, my children love it when myself or my husband sit by the bed after their bedtime routine and the lights have been switched off.

Nowadays, I remain for four minutes at their bedside. Emma wants me to be there as many minutes as her age (she is four as I write this chapter). And my son wants the time to be equally distributed, so he suggested four minutes for me to stay at his bedside as well, whenever he wishes and I am able to. I take my e-reader, set the timer to four minutes, hold each of their hands (if they wish so) for four minutes and read. We all enjoy this quiet time.

The timer, in fact, is one of the tools we use most frequently in our household. For example, we have an agreement with our son that he spends the same (or more) time off screen as on screen. So he sets the timer for thirty minutes when both playing games on the iPad or his school computer, and when playing in his room, outside, or reading.

As to the feedback system and recording of points described above: I don't use these anymore and instead use the approach described in chapter 20.

One of the reasons I no longer use the 5 Minute Perseverance Game feedback system is that it is not suitable for turning your whole life into games. I discovered that the lists of projects and activities I dealt with within any given month could become enormous (as it was in August 2017; see chapter 8, section 3).

As a result, the process of recording all the points turned into an escape-to activity, rather than supporting me in having fun in what I did. I started spending too much time on figuring out in which project I had earned a point (if I didn't record the point immediately after each step in the project or activity). I remember being frustrated with myself for not being diligent enough in recording my score, which meant that I "fell out" of the game and wasn't enjoying it anymore.

Besides that, there were days when I didn't have or need to do anything for a specific project, so the lack of a point wasn't due to my procrastination, but merely due to the absence of available tasks in that project. The design of the feedback system described in this chapter doesn't take this into account.

However, this framework is ideal for turning single projects into games (especially those that take a long time to accomplish), and also when you first start turning your life into games.

7. Images, results, and examples of the feedback system and points gathered

The picture below shows the points I earned in June 2017. I had fifteen different projects (project areas) or activity games running in parallel:

1. New projects (pitching for new consulting projects).
2. Working on my book *Cheerleading for Writers*.
3. BRWG CPF Work (Change Proposal Form = CPF submission and work for the international working group (Business Rules Working Group = BRWG) I was leading in the S1000D community at that time; I mentioned both the group and the specification, along with its community, in chapter 15, section 4).
4. BRWG and other S1000D work (this included revising and posting minutes of the meetings, updating action lists, and communication within this technical community).
5. Book update and marketing (this included marketing for my business Optimist Writer).
6. 5MPG blogging (5MPG = 5 Minute Perseverance Game; i.e. this was blogging about the experiences I had playing the self-motivational game described in this chapter).
7. S1000D & Business Blog (these were not the S1000D community work, but the articles I was publishing on my blog about S1000D and also business development).
8. Learning Danish.

9. Learning Chinese (writing Chinese characters).
10. Meeting and communicating with friends and family.
11. Family and personal administrative matters, as well as those for my business.
12. Household and decluttering.
13. Sports.
14. Minimum 6 hours sleep.
15. Something for fun.

The days on the picture were crossed out one-by-one as I recorded the results in a Microsoft Excel file. At the end of each month (here, June 2017), I calculated the score for each week, for the whole month, and per project.

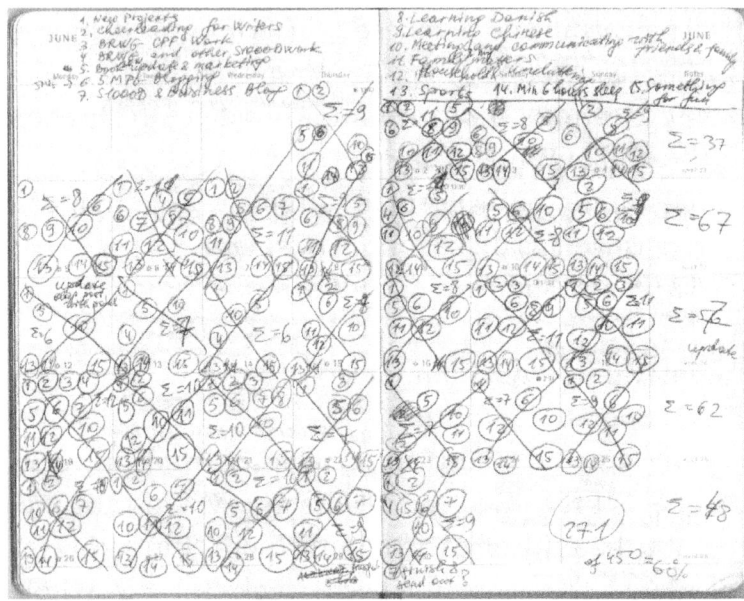

Until early December 2017, I was updating an Excel file with the name: Vicas-5MPG-stats-20171201-1.xlsx, which stands for Vica's (short for Victoria's) 5 Minute Perseverance Game statistics. Here is the table for June 2017:

Self-Gamification Happiness Formula

Day/Project	1	2	3	4	5	6	7	8	9	10	11	12	13	14	15
1	x	x			x	x				x	x		x	x	x
2	x	x			x	x		x	x	x	x	x	x		x
3					x	x		x	x	x			x	x	x
4		x				x		x		x	x	x	x	x	x
5	x					x		x	x	x			x	x	x
6	x			x	x	x	x			x	x	x	x		x
7	x	x			x	x	x	x	x		x		x	x	x
8	x				x	x		x	x		x	x	x		x
9	x			x	x				x	x	x	x	x	x	x
10					x	x				x	x	x	x	x	x
11		x			x	x				x	x	x	x	x	x
12	x				x					x			x	x	x
13	x			x	x					x			x	x	x
14	x			x	x					x			x		x
15	x	x			x					x	x	x	x		x
16	x				x	x				x	x	x	x		x
17	x	x	x			x		x	x		x	x	x	x	x
18	x	x	x		x	x				x	x	x	x	x	x
19	x	x	x	x	x	x	x			x	x	x	x		x
20	x	x			x	x				x	x	x	x	x	x
21	x	x	x		x	x	x	x		x			x		x
22	x		x		x	x							x	x	x
23	x				x					x	x	x	x		x
24	x				x					x		x	x	x	x
25	x	x			x					x	x	x	x	x	x
26	x	x			x	x				x	x	x	x	x	x
27	x	x			x	x				x	x	x	x	x	x
28	x	x		x	x	x				x		x	x	x	x
29	x	x			x	x					x		x	x	x
30	x	x		x	x					x			x		x
sum	26	17	5	6	22	26	9	9	7	25	20	19	30	20	30
%	87	57	17	20	73	87	30	30	23	83	67	63	100	67	100
Project	1	2	3	4	5	6	7	8	9	10	11	12	13	14	15

References:

*	https://www.victoriaichizlibartels.com/5-minute-perseverance-game/
**	https://pomodoro-tracker.com/

Chapter 19. Project ("Crush") Management Game

"Without leaps of imagination, or dreaming, we lose the excitement of possibilities. Dreaming, after all, is a form of planning." — Gloria Steinem

1. About the Game

This game was a consequent development, after having applied the 5 Minute Perseverance Game to multiple projects. As I described in chapter 8, section 3 and chapter 18, section 6, I first tried to turn my whole life into games in August 2017, but twenty-one projects was too many and I couldn't possibly have attended to all of them every day.

So at the end of August 2017, and shortly before the September 2017 round began, I asked myself how I could incorporate every area of my life into games. I came up with the idea of defining project and activity areas. I call these groups interchangeably "areas" and "categories." I use "area" more often, but feel free to use whichever feels right for you.

In this design, I tested eight, six, and four areas. If a project was urgent (with a deadline) and required more of my attention, then I dedicated an entire area to it.

In general, my day — when I applied this framework — resembled the fitness program TruFusion, which I referred to in chapter 12, section 5. The difference was that my various "work-out" styles were different projects and activities.

The word "Crush" in the title — and I initially called this design "Project Crush" — came from the invitations I was getting from my friends who played Candy Crush Saga on Facebook (see chapter 3, section 4 and chapter 12, section 4). I didn't want to play the game itself, but the concept of points popping up when a certain number of the same type of candies are grouped, intrigued me and gave me an idea.

I added a bonus system. If I completed a task and delivered something to a customer, project partner, editor, family member or a friend, then I got points. I got even more points if I managed to attend to projects and activities in all areas or categories for the day.

Later, as I was planning one of the upcoming rounds of the "Project Crush" game, I realized that what I was doing was project management, which I enjoyed now and had resented before. Thus it was essential for me to add the word management into the title of the game.

This design also helped me to create a short game variant, the "Project Booster," I often use for those projects and activities I am scared of and resent most, but want to get going (see section 7 below).

2. Goal

The goal is to gather as many points as possible for each project or activity area, as well as the total (both with and without taking bonus points into account).

In contrast to 5 Minute Perseverance Game there is no maximum number of points you can earn per project/activity or project/activity area, except for any you have explicitly limited the number of points per day for (see item 6 of the list "Before the monthly round — Preparing the game field" in section 3 below).

3. Rules

Before the monthly round — Preparing the game field:

- Make a list of all projects and activities (including those for developing healthy habits and well-being).

- Identify those projects and activities that will require more of your attention. Try not to define more than one or two of these for each month. (See also the contemplations on "ambition projects" in chapter 15, section 16 and chapter 20, section 5.)
- Group the rest of the projects and activities by whatever logic makes sense to you. Please note that your understanding of how to group them best will change from month to month. And there doesn't always have to be a common theme to them (such as grouping well-being activities, projects at work, or time with your family and friends) — you might also group them according to the amount of work you need to invest in each area, so that you have the chance to earn at least one point in each area every day. Do what feels best for you now.
- Assign a number from one to four, one to six, or one to eight to each group or project and activities, you have identified. I don't recommend defining more than eight areas per day. The Balance Game (chapter 20), which was based on this framework, has only four categories, which I think is enough. An odd number of areas is also possible, I just found it more appealing to use an even number when I drew the game field for each day.

- For now, choose what the kaizen-step will be for each project in each project and activity area or category. It could be a paragraph of text for your report or work-in-progress, or five minutes of your time on that project. Make sure that the steps are small and effortless. So don't say "writing a page" (because some pages can be tough to write); or "going through one chapter of the language textbook," which could also turn out to be enormous, depending on your language skills and the length of chapters in the book. The smaller the step, the better. When in doubt, use time limits to set up the length of these kaizen-steps. You can adjust this parameter for each project once you start testing your self-motivational games (i.e. start work on the project in the given round). But try to make these adjustments minimal, and only do so in the first few days of your game round.
- Decide for which projects or activities you want to limit the number of points you can earn each day. This is best done for those escape-to activities that you both need and love to do. For me, this is reading. I need to read for my work, but I sometimes find myself stubbornly continuing to read, despite other projects and activities "calling my name."

Self-Gamification Happiness Formula

- Draw a template for your daily feedback. You need to have one larger field for recording your bonus points, and four, six, or eight equally sized fields to register your scores for each project/activity area.

Here is a one-day example template defining six project/activity areas to attend to daily for one game round (for example, a month):

1	2	3
4	5	6
Bonus area		

[A side-note: I used a monthly calendar and drew this output for each of the days (see the picture below), but when you record all the points of your projects you might find that the space for a day in a monthly calendar isn't enough. You could therefore use a daily or weekly planner instead. I now use a weekly planner to record points (one point = ten minutes) in the Balance Game (see chapter 20).]

While playing:

- At the beginning of each day (or the evening before) jot down the to-do list for today in your To-do Game Book and list all the projects and activities for each of the four, six or eight areas you decided on when designing this round of your project management game. Record at least one project or activity per area. But make sure not to overload yourself. Better to jot down fewer items on your list than more. If you manage to do more than planned in your to-do list, then you will get more points. Remember to take into account, or even better schedule, some "breathing out" time (Chapter 9, section 3).
- Choose the project and activity area you are going to attend to next.
- Choose the project or activity in this specific area you are going to work on next.
- Prepare everything you need to work on your project.
- Work on your project and perform the kaizen-step you decided on previously. You have to be doing actual work on the project (such as, for example, writing your report.) Thinking about and researching for the project doesn't count. A small caveat to that: short searches online for a word, phrase, or fact, and then returning to your project, counts, of course. What doesn't count is stopping work on the

project for a more extended period and, for instance, reading on the topic for hours. The research part could be a game on its own.
- Record a point for each step, of each project/activity, in each project/activity area.
- Record your bonus points when you reach certain levels in your self-motivational games (see section 4 below).
- At the end of each week and at the end of the whole round see how many points you gathered.

4. Feedback system
You earn:
- *One point*, for each step, of each project/activity, in each project/activity area.
- *Five points*, if you complete a task and deliver something to your customer, project partner, editor, family member, or a friend. This could be an extended e-mail, a report, your manuscript, or a quilt you made for your friend's newborn. You get the bonus points on completion day. You might have been working on this project for quite some time, but to celebrate the job being done, you get the five points on the day you finish and deliver it.
- *Ten points*, if you manage to work on one full set of projects or activities in the areas you have

defined. It means that if you have six areas for this round, for example, then for each set of points (one point in each of six areas) you get ten bonus points. Let's take a concrete example. Let's say you have the following results at the end of your day: area 1 — four points, area 2 — six points, area 3 — eight points, area 4 — two points, area 5 — five points, area 6 — nine points. Then you will get two times ten points because there are at least two full sets of points done in each area (the least points you collected was two, in area 4 of your projects and activities).

5. Tactical Variants
Number of projects

The design of this framework is very flexible and depends strongly on how you plan your project and activity areas for each round.

Numbers assigned to projects

If you have a project running over several months and you find yourself getting "bored" with the feedback system, then you can also give your projects varying numbers. It is like shuffling cards for the new round. This will help your brain to practice being present and not nudge you to record the score immediately because you want to be done with it.

Duration of one move/step

The length of one move/step also depends on the design of each round and each project. The primary criterion is to make this step as small and as effortless as possible.

Length of a game round

As with 5 Minute Perseverance Game, I recommend monthly rounds here too, especially when you test this framework for the first time. You need to get a good feel for it. Make notes on what you like in this design, and what you would want to change. Weekly rounds are also possible, or you can have both weekly and monthly rounds. You can use an Excel file, for example, to record your daily, weekly, and monthly results, and to follow your progress for more extended periods, like a year. But don't have only yearly rounds - you need to have the finish line in sight (see more on this in chapter 12, section 3).

Bonus points

You can play with the number of bonus points here. I initially gave myself more points for completing a task than for attending to all project/activity areas in any given day. But a month later, I decided to change that and defined the feedback system described above. I did that because completion of some tasks was simple (perhaps owing to my light and gameful approach), but managing to attend to all areas felt like a higher level in a game. I mentioned this modification in the design in chapter 12, section 9.

Scores and statistics

If recording your score and watching it change over the days within your monthly (or longer) game rounds as you attend to your projects, contributes to your motivation and is fun for you, then go ahead and create spreadsheets for the statistics in your self-motivational games. But if this turns into an escape-to activity, then observe that you are taking your game too seriously and might not be "playing it," in other words, not seeing the whole process as a game anymore. Another idea is to limit your recording to a week or even a day. I now have daily rounds in the Balance Game, although since I record my score in a weekly planner, I have an overview of the progress in any given week. See more in chapter 20.

6. Notes on the current use of this design

There were some drawbacks to this design.

Since there was generally no limit to gathering points (only for one or two single escape-to activities), I noticed that I started putting pressure on myself to attain more. Even for taking a break. Somehow there was never enough time for anything: not for work, relaxing, or taking time for loved ones. I saw that I started judging myself for gathering more points in one project than another.

Another problem was that the steps in various projects were fundamentally different. In some cases I set a timer, in others I gave myself a point per written paragraph or even sentence, or a PowerPoint slide created. So my attempts to compare one project with another, and try to justify my dismay at managing to work on one thing and not another, was neither fair nor honest.

The solution was to allocate all points based on a certain amount of time. That is how the Balance Game was born (see chapter 20).

Even if I don't use the Project ("Crush") Management Game design anymore, I still use a small variant of this game to boost my flow in a stalling project, or one that scares me but I still want to pursue. There is always one such project every once in a while. See the next section.

7. A small, swift variant of the Project ("Crush") Management Game — Project Booster
About this little game

The first time I applied it was when I was struggling with incorporating the self-edits, I made on paper into my book project on the computer. I mentioned this story in chapter 15, section 10. I procrastinated over the task for several days, despite wanting to make progress on the book and having a deadline for finishing it.

I could see the reason for it. The manuscript was overloaded with hand-made marks, and the whole process just seemed too overwhelming. After contemplating how I could support myself to get the work flowing, I had the idea of taking a piece of paper and keeping a tally — jotting down one line (point) for each paragraph of incorporated changes. I loved when I crossed the four short lines to mark the fifth point, and then strike through the next set of four short lines to indicate the tenth point, and so on.

At some point, I stopped jotting down the points, because I was enjoying the process. The reducing number of pages I still needed to modify was also a great (and encouraging) feedback system in this little game, which I now call the "Project Booster."

Whenever I need a boost, both in my mood and my project, I bring this one out.

Goal

Get a project flowing and being fun.

You could measure this by how few points you managed to gather up until it became fun to do, but this could add pressure and make you resent the accumulating points on your scrap of paper.

Another possibility of setting the goal here is to gather as many points as possible in a given time. I sometimes set the timer to ten or more minutes and check how many paragraphs I can edit, or how many words I can write, in that time. You can also set the timer to twenty-five minutes (as in the Pomodoro system; see references in chapter 18).

Rules

- Get ready to boost your project.
- First, decide on the size of the smallest step that would pose no effort for you. Don't forget to be both honest and kind to yourself.
  - Another time I had to do edits I thought that one page a day wouldn't pose any difficulties for me. But after resisting this task for some time, I realized one page was too daunting. I asked myself, "What about one paragraph, and then you can record a point, take a break or do something else, and later edit another?" I observed myself sighing with relief and felt a twinge of a smile on my lips. Yes, this was better. I was immediately curious about how many paragraphs I could manage before I stopped having fun. Something unexpected happened. With every point gathered and every edited paragraph crossed-out on the manually edited pages, my experience of fun for the task increased exponentially, and I

managed to incorporate edits for more than one page a day, and in a couple of days was done with the whole assignment.
- Start your computer, or another device, or get the tools you need for your project. Put a notebook or a sheet of paper and a pen beside you. Don't forget the timer.
- Set a timer to the chosen period and start playing.

Feedback system

This is the sheet of paper on which you record each point for each tiny bit done in the project.

Tactical Variants

I can't think of any. But if you do, then adjust to whatever is most fun for you.

Notes on the use of this design

A friend used the 5 Minute Perseverance Game to motivate herself to redecorate her house. Now that I think about it, she applied the Project Booster, although I didn't have this name at the time. She simply told me that she got inspired by the 5 Minute Perseverance Game to paint the walls in her house. The task always took more than an hour per room, because she also needed some time to prepare the actual "move" of painting, but the thought "I will invest five minutes and then see how that goes," and the point earned (even if she didn't record them) motivated her to keep going, and to make considerable progress every day. She told me that she had much fun in the process too.

8. Images, results, and examples of the feedback system and points gathered

The photos below show the feedback system and the points earned for December 2017 and January 2018. In the latter, I attempted to limit the reading of each book I took into the game to a maximum of two points a day. But I had difficulty limiting the number of books to read. I refused to reduce my list any further than eight groups (!) of books (and one periodical). But fortunately as you can see on the second picture, I didn't always escape into reading, or more precisely, I didn't earn all possible points for reading and instead gathered points for other projects too. The total in January 2018 was higher than in December 2017 (although the comparison between the two is unfair, because of the holiday season in December).

Here are the project and activity areas I defined for December 2017:
1. Finish the first drafts of two books (works-in-progress), which were both about 80% done by the start of the December 2017 round.
2. Book marketing.
3. Training and consulting projects.

4. Tools page (data I offer for sale on my website) development.
5. Family, my business, and other admin matters.
6. Free time, fun, health and movement.
7. Voluntary work (technical and creative).
8. Other writing projects (this is mainly to catch any freely floating ideas and stop them going unnoticed).

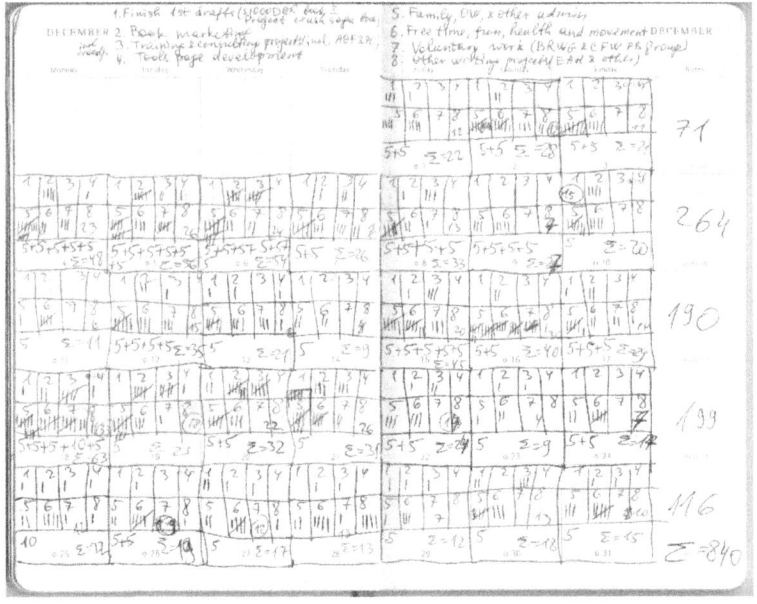

Here are the project and activity areas I defined for January 2018:

1. *SG-Book* (Note: this book here; SG = Self-Gamification) and the crowdfunding

campaign connected to it (I mentioned this campaign in chapter 15, section 2).
2. *S1000D-Book* and all S1000D related work (including BRWG); I mentioned my S1000D books, the working group, and the specification, along with its community, in chapter 15, section 4.
3. *International startup report/book* (actual writing); this is related to an initiative by the consultant who helped me when I started my business two and a half years prior.
4. *Everywhere at Home* (a memoir collection I worked on at that time).
5. *A President's Sister* (writing the second book in the series "A Life Upside Down").
6. *Family & OW Admin, AOF & other* (Optimist Writer = my business; Admin = administrative work; AOF = an evening school in Aalborg, the city where I live; other = other projects not listed above).
7. *Free Time, Health, and Movement* (doesn't include reading).
8. *Reading* (various books, including Writer's Digest Magazine; in eight groups).

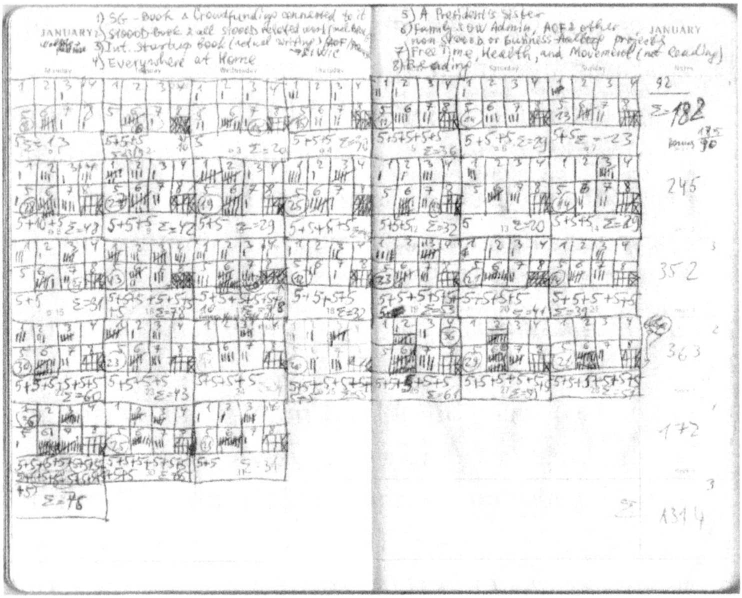

Chapter 20. Balance Game

"Balance is not better time management, but better boundary management. Balance means making choices and enjoying those choices." — Betsy Jacobson

1. About the Game

This design helped me to become more aware of how I spend my day (and my life) and to be more deliberate about it. Thus, initially, I called it "Making More Time Count Game."

But shortly afterwards I recognized that it helped me to find the balance between commitments, leisure, dreams, passion, wellness, enough movement and sleep, and other aspects that contribute to all the areas of my life. It is about keeping balance in each moment, whatever I am up to, and having a balanced — both exciting and relaxed — life. This is why I now call it the "Balance Game."

After designing, testing, and adjusting it, I think that the Balance Game is especially suitable for ambitious and active people, for example, entrepreneurs.

My rounds used to be monthly (see chapters 18 and 19). Then they were week-long, and now my game rounds are a day long. I rarely compare the points collected on different days. I am just interested in obtaining all possible (five) stars.

To understand fully how this framework works, please read chapter 19, because the Project ("Crush") Management Game is where the Balance Game has its origins.

The difference now is that the areas are more rigidly defined. They are the same every month. There is a maximum number of points to be earned, but not per project. I can earn more than one point per day per project, up to a maximum for each day: one point per ten minutes, resulting in six points per hour, leading to a maximum of one hundred and forty-four points per day (twenty-four hours).

2. Goal
The goal is to gather five stars in any given daily round of the game. (See section 5 below for an additional goal arising from the add-on feedback feature with asterisks.)

3. Rules
Please note that I designed these rules for my specific self-motivational games. I will indicate more generic terms were possible. But in general,

the rules for how a star can be gained in each project/activity area are specific to me and should only serve as inspiration when you design your own Balance Game.

There are four areas/categories of projects and activities in this game (and in my life, as I see it today):

- *Area 1:* Passive income* projects and activities (my books, online courses, data I offer for sale on my website, and marketing work connected to them, including updating my website); for you, these could be creative projects (both at work and home).
- *Area 2:* Active income** projects (consulting, coaching, teaching, and other freelancing) and any other work I do on my computer, including administrative work of both a personal and business nature (such as book-keeping for my company, private online banking and answering e-mails and direct messages on social media).
- *Area 3:* Anything I do away from my computer: these include spending time with my family and friends, wellness, accompanying my children or my mother to the doctor's, household chores, reading, and many more. If I watch a video or film online with my family, then I record them here in category 3. I also log points here when I surf or watch videos online, or am on social

media when not related to my work. The star for this category is given for specific activities (see section 4), rather than an amount of time. This helps me to be more and more purposeful about being online.
- *Area 4:* Sleep.

Before the daily round — Preparing the game field:
- Update the to-do list for the next daily round to play. Use the To-do Game Book (see in chapter 11, section 2, activity 2 what that Game Book is).
- Prepare the feedback system in the Points and Stars Game Book (see its definition in chapter 11, section 2, activity 2) for the next daily round. Split the day entry in the weekly calendar into five fields. Four smaller ones to record points for each project/activity area and one larger one to mark the time that you stopped playing one project or activity in one area and started another.
- Optional fields: I also used to draw two smaller boxes to record the total score, and the possible number of points for that day (determined by the time I went to bed). The latter number could be more or less than one hundred and forty-four points because I don't go to bed at the same time every day. For some time, I left these optional

fields empty, because they didn't affect or help me in any way to reach my daily goal of getting five stars. Now I use this space for the new tactical variant with the asterisks (see section 5 below).

While playing:
- Mark the time when you start your day.
- Record points for sleep. Give yourself a star if you gathered enough points. See section 4 below for further rules on this.
- Choose the project and activity area you are going to attend to next.
- Choose the project or activity in this specific area you are going to work on next.
- Prepare everything you need to work on your project.
- Work on your project. You can either put a timer on for the time you wish to work on it, or work on a task of your choice without setting the timer. In the latter case record the time when you start and stop working on the project. The same rules apply here as in the previous two frameworks, described in chapters 18 and 19: you have to be doing actual work on the project. Thinking about and researching for the project doesn't count. A small caveat to that: short searches online for a word, phrase, or fact, and

then returning to your project, counts, of course. What doesn't count is stopping work on the project for a more extended period and, for instance, reading on the topic for hours. The research part could be a game on its own.

- Record the points for the time spent on the project in one go. This can be a minimum of one point, corresponding to ten minutes.
- Record the time when you record the points. This point in time can either be when you move to another project or activity or take a small break to see how you are progressing. The time is rounded up to a full ten minutes. For example, 7:44 a.m. will be rounded to 7:40 a.m., and 4:55 p.m. will be recorded as 5:00 p.m. [A side-note: this approximation helped me relax more about recording the score and not take it too seriously.]
- Draw a star in each category as soon as you have gathered the necessary points or accomplished all you wanted to do to get them (see section 4 below).
- At the end of each day, check how many stars you have earned. If you collected a star for each of the four project or activity areas, then you get the fifth star as well. Color them in to make them more visible in your Points and Stars Game Book. Take pride in your achievements today. You can also make a little celebration out of the

star drawing procedure. My eight-year-old son sometimes draws the outlines for the stars, and my four-year-old daughter colors them in pink. These few-minute long celebrations are an immense joy for all of us. And even when my children don't want to help me with drawing and coloring stars, any time I do it myself I remember the sweet moments when we did it together, especially the first time.
- Take a look at the clock when you go to bed. Mark the time in your Points and Stars Game Book if you need to. You can also calculate the points you will earn by sleeping from that point in time until the alarm goes off the next morning. I like thinking of this number when I put my head on the pillow, and I remember it in the morning when the alarm goes off, or if I wake up a little earlier. So far I have never forgotten how many points I've got for sleep, if I noticed what time I went to bed and the time when I woke up. And since playing this game, I have rarely forgotten to take a look at the clock.

4. Feedback system
On weekdays:
I earn a star:
For the project/activity area 1 or 2:
- If I achieve ten points or more in either of them.

- If there is a project in either area/category that requires more time (such as a writing project with a deadline (area 1), a consultancy appointment (area 2), or a more extended visit to the doctor (area 3)) and gets twenty or more points (twenty points corresponds to three hours and twenty minutes), then I collect a star for only three points in categories 1 or 2.
- If there is too little to do for area 2 (consulting, teaching, and other freelancing projects, plus admin and online banking) on any given day, then three points are enough to earn a star. Three points (equivalent to thirty minutes) can also be reached by answering e-mails or other similar tasks.

For area 3, the following needs to be done to collect a star:

- Eye gymnastics (indicated with an "E" in the feedback system): at least three different exercises, with, initially ten, now fifteen repetitions each.
- Straight posture (indicated with "SP" in the feedback system): practiced for at least thirty seconds every day.
- Work-out (indicated with a "W" in the feedback system): perform a combination of yoga and work-out exercises for at least ten minutes a day.

For area 4, I get a star if I sleep for more than seven hours a day. This corresponds to forty-two points.

- If I sleep for six and a half hours (thirty-nine points) at night and then have a thirty-minute (three points) nap during the day, then this would count too.
- If I wake naturally up to twenty minutes before my alarm goes off, when I have set it for seven hours after going to bed, then I still get forty-two points.
- If I wake up an hour earlier, then I go back to sleep and wake up with the alarm. It is crucial that I dedicate enough time to a good night's sleep and feel rested when I wake up.
- However, if I set the alarm to ten minutes less than seven hours because I went to bed a bit later, then I don't get a star. There are limits to flexibility here, as in any other game.

On weekends and holidays:
I earn a star:
- *For the project/activity categories 1 or 2* if I earn *no more* than ten points. The exception here is the "ambition project," which I address in section 5 below and in chapter 15, section 16.
- *For category 3,* the same rules apply as on weekdays.

- *For category 4*, the same rules apply as on weekdays.

5. Tactical Variants
Strategic approach

If I work on my writing or other projects from the passive income category away from my computer (with a notebook and pen, or editing the manuscript on paper) then I can choose to record these in either area 1 or 3, to increase my chances of collecting a star. On weekdays, logging them in 1 makes more sense since the higher the score, the greater the likelihood of obtaining a star. On weekends, however, where I get a star for *not* doing too much in that category, recording those away-from-the-computer points in 3 makes more sense.

One big project game on the weekends and holidays

If there is a category 1 project I am very passionate about, I can still earn a star in this area despite working on it during weekends or holidays and exceeding ten points. The important thing is that I don't collect more than ten points on other projects or activities in this category. There should only be one (or two at a push), exception ("ambition") projects, especially on weekends. (See also chapter 15, section 16 and item 2 in chapter 19, section 3.)

The number of "ambition projects" on weekdays can increase slightly, but it has never been higher than five so far since I introduced this design. I recommend minimizing the number of "ambition projects," so that you are not tempted to increase the pressure you put on yourself, and instead give yourself enough time to be creative in the projects you are up to now.

On weekdays, your "ambition projects" add to the fun of collecting stars. They might vary between weekdays and weekends (for example, developing an online course during the week, and plotting a novel on the weekends), or on different days in general.

Combining with other games

The Balance Game is the main framework I currently use. Its feedback system is the only one I maintain. I play this game every day, and for the whole day. But there are also other, usually very short games, I play during the day:

5 Minute Perseverance Game (chapter 18, section 6): A timer is an essential tool for me, and I use it often when I notice myself procrastinating about something. So I say to myself, "Play for just 5 (or 10) minutes and then you can play another game." This helps me to move the task forward and resist it less.

Project Booster (see chapter 19, section 7): I apply this primarily to larger or trickier (those I procrastinate about) tasks that I need to complete in a short period. And I often try it after or along with the 5 Minute Perseverance Game (such as setting the timer). If I log my score on a separate sheet of paper and not in frames of the Balance Game, then I discard that piece of paper at the end of the day.

Special bonus stars (asterisks = "") for doing some things before others* (see also chapter 12, section 12): This is one of the latest add-ons to this design. I get an asterisk if, after working on my projects for a while, instead of watching random videos on YouTube (escape-to activity), I stand up, leave my computer, and do something else (a household chore, yoga + workout, reading, drinking a cup of coffee, or anything else to recharge), before returning to the project. I get an asterisk in a circle if I do my workout before dinner. And I get the third type of asterisk, one in a square, if I go to bed before 10 pm. If I manage to collect all three kinds of asterisks, I get the fourth one, an asterisk in a triangle. There is a difference between this system and the one with the stars (described in section 4 above): while I collect the stars depending on *what* I manage during the day, the asterisks of various types are awarded according to *when* I do things.

Self-Gamification Happiness Formula

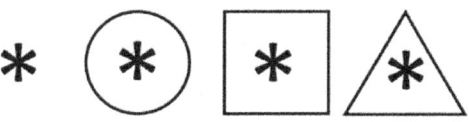

Role-Playing Games (RPG)***: In chapter 11, section 1, I mentioned that I sometimes imagine myself being Super Mario or another character in a video game on a quest, especially when I observe myself judging the current moment of my life or what I am up to as not being good enough.

Another great role to play — and you might have heard of this before — is to take on the part of a person you want to be (or daydream about being), and to behave as such. So I ask myself, when I feel in doubt about where I am heading, who do I want to be in my dreams? The answer is always to continue being a writer and an online instructor. When I look at my dreams and goals for writing, then the answer is like a pendulum moving between a mid-list and bestselling author. But when I ask myself how I would behave if I reached that dream, the answer is always the same: I would do what I most wanted to do; try to add value in whatever I did; and seek ways to make everything fun. And if there was something I didn't like doing, I would either bring elements of fun into it, or ask someone else to do it for me and pay for that service. This approach is often helpful for me, to keep my dreams and goals in focus, and to make my next smallest and most effortless steps toward them.

As I recounted in chapter 12, section 9, I recently started using the SuperBetter approach by Jane McGonigal (mentioned in chapter 2, section 3) to bring more fun into navigating my various food sensitivities and intolerances. But, due to the reasons described in chapter 12, section 9, I do not take the definitions of villains, allies, and power-ups too seriously. Nor do I collect any points in this Role-Playing Game — I keep my score in the Balance Game. In other words, I use my Balance Game scoring system to keep score of all my games (if they are designed to allow me to do so), and this has worked so far. I think one of the main reasons I play this short Role-Playing Game is that it is much more fun to declare myself a hero than a victim of the food intolerances, and to add labels like "bad guys" and "good guys" to the products, instead of "things not to eat" and "things that are allowed." I also observe my self-judgment disappearing when I discover that I am thirsty, and think of drinking water as a power-up. I drink it, feel how the fresh water caresses my throat, and think with a grin "Power Up!" or a version of "Now I am more powerful than a moment before."

6. Notes on the current use of this design

I tested this design in September 2018 (a year after I started playing Project ("Crush") Management Game; chapter 19), and started attributing one point to ten minutes. On December 30th 2018 I added the stars to my feedback system, to mark rewards for achieving specific goals.

I feel very comfortable with it now and have fun playing it. The addition of ambition projects brought dynamism and excitement to the feelings of balance and well-being. I enjoy this combination very much. The newest add-on with the asterisks supports me in keeping my escape-to activities at bay, and in performing what I want to do *when* I want to.

I can't say now how this framework will change with time, or whether I will create an entirely new one, based on this one or not.

For now, I can say that this framework and its design evolve continuously, and I have immense fun adjusting the game plan. It becomes incrementally more multidimensional and sophisticated, in an exciting way. I notice many new nuances to my projects and activities and how I can accommodate them in the rules of this game (such as with the previously mentioned sleep, and how points are assigned on weekdays vs. weekends and holidays).

[A side-note: The asterisk in the square hasn't worked very well during the first couple of days of testing, so I will need to figure out how to either motivate the player in me to get more of them (by more often going to bed before 10 pm), or ask the designer in me to adjust the rules.]

This self-motivational game design is a product of self-gamification. The original framework and the more sophisticated model of today were born out of awareness and developed step-by-small-step. The whole process felt like a big, fun game. And still does.

I will continue playing and see what happens. Curiosity and fun will continue to help me find the best way both in designing and playing it.

7. Images, results, and examples of the feedback system and points gathered

The photographs below show the feedback system and the points earned for some of the days of this year, as I played the Balance Game. You can see the pink (or gray, if you read this in paperback or on a gray-scale rendering e-reader) stars and also that I don't manage to gather all five stars every day. But I am happy to say that I achieve most of them (see below, after the images, the results of my first three months playing the Balance Game).

Self-Gamification Happiness Formula

This was the first time I have ever had so many days in a row of getting enough sleep and taking care of my health. But I still have room to improve in this game, because even though I once got five stars for eleven days in a row, I am yet to have a full week from Monday to Sunday with all five stars.

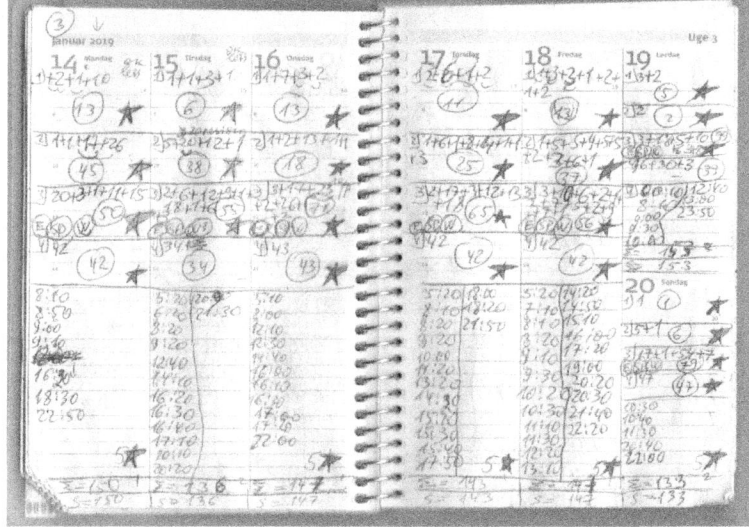

The photograph below shows the inclusion of the "ambition project," which at the point of putting these words on the computer screen is writing this book. You can see it by the abbreviation SG standing for "Self-Gamification" at the top of the picture.

You can see the asterisks in action at the bottom of the photograph below. The asterisk in the square (see what it means in section 5 above) is a tough one to collect. ;)

Self-Gamification Happiness Formula

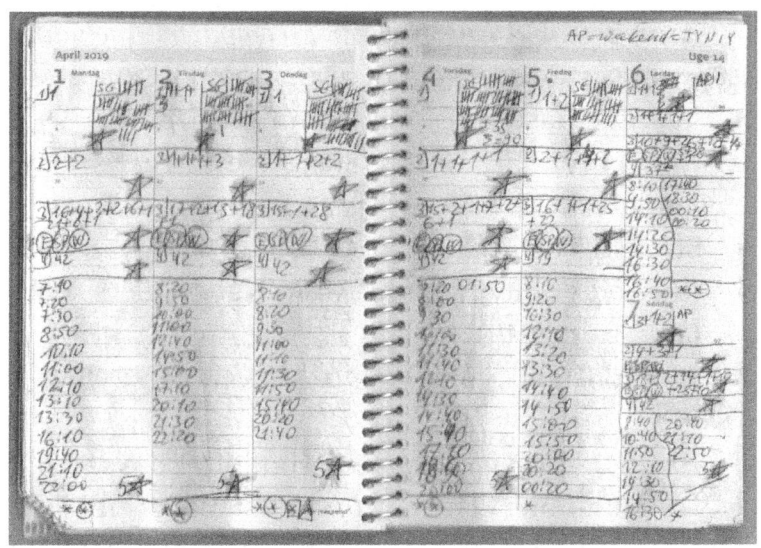

<u>Results for the Balance Game from December 30, 2018 to March 30, 2019 (Total: 91 days)</u>

Collecting stars in general:

5 stars: on 63 out of 91 days = 69%

4 stars: see 5 stars (since if I gather a star in each of the four project/activity areas, I get the fifth star)

3 stars: on 26 out of 91 days = 29%

2 stars: on 2 out of 91 days = 2%

1 star: on 0 out of 91 days = 0%

Collecting stars per category (or specific activity):

Area 1 — Passive income: a star on 91 out of 91 days = 100%

Area 2 — Active income and administrative work: a star on 91 out of 91 days = 100%

Area 3 — Away from my computer (including wellness): a star on 83 out of 91 days = 91%
- Eye gymnastics (E): on 90 out of 91 days = 99% (the only day missed was New Year's day, January 1, 2019)
- Straight Posture (SP): on 90 out of 91 days = 99% (the only day missed was New Year's day, January 1, 2019)
- Workout and yoga (W): on 83 out of 91 days = 91%

Area 4 — Enough sleep: on 69 out of 91 days = 76%

[A side-note: There are no statistics for the asterisk add-on scale since I am in the testing phase and it is very new. However, it works well in helping me *not* to escape from what I want (and commit) to doing, and to do work-out and yoga before dinner time, as the asterisks (with and without the circle) collected in the week of testing this add-on show in the photograph above.]

Glossary and References:

* "Passive income is income resulting from cash flow received on a regular basis, requiring minimal to no effort by the recipient to maintain it." (https://en.wikipedia.org/wiki/Passive_income)

** "Active income refers to income received from performing a service. This includes wages, tips, salaries, commissions and income from businesses in which there is material participation. For example, an accountant who works for a monthly paycheck receives active income." (https://www.investopedia.com/terms/a/activeincome.asp)

*** "A role-playing game (sometimes spelled roleplaying game; abbreviated RPG) is a game in which players assume the roles of characters in a fictional setting. Players take responsibility for acting out these roles within a narrative, either through literal acting, or through a process of structured decision-making regarding character development. Actions taken within many games succeed or fail according to a formal system of rules and guidelines." (https://en.wikipedia.org/wiki/Role-playing_game)

Conclusion

"Life is a game and you are the player. As you master the game, so you also create it." — Jay Woodman

Congratulations! You now turn your life (or at least parts of it) into engaging, exciting, and fun games.

You learned so many things since you first started reading this book.

You learned about *self-gamification*, which is an approach that brings together the ability to be aware (that is honest, kind, and non-judgmental toward yourself and others), to make small and effortless steps towards your goals, and last but not least, appreciate each of these small steps in the fun feedback system of your self-motivational games.

As a result and after starting to practice self-gamification, you have been both honest and kind to yourself. You have learned to identify the most appropriate next steps towards your goals and dreams. You have designed your own self-motivational games for projects and activities, independent of whether you think you love doing

Self-Gamification Happiness Formula

or have to do them. And you have more and more fun in the process.

You might be using the game plans of others, but you adjust them and do what's best for you.

I recently contemplated why I don't use any of the many beautiful and skillfully designed diaries that are on sale in bookstores and online, and in many different languages. I looked into some of them online recently. They have habit trackers and places to record goals, to-do lists, and also what we are thankful for. I wondered why my hand-written and very simplified feedback system with self-drawn and colored stars suited me more.

The first answer that came to mind is that I created it myself for my own needs. Yes, *being both the designer and player* of my games is what empowers and encourages me, helping me to keep playing and have no intention of giving up.

You are now the designer of your life and not its victim. You have tasted fun while playing and developing your project and project management games, and they now excite you.

Before you go, a quick question.

Were the expectations that you had at the beginning of this book satisfied?

Take a look at the expectations you formulated after reading the introduction. Were they satisfied? If yes (however partially or hopefully even more), then how? Is your view of yourself and the world around you different now than it was? If yes, how?

Use the lines below (or a notebook, if you are reading this on an e-reader) and a pen to jot down your answers:

_____
_____
_____
_____
_____
_____

And now, all there is left for me to do is to wish you the following:

Enjoy your self-motivational games! Enjoy your life!

And have fun designing, playing, and living!

Self-Gamification Happiness Formula

Two More Quotes About Happiness

[A side-note: I first discovered these quotes on a blouse I bought. I feel they say everything, and are the perfect conclusion to the quote I opened the book with, which stated that happiness is a way.]

"Be content with what you have; rejoice in the way things are. When you realize there is nothing lacking, the world belongs to you." — Lao Tsu

"Happiness is a choice, not a result. Nothing will make you happy until you choose to be happy. No person will make you happy unless you decide to be happy. Your happiness will not come to you. It can only come from you." — Ralph Marston

Recommended Reading

"If you don't like to read, you haven't found the right book." – J.K. Rowling

To keep this list as concise as possible I have only listed fifteen entries, which I highly recommend. But I also encourage you to check out the other books and resources I referred to and quoted throughout the book.
1. *Being Here: Modern Day Tales of Enlightenment,* Ariel and Shya Kane, 2007
2. *Being Here...Too: Short Stories of Modern Day Enlightenment,* Ariel and Shya Kane, 2018
3. *Practical Enlightenment,* Ariel and Shya Kane, 2015
4. *Working on Yourself Doesn't Work: The 3 Simple Ideas That Will Instantaneously Transform Your Life,* Ariel and Shya Kane, 2008
5. *One Small Step Can Change Your Life: The Kaizen Way,* Robert Maurer, 2014
6. *Mastering Fear: Harnessing Emotion to Achieve Excellence in Work, Health and Relationships,* Robert Maurer, 2016

7. *Leap Year: How small steps can make a giant difference,* Helen Russell, 2016
8. *The Game Inventor's Guidebook: How to Invent and Sell Board Games, Card Games, Role-playing Games & Everything in Between!,* Brian Tinsman, 2008
9. *Theory of Fun for Game Design,* Raph Koster, 2013
10. *Lifelong Kindergarten: Cultivating Creativity through Projects, Passion, Peers, and Play,* Mitchel Resnick, 2017
11. *Reality Is Broken: Why Games Make Us Better and How They Can Change the World,* Jane McGonigal, 2011
12. *Actionable Gamification: Beyond Points, Badges, and Leaderboards,* Yu-kai Chou, 2015

The following books are not referenced in *Self-Gamification Happiness Formula: How to Turn Your Life into Fun Games,* but you might find they enrich your experience of sharing self-gamification and taking responsibility for living a profound life.

13. *The Go-Giver: A Little Story About a Powerful Business Idea,* Bob Burg and John David Mann, 2010
14. *The Go-Giver Influencer: A Little Story About a Most Persuasive Idea,* Bob Burg and John David Mann, 2018

15. *The Latte Factor: Why You Don't Have to Be Rich to Live Rich*, David Bach and John David Mann, 2019

Dear Reader, Thank You!

First of all, thank you very much for purchasing and reading *Self-Gamification Happiness Formula: How to Turn Your Life into Fun Games*!

I hope you enjoyed reading this book as much as I loved writing it.

This might be the most important book I ever write in my life. I thoroughly enjoyed writing it. I fretted, I grew, I learned. I turned it into a game and played. And I did everything I could to be excellent in this game. But best of all, I got to encourage and empower others. I hope you felt empowered by the end of it, or even before.

If the book stirred you in any way, I would like to ask you to take a moment and leave an honest review on the retailer site where you purchased it. You can use, for example, the notes you made on whether or not it met your expectations. You can find the list of retailers on the web-page for the *Self-Gamification Happiness Formula: How to Turn Your Life into Fun Games* (https://www.victoriaichizlibartels.com/self-gamification-book/).

Your feedback will help me to improve the content I create, and it will help other potential readers discover this book.

If you loved this book and what you learned here, then please share it with others, so that they can also profit from the self-gamification synergy. You could consider giving it as a gift, or share it with them via the link above.

Thank you very much for your help and support!

But please don't go yet — I have a few more things that I'd like to address.

Thanks again for reading my book! It means a lot to me. I am continually working on creating more content on the topic of how to become an expert designer and player of the game called life. So, I would like to invite you to take another moment to sign up to my blog and occasional email update. You can unsubscribe at any time. You can sign up here: https://www.victoriaichizlibartels.com/subscribe-to-victorias-blog/.

And last but not least, you can join the self-gamification community. There are various options for doing so. Please visit https://www.victoriaichizlibartels.com/community/ to find out more.

Acknowledgments

"In the end, though, maybe we must all give up trying to pay back the people in this world who sustain our lives. In the end, maybe it's wiser to surrender before the miraculous scope of human generosity and just to keep saying thank you, forever and sincerely, for as long as we have voices." Elizabeth Gilbert, *Eat, Pray, Love: One Woman's Search for Everything*

This book wouldn't be what it is, nor have been such a pleasure to write, without the help, support, and work of many brilliant people. I will try to mention everyone, but if I have forgotten anyone, please feel included. My experience of developing, practicing, and sharing self-gamification profited immensely from the feedback I got. I am also immensely grateful for the richness of information and inspiration available in the world, and to everyone that shares the wealth of their wisdom with others.

First, I would like to thank Ariel and Shya Kane, the award-winning authors, seminar leaders, radio show hosts, business consultants, and dear friends, for all you do. I have profited immensely from the many resources that you offer to empower and encourage your listeners, readers, seminar participants, clients, and friends. Self-gamification would not exist without your definition of awareness. I previously would not have imagined looking into anthropology, about which, inspired by your work, I am in the process of learning more.

I am also grateful to Robert Maurer and all his books on kaizen. They were a huge support in understanding how my brain functions and why I procrastinate over the things I want to pursue.

I am also indebted to the experts in the game and gamification design field. Thank you so much for joining in the conversations I started on social media. And thank you also for the resources you provide and share. Special thanks to Yu-kai Chou, one of the gamification pioneers, for the live chat online. I was honored and humbled when you asked me for an interview to talk about gamification as a lifestyle.

Many thanks to Line Weiss Christensen for being the friend who pointed out to me that the 5 Minute Perseverance Game was none other than a gamification approach. From you, Line, I heard the word "gamification" for the first time, and on that day the exciting adventure of this book began.

I was thrilled when Mikkel Lund, who is now a gamification consultant, project manager, and digital designer, asked me to share my expertise in self-gamification while he was writing his master's thesis on gamification. Thanks to your questions and the fun chat we had over coffee I became aware of the two sub-types of escape-to tasks. Thank you very much for that.

Big thanks also to Giselle Christoffersen, an inspiring psychologist who uses gamification and serious games to motivate, engage, and change behavior, for our exciting exchange on gamification and its potential, and for co-organizing the "Gamification Aalborg" interest group on Facebook with me.

I am incredibly grateful to Leah Schneeflock for supporting me during the crowdfunding campaign I launched for this book in 2018. Your advice added to the fun in the process and I still love the tag-line you came up with from the material I sent to you: "'Candy Crush' meets 'Big Magic'." Even if I didn't use it in the book, I tapped into the spirit of this tag-line while writing it.

Many thanks to my fellow crowd-funder and supporter of the idea for this book at Inkshares.com (where I started the crowdfunding campaign), Rose Jermusyk, for helping me identify that it was going to be a combination of a guidebook, memoir, reference book, and essay/case-study anthology.

Huge thanks to Tammy Lain, Annie Pinnock, all the students on the Udemy motivational online course and the live AOF course in Aalborg (as well as the organizers of the latter: Tak, Lone og Ditte!), followers of my posts on self-gamification on social media, and friends, who share with me the experiences they have while turning their lives into games. Your feedback enriched the parts of the book where I address the lessons learned. I also learned a great deal from the questions you asked about how I turn my life into games and how you can do the same.

Special thanks to my dear friend Auria Paz Aguilar. You are not only my student on Udemy and publicist for my books and online courses, but you are also a cheerleader for self-gamification and the messages I convey with my business. Thank you so much for all you do! I am utterly excited to continue working with you and for both our companies to grow stronger and bring more and more value to our customers.

I am delighted with how this book turned out. And this is very much due to support and help from Sarah Le-Fevre, an expert in games-based learning design and delivery, and Lego Serious Play facilitator. Dear Sarah, thank you so much for agreeing to the idea of reading each other's books chapter by chapter. I learned so much from our exchange. Your input from preface until the end affected the content, and especially the practical part of the book, immensely and positively. Thank you so much for letting me know what resonated with you and how applying the ideas from this book helped you with your projects, activities, and life. Due to your advice and encouragement, the writing flew much more fluently toward the end of the book.

I have to thank my dear friend Heike Werntgen for the unique art she created for the *Self-Gamification Happiness Formula* book cover. Your beautiful and happy art inspired the final title of the book, as well as the creation of the formula.

I am immensely grateful to Alice Jago for editing this book, making it sound beautiful and easier to read. And for making such a beautiful book cover out of Heike's art. I am thrilled that we already have plans to work on more projects together. I love working with you, Alice!

My deepest gratitude goes to my mother, Veronica, my sister, Svetlana, and my niece, Mihaela, for their love and support and for being interested in my quirky self-motivational games. I would also like to express my gratitude to my husband's family, especially his parents, Gundel and Roland. Together with my mother, my sister, her husband Poul, my niece and her beautiful family with husband Jens and sweet daughter Vera, they cheer and support me on my entrepreneurial adventure.

And now to the sweetest bit. Dearest Michael, Niklas, and Emma, this book is devoted to you, not just because you are my favorite gamers in the world. You brighten up my day, you challenge me in the most exciting and brilliant ways, you encourage me, you try out my gameful suggestions, and you always wish me luck, success, and fun with my projects. You are as much a part of this creation as I am. Without you, this book (or any of my heart's projects) would not be a reality. I love you!

About the Author

Victoria Ichizli-Bartels lives her life as if it were a game and never wants to stop playing. Author of *5 Minute Perseverance Game* and instructor of the online course *Motivate Yourself by Turning Your Life Into Fun Games,* this book is Victoria's third work on self-gamification, an innovative method for approaching your life as games and having fun in the process.

Victoria is a writer with a background in semiconductor physics, electronic engineering (with a Ph.D.), information technology, and business development. While being a non-gamer, Victoria came up with the new term *self-gamification*, a gameful and playful self-help approach bringing anthropology, kaizen, and gamification based methods together to increase quality of life.

Victoria was born in Moldova, lived in Germany for twelve years, and now lives in Aalborg, Denmark, with her husband and two children.

Visit or contact Victoria at victoriaichizlibartels.com or optimistwriter.com

Victoria Ichizli-Bartels

Also by Victoria Ichizli-Bartels

Fiction
Books

Between Grace and Abyss: A Short Story
(Also available as a free e-book upon subscription to
victoriaichizlibartels.com or optimistwriter.com)

Nothing Is As It Seems: A Novelette
(The e-book is permanently free)

Seven Broken Pieces: A short story
(Prequel to series "A Life Upside Down")

A Spy's Daughter: A novella
(Book 1 in series "A Life Upside Down")

The Truth About Family:
A novel inspired by true events

Motivational
Books

Cheerleading for Writers:
Discover How Truly Talented You Are

Turn Your No Into Yes:
15 Yes-Or-No Questions to Disentangle Your Project
Free e-book

ഔ 480 ര

Self-Gamification Happiness Formula
(Available upon subscription to victoriaichizlibartels.com or optimistwriter.com)

5 Minute Perseverance Game:
Play Daily for a Month and Become the Ultimate Procrastination Breaker

Online Course
Motivate Yourself by Turning Your Life Into Fun Games: Practice Self-Gamification, a Unique Self-Help Approach Uniting Anthropology, Kaizen, and Gamification
https://bit.ly/2QDpbbw

Business Books
Take Control of Your Business:
Learn what Business Rules are, discover that you are already using them, then update them to maximize your business success

Resources
The Business Rules Memo
https://www.victoriaichizlibartels.com/s1000d-navigation-maps/#BrMemo

S1000D Books
brDoc, BREX, and Co.: S1000D Business Rules Made Easier

S1000D® Issue 4.1 and Issue 4.2 Navigation Map:

Victoria Ichizli-Bartels

552+87 and 427+90 Business Rule Decision Points Arranged into two Linear Topic Maps to Facilitate Learning, Understanding, and Implementation of S1000D®

S1000D Issue 4.1 Untangled:
552+ Business Rules Decision Points Arranged into a Linear Topic Map to Facilitate Learning, Understanding and Implementation of S1000D
(unpublished, replaced by *S1000D® Issue 4.1 and Issue 4.2 Navigation Map*, see above)

Data Sheets and Templates

S1000D® Navigation Maps
https://www.victoriaichizlibartels.com/s1000d-navigation-maps/

Made in the USA
Las Vegas, NV
26 May 2025